Barbara
Ox

Holy Russia a

Holy Russia and Christian Europe

*East and West in the
Religious Ideology of Russia*

Wil van den Bercken

SCM PRESS

Translated by John Bowden from the Dutch *De mythe van het Oosten. Oost en West in de religieuze ideeëngeschiedenis van Rusland*, published 1998 by Uitgeverij Meinema, Zoetermeer, The Netherlands.

0 334 02782 9

This edition first published 1999 by
SCM Press
9–17 St Albans Place London N1 0NX

SCM Press is a division of
SCM-Canterbury Press Ltd

Printed in Great Britain by
Biddles Ltd, Guildford and King's Lynn

For Raja, light from the East

No! The West cannot be in the East,
The sun cannot set where it rises

(Michail Pogodin, 1845)

What is the meaning of East and West
if the world is round?

(Proverb)

Transliteration

In the dilemma over what transliteration to use for Russian names and book titles I have opted for the international scholarly transliteration, because that is the only consistent one. However, geographical names and names of well-known tsars are in the usual English spelling. The international transliteration is pronounced as follows:

č as ch
ch as kh
š as sh
šč as shch
ž as zh
c as ts
e as ye
ë as yo

The apostrophe after a consonant replaces the Russian 'soft sign' and means that the consonant has to be pronounced with a slight ye-sound.

Contents

Introduction

Myths of the West and the East

For a long time the idea prevailed in mediaeval historiography that civilization moved from the East to the West by way of successive world empires: from Babylon to Egypt, on to Greece, then to the Roman empire and finally to the Frankish and German empire. Christian salvation history was also put in this perspective, producing a kind of salvation geography, a movement of Christian salvation history which improved in quality from East to West.[1] The westward movement of salvation ended in the empire of Charlemagne or the German emperors, which was the *imperium Christianum* predestined by providence. The twelfth-century chronicler Otto of Freising sums up this view in his statement that 'one should not be amazed that power and science have transferred from the East to the West, since the same thing has happened with regard to religion'.[2] Many writers and theologians after him saw the same divine predestination in the history of the West.

In Protestantism, eyes were turned away from the East even more strongly than in Catholicism.[3] In principle that was the case in Puritan Protestantism, where there is a continuation of the westward movement from the European continent to England and from there to the United States of America, 'God's own country'. J. W. Schulte Nordholt, an expert on America, called this 'the myth of the West', and analysed it in a book of the same name.[4] He did so from a Western, self-critical standpoint.

A large part of the European population had never believed in the Western-orientated view of religious history, namely the Eastern Orthodox part, Russia and the Ukraine. However, contrary to Schulte Nordholt, it did not reject this vision on the basis

of a critical historical standpoint, but from an ideological and
religious view of history that was directed eastwards. Schulte
Nordholt indicates this Russian notion at the end of his book,
but does not go into it more closely. His task was to show
how much the religious gaze was fixed on the West, and here
he succeeded admirably. The many remarks by English and
American writers, clergy and politicians which he quotes are
disconcerting in their religious naivety and nationalistic presup-
positions. The idea that Christianity also developed eastwards
did not appear at all in this view of the world.

But even without a Western ideological perspective on
Christianity, the Eastern Orthodox world of Christianity proves
to be an unknown and in any case neglected factor in the historical sense of Christian identity among Europeans. The majority
of textbooks on European church history or even the history of
religious art allow only a marginal position to Russia and the
Balkans; the notable exception here is the 1984 work by A.
Angenendt about the conversion histories of the mediaeval
European rulers.[5] Angenendt rightly takes the Slav world, not
only that of the Poles but also that of the Bulgarians and the
Russians, with Europe, even with the *West*, as is clear from the
sub-title of his book.

However, in general 'Christian Europe' is understood to be
Western and Central Europe, which ends with Poland and
Hungary. The Christianization of Poland and Hungary in the
tenth century is regarded as a religious and political milestone
in the Christianization of Europe, but the Christianization of
Kievan Russia which took place at the same time and the
earlier Christianization of Bulgaria find no place in the historiography of the idea of Europe. This emerges for example from the
study by Rolf Förster: 'Around the end of the first millennium
the "West" was finally developed with the Christianizing of the
Poles, the Hungarians and the three Scandinavian kingdoms.'[6]
And the author makes this statement with reference to Europe
before there was any schism between Latin and Orthodox
Christianity and when the Kievan rulers married their children to
European royal families.

Russia also remains out of the picture for centuries even in the recent Dutch studies by P. Rietbergen and P. van den Boer on 'the idea of Europe', although the authors fully recognize the decisive role of Christianity in the rise of mediaeval Europe.[7] As a result these studies remain traditionally one-sided (or Westernized), informative though they are.

For centuries Russia and its Orthodox Church have existed beyond the Christian horizon and the cultural consciousness of 'Europeans', although they were part of so-called Christian Europe. That already dates from the early Middle Ages. In the Middle Ages what was then Russia, called *Rus'*, with Kiev as its capital, was not unknown to the great mediaeval chroniclers like Thietmar of Merseburg, Adam of Bremen and Helmold of Bozau.[8] But their accounts of *Rucia, Ruscia, Ruzzia, Rugia, Rutenia, Rossia, Russia,* the various Latinized forms of the Slavonic *Rus'*, are fragmentary. A case in point is Helmold of Bozau's observation on Russia in his *Chronica Slavorum* (Chronicle of the Slavs, 1170). In the first chapter he introduces the Slav peoples, from the Baltic to the Black Sea, and says of them and Russia:

> All these nations, with the exception of the Prussians, adorn themselves with the name of Christianity. It is a long time ago, since the land of the Russians adopted the faith . . . I have not the faintest idea, however, by what teachers it was converted to the faith, except for the fact that it seems that in all their observances they follow the Greeks rather than the Latins. For it is only a short distance across the Russian sea to Greece.[9]

After the national conversions in the ninth and tenth centuries the identification of Catholic Europe with the *corpus Christianum* became a matter of course. All the European kings defended true Christianity in their own way, within that unconscious and zigzagging concept of westward-oriented Christianity and civilization which started with Charlemagne as the *devotus ecclesiae defensor*, and continued by way of the German *piissimus rex* and *Christianissimus imperator* of the empire which was still called 'holy', the Spanish *reyos catholicos* and the English *defender of the faith*.

Meanwhile Kievan Russia with its own religious and historical perspective was ruled by a prince 'beloved of God', who later in the Moscow empire was to become the 'orthodox and most pious' tsar and 'protector of the faith', and in whose empire was to be formulated the view of the eastward movement of Christianity and civilization. This was the origin of what by analogy with Schulte Nordholt's title may be called 'the myth of the East'.

The Western myth envisages a Christian one-way traffic from Jerusalem through Rome to the Holy Roman Empire, followed by a Catholic variant from Spain to the New World, or a Protestant variant from England to the United States. The Eastern myth follows the route from Jerusalem to Constantinople to Kiev to Moscow. In nineteenth-century pan-Slavic thought this myth is given scholarly form by Nikolaj Danilevskij in the idea that Slavic-Orthodox civilization is replacing Roman-German, Catholic-Protestant civilization.

So the Christian epicentre is situated in various places during history. Even today, Protestant fundamentalists in America imagine their country to be the gate to the kingdom of God, whereas Orthodox nationalists in post-Communist Russia regard their country as the place of Christ's second coming, and as a stronghold against materialistic America and the atheistic West.

Viewed from the perspective of the phenomenology of religion, both myths are forms of ideologizations of Christianity. Throughout history Christianity has fulfilled an ideological function in ever-changing places, varying in intensity from innocent religious romanticism or cement for a national sense of identity in order to be able to hold its own over against foreign rulers to the nationalistic religious self-glorification and political usurpation of Christianity.

The identification of Christianity with a nation, state or empire is contrary to the very nature of Christianity, which is supranational. The keynote of the entire history of Christianity, however, is the struggle between the universal, supranational character of Christianity and its ties with a political or cultural entity. That is the paradox of Christian Europe, which divides this Europe at the very point which is a common element in the genesis of the cultural history of Europe.

Christianity as the sacralization of a sense of nation is again playing a role in present-day Russia, which is looking for a new national identity. Many writers and presenters inside and outside the church are referring back to the religious and ideological images of the past, using them to distinguish Russia from the rest of Europe. That makes the present study topical.

However, I equally see the topicality of this book in its implicit demonstration of the common historical roots of Christianity in Russia and the Ukraine and Europe. This makes it possible to emphasize in the discussion of the future of Europe that Russia belongs to Europe. For that is the paradoxical conclusion of this study: despite the fact that for centuries Russia has opposed the West in terms of religion and ideology, it has always continued to belong to the sphere of European culture. That is witnessed to not only by the cultural phenomenon of the mediaeval chronicles in Russia but also by the correspondence between the religious and ideological self-images which have been formed in Russia and Western countries. And even after the cultural division brought about by the Renaissance and humanism, Russia remained within the European sphere, difficult though that is to define. That is why with its explosion of literary creativity in the nineteenth century it could so quickly gain its place in European culture and even bring this to new high points.

The division of the book

Chapters 1 and 2 investigate Russia's view of its own conversion on the basis of the two historical documents which describe the introduction of Christianity into Russia: the earliest Russian chronicle, *The Narrative of Bygone Years,* and the eleventh-century treatise by Ilarion of Kiev, *On the Law and Grace.* Large parts of these documents are given in translation: this is literal, because the precise words with which Russia described its Christianization and religious self-image are important.

Chapter 3 compares Russia's very distinctive account of its conversion with the 'nationalistic' accounts of the conversion of Western and Eastern European countries; here there are numerous quotations from mediaeval European chronicles. These first three chapters are not concerned to reconstruct the actual process of conversion, but to give an analysis of the way in which it is described in the various national chronicles.[10]

Chapter 4 describes the origin of the Russian religious and ideological myth in the fourteenth and fifteenth centuries at the time of the Tatar domination and the political rise of Moscow.

Chapter 5 describes the development of the myth in the sixteenth century, under Ivan the Terrible, and during the church schism of the seventeenth century.

Chapter 6 shows the secular transformation of the religious and political myth in eighteenth-century Petersburg Russia.

Chapter 7 describes the breakthrough of Russia's religious and ideological view of itself in the person of the nineteenth-century philosopher Čaadaev, the first Russian to think in generally philosophical terms.

Chapter 8 gives a survey of the different Slavophile tendencies in the nineteenth century which in a gradually differing manner emphasize the special character of Russia as compared with Europe.

With the nineteenth-century debate between Slavophiles and those inclined towards the West, the Russian conflict over identity was in fact resolved: by the passion and the intellectual concepts with which the two parties carried on the dispute they demonstrated, one voluntarily and the other somewhat involuntarily, that Russia already forms part of Europe.

The Entry of Kievan Russia into the Christian World

Among the narratives of the conversion of the European peoples in the early Middle Ages, that of the Russians is by far the most attractive. The narrative is moving in its religious spontaneity and phenomenological simplicity, but at the same it is full of deep theological texts and throughout it is composed in an attractive literary style. Whether from the perspective of church history or missiology, the narrative is unique in the history of the Christianization of Europe.

The real course of events in Russia's transition to Christianity was definitely less unique, less rapid and more prosaic than the narrative suggests. There was a good deal of political calculation on the part of prince Vladimir, before he changed from a defender of paganism into a promoter of Christianity, from the owner of eight hundred concubines into the monogamous husband of a Byzantine princess; in short, before he became 'holy and apostolic'. However, what we are interested in here is not a historical reconstruction of events but the chronicler's perception and its continued effect on Russian religious self-awareness. When the monk Nestor wrote his chronicle, he strove to express the religious and historical self-awareness of his newly converted nation.

First a remark about the chronicler himself. Whether he was called Nestor, and thus was the same person as the author of some lives of the saints, is not certain. However, at all events he was a monk of the Kievan Caves Monastery. I imagine him in a

cell like the monk-historian Pimen in Puškin's *Boris Godunov*,
who had the same sense of history and duty.

> One last narrative
> and my chronicle is finished.
> I have fulfilled the obligation imposed by God
> on me, a sinner. With good reason the Lord
> has let me bear witness for many years
> and has made me wise in the art of books.
> One day a diligent monk
> will find my zealous, anonymous work.
> Like me, he will light his lamp
> and, after brushing the dust of centuries from the volumes,
> he will transcribe the true stories,
> so that the descendants of the Orthodox shall know
> the past fortunes of their land . . .

Five hundred years lie between Nestor and Pimen, but monastic
life will not have changed much in that time. And the chronicling
of Russian and Western monks did not differ much in the
eleventh and twelfth centuries. The literary work of the Russian
monks shows the great importance of the church for the beginning of Russian culture and also the parallels with the monasteries elsewhere in Europe. That indicates unmistakably that
Russia shared in the creation of a common Christian culture in
mediaeval Europe, even though at the time people were not
aware of it either in Russia or in the West.

An examination of the faiths

The Nestorian Chronicle, *The Narrative of Bygone Years*
(*Povest' vremennych let*), is the oldest Russian chronicle and
deals with the history of the origin of the world and of Russia.[11]
The short section on world history is based on the Byzantine
world chronicle by Gregory Hamartolos. The *Povest'*, which
from now on I shall refer to by its traditional name, the
Nestorian Chronicle, has the Slav people deriving from one of

the seventy-two nations which, according to the Bible, were spread over the earth after the Tower of Babel. The chronicle ends in 1116, but some parts come from the end of the eleventh century.

The narrative of the conversion of prince Vladimir and his empire is written under the years 6494 to 6496 inclusive, according to the Byzantine era from the creation of the world, or the years of the Lord 986 to 988 inclusive. Russia needed two or three years to make its choice of a new faith to replace paganism, which was felt to be unsatisfactory. And a choice it was. That is precisely what is special about this conversion: it was a well-considered adoption of Byzantine Christianity.

Vladimir had the existing monotheistic religions investigated for their suitability for Russia. It was an 'examination of the faiths' (*ispitanie ver*), as it is called in the Chronicle. It was not a chance adoption of any new religion offering itself to the pagan Russians, but a conscious choice.

The initiative remained in the hands of the Russians, although they reacted to influences from abroad. Vladimir saw new religions come into being on the borders of his empire. Shortly before him, the Polish and Hungarian peoples had adopted Latin Christianity, the Bulgarian people in the Balkans Byzantine Christianity, the Bulgarians on the Volga Islam, and in the ninth century the Khazars, living north-west of the Caucasus, were the only non-Jewish people in history to accept Judaism as their state religion.

For one reason or another Vladimir concluded that paganism was no longer satisfactory as a spiritual cement for his people. The conclusion that polytheism was outmoded was already overdue, for Vladimir's grandmother, the regent Olga, had already embraced Christianity in 955. According to the Nestorian Chronicle she applied her powers of persuasion to win her son Svjatoslav over to the new religion,

but he would not listen to her suggestion, though when any man wished to be baptized, he was not hindered, but only mocked. For to the infidels, the Christian faith is foolishness

... But he did not heed her exhortation, answering, 'How shall I alone accept another faith? My followers will laugh at that.'[12]

At first Svjatoslav's son, Vladimir, was also a confirmed adherent of the tribal god Perun. He even tried to reorganize the pagan cult, apparently as a reaction to a growing Christian infiltration into his empire. It was no longer possible to counter this completely, because the Byzantine empire was so close. Even before Olga, there was already a small Christian community in Kiev, for in a peace treaty with Byzantium in the year 945 a distinction was made between pagan and Christian Russians. The former, which included 'the prince and his men', confirmed the treaty with an oath by their god Perun, and the others, 'those who had been baptized', took a Christian oath.[13]

The Chronicle states that in 986 there were canvassing visits by representatives of the three monotheistic religions: Islam, Judaism and Christianity, Latin as well as Greek. In order to do justice to the specific character of the narrative I shall quote the long fragment of the chronicle concerned in a literal translation, including the syntactical inconsistencies, like a sudden transition from the plural to the singular or vice versa.

In the year 6496 (= 986), Vladimir was visited by Bulgars of Mohammedan faith, who said, 'Though you are a wise and prudent prince, you have no religion. Adopt our faith, and revere Mahomet.' Vladimir inquired what was the nature of their religion. They replied that they believed in God, and that Mahomet instructed them to practise circumcision, to eat no pork, to drink no wine, and, after death, promised them complete fulfilment of their carnal desires. 'Mahomet,' they asserted, 'will give each man seventy fair women. He may choose one fair one, and upon that woman will Mahomet confer the charms of them all, and she shall be his wife. Mahomet promises that one may then satisfy every desire, but whoever is poor in this world will be no different in the next.' They also spoke other false things which out of modesty may not be written down. Vladimir listened to them, for he was fond of women and indulgence, regarding which he heard with pleasure. But circumcision and abstinence from pork and wine were disagreeable to him. 'Drinking,' said he, 'is the joy of the Russes. We cannot exist without that pleasure.'

Then came the Germans, asserting that they were come as emissaries of the Pope. They added, 'Thus says the Pope: "Your country is like our country, but your faith is not as ours. For our faith is the light. We worship God, who has made heaven and earth, the stars, the moon, and every creature, while your gods are only wood." Vladimir inquired what their teaching was. They replied, 'Fasting according to one's strength. But whatever one eats or drinks is all to the glory of God, as our teacher Paul has said.' Then Vladimir answered, 'Depart hence; our fathers accepted no such principle.'

The Jewish Khazars heard of these missions, and came themselves, saying, 'We have learned that Bulgars and Christians came hither to instruct you in their faiths. The Christians believe in him whom we crucified, but we believe in the one God of Abraham, Isaac, and Jacob.' Then Vladimir inquired what their religion was. They replied that its tenets included circumcision, not eating pork or hare, and observing the Sabbath. The prince then asked where their native land was, and they replied that it was in Jerusalem. When Vladimir inquired where that was, they made answer, 'God was angry at our forefathers, and scattered us among the gentiles on account of our sins. Our land was then given to the Christians.' The prince then demanded, 'How can you hope to teach others while you yourselves are cast out and scattered abroad by the hand of God? If God loved you and your faith, you would not be thus dispersed in foreign lands. Do you expect us to accept that fate also?'

Then the Greeks sent to Vladimir a philosopher, who spoke thus: 'We have heard that the Bulgars came and urged you to adopt their faith, which pollutes heaven and earth. They are accursed above all men, like Sodom and Gomorrah, upon which the Lord let fall burning stones, and which he buried and submerged. The day of destruction likewise awaits these men, on which the Lord will come to judge the earth, and to destroy all those who do evil and abomination. For they moisten their excrement, and pour the water into their mouths, and anoint their beards with it, remembering Mahomet. The women also perform this same abomination, and even worse ones.' Vladimir, upon hearing their statements, spat upon the earth, saying, 'This is a vile thing.' Then the philosopher said, 'We have likewise heard how men came from Rome to convert you to their faith. It differs but little from ours, for they celebrate the communion with wafers, called *oplatki*, which God did not give them, for he ordained that we should celebrate the communion with bread. For when he had taken bread, the Lord gave it to his disciples, saying, 'This is my body broken for you.' Likewise he took the cup, and said, 'This is my blood of the New Testament.' They do not do this, for they have modified the faith.' Then Vladimir remarked that the Jews had come into his presence and had stated that the Germans and the Greeks believed in him whom they crucified. To this the philosopher replied, 'Of a truth we believe in him. For some of the prophets foretold that God should be incarnate, and others that he should be crucified and buried, but arise on the third day and ascend into heaven. For the Jews killed the prophets, and still others they persecuted. When their predictions were fulfilled, our Lord came down to earth, was crucified, arose again, and ascended into heaven. He awaited their repentance for forty-six years, but they did not repent, so that the Lord let loose the Romans upon them. Their cities were destroyed, and they were scattered among the Gentiles, under whom they are now in servitude.'

Vladimir then inquired why God should have descended to earth and should have endured such pain. The philosopher then answered and said, 'If you want to hear the story, I shall tell you from the beginning why God descended to earth.' Vladimir replied, 'I would very much like to hear it.' And the philosopher began his narrative.

This is followed by the philosopher's exposition, running to twelve pages, of the history of salvation from the creation of the world to the coming of Christ. Theologically speaking, the Greek philosopher's exposition is an important part of the conversion narrative. It shows that, apart from all the primitive arguments, based on superficial observation, with which other religions are rejected, aspects of Christianity related to the content of faith do play a part. In fact Vladimir is given his first lesson in religion here.

The Greek philosopher's final argument, however, is quite a practical and theological one, namely the retribution at the Last Judgment. The philosopher illustrates this by means of a tapestry on which the Last Judgment with heaven and hell is embroidered. He explains it:

'When the apostles all over the world taught faith in God, we Greeks also accepted their teaching; the whole world believed their teaching. God has also established a day when he will descend from heaven and judge the living and the dead and will recompense each according to his deeds: for the righteous the kingdom of heaven, of inexpressible beauty, joy without end and immortal life; for the sinners a fiery torment, a worm which never gives rest and endless torments. These shall be the torments of those who do not believe in our God Jesus Christ: those who are not baptized will be tormented in the fire.' When he had said this, the philosopher showed Vladimir a tapestry on which the judgment of God was depicted, with the righteous going joyfully to paradise on the right and the sinners on the way to torment on the left. Vladimir sighed and said: 'Those standing on the right are having a good time, but woe betide those standing on the left.' The philosopher said: 'If you want to stand with the righteous on the right side, then have yourself baptized.' Vladimir stamped this thought on his heart and said: 'I shall wait a little', for he wanted to examine all faiths. And Vladimir gave him many gifts and had him escorted with great honour.

Vladimir is impressed. But his answer to the urging of the Greek

that he should be baptized is almost laconic: 'I shall wait a little.'
For first he wanted to investigate other faiths.

This happens one year later. Vladimir discusses with his
advisers the visits of the representatives of the various faiths
and indicates that he was highly impressed by the Greeks. The
advisers, however, strike a note of warning, for, as they say,
'nobody scoffs at his own law'. In other words, everybody
propagandizes for himself. Their advice, therefore, is to go and
have a look among the various peoples and study their cults.

So the Russians set out on their tour of the churches. They do
not, however, go to the Khazar Jews. They make an assessment
of the three other religions on the basis of the services they attend
in church and mosque. The Bulgarians drop out of the competi-
tion because of the 'gloom and stench' in the mosque, and so do
the Latins, 'because there was no beauty in their churches'. So the
Greeks won with flying colours, literally and figuratively. The
Russians were overwhelmed by the Orthodox worship in Hagia
Sophia in Constantinople.

In the year 6495 (= 987). Vladimir summoned his boyars and
elders together and said to them: 'Behold, the Bulgars have
come to me and said: "Accept our Law." After that the
Germans came and they praised their law. After them came the
Jews. After all these came the Greeks who scorned all laws but
praised their own, and they spoke a great deal and told of the
whole world from its beginning. They spoke in a way that
could be understood and it is marvellous to hear them and
everyone listened to them readily. They also told of the existence of another world and said: if anyone is converted to our
faith then when he dies he will rise again and will never die for
eternity; if he accepts another law, he will burn in fire in the
other world. What do you think? What is your answer?' And
the boyars and the elders said: 'Know well, prince, that no one
scorns his own law but praises it. If you really want to attain
knowledge, then you have men before you: send them out and
discover what their religion is and how each one serves its
God.' Their answer pleased the prince and all the people. They

chose capable and understanding men, ten in number, and said to them: 'Go first to the Bulgars and investigate their faith.' They departed, and when they had arrived among them they saw their unclean deeds and the bowing in the mosque. After that they returned to their land. And Vladimir said: 'Go also to the Germans, see how it is with them and go from there to the Greeks.' They came to the Germans and after they had seen their worship they went to the imperial city and went to the emperor. The emperor asked them why they had come. They told him all that had happened. When the emperor had heard that, he was glad and showed them great honour that day. The next day he sent a report to the patriarch and said: 'The Russians have come to investigate our faith. Adorn the church and the clergy festively and do you yourself put on episcopal vestments, so that they may see the glory of our God.' When the patriarch had heard that, he ordered the clergy to convene and they celebrated the feast day according to their custom and burned incense and brought together singing and choirs. He went to church with the Russians and people gave them room and showed them the beauty of the church, the singing and the episcopal worship with the assistance of the deacons and told them about the service of their God. And they were enraptured; they marvelled and praised their worship. And the emperors Basil and Constantine summoned them and said to them, 'Go to your land', and they let them go with many presents and much honour. And they returned to their land.

Prince Vladimir summoned his boyars and elders and said to them: 'Behold, the men whom we sent have returned; let us hear what they have experienced.' And he turned to those who had been sent out: 'Say what happened.' They said: 'We went to the Bulgars, and saw how they bow in their temple and stand there without a girdle. Once a person has bowed, he goes to sit down and looks now this way and now that, like one possessed. And there is no joy among them, only sombreness and a great stench. Their law is not good. And we went to the Germans and saw much worshipping in their churches, but we did not see any beauty among them. Then we went to the

Greeks and they brought us to the place where they serve their God and we knew not whether we were in heaven or on earth. For on earth there is no such splendour or such beauty, and we are at a loss how to describe it. We only know that God dwells there among men, and their service is fairer than the ceremonies of other nations. For we cannot forget that beauty. Every man, after tasting something sweet, is afterward unwilling to accept that which is bitter, and therefore we cannot dwell longer here.' Then the boyars said, 'If the Greek faith were evil, it would not have been adopted by your grandmother Olga, who was wiser than all other men.' Vladimir then inquired where they should all accept baptism, and they replied that the decision rested with him.

The liturgy in the monumental Hagia Sophia, a building which still impresses even the modern spoilt tourist, must indeed have made an overwhelming impression on the barbaric Russians, who did not even have stone buildings in their own country. And the service itself, with hundreds of candles reflecting on the golden mosaics, with the spell-binding hymns sung by large choirs, with the crowned patriarch and the metropolitans in princely vestments, with the entire space filled with the fragrance of incense, must have been a cultural shock for the Russians, who were accustomed to idolatrous cults with human sacrifices, performed before sacred trees or primitive wooden images. Their amazement is reflected in the words with which they reported to Vladimir: 'and we knew not whether we were in heaven or on earth. For on earth there is no such splendour or such beauty, and we are at a loss how to describe it.'

Thus for the Russians the aesthetic argument became the deciding factor in the choice of a new faith. This confrontation with a splendour which was quite new to them has undoubtedly taken place, if not during an explicit expedition concerned with faith, then certainly during a trade or diplomatic visit to Constantinople. The elaboration of the aesthetic argument in the Russian conversion story is literary imagination on the part of the chronicler, which as such is also an aesthetic act. But the predilection for liturgical splendour would remain a typical characteristic of Russian Orthodoxy.

The story of the examination of the faiths is very special from a literary-historical point of view. We do not find it in any other conversion of a European people. It is typical of Russia, which was confronted at its frontiers with other monotheistic state religions than Christianity. However, the literary procedure of a comparative religious examination by a prince or king looking for a new religion for his people is not entirely unique to Russia. It seems also to have occurred in the case of the Khazars, a Turkish people which in the end adopted Judaism. This story is related in the ninth-century Slavonic Life of St Cyril, or Constantine the Philosopher, as he was called by his secular name and profession.[14] In the early 860s this Greek scholar had travelled with a Byzantine government delegation to the Khazars, at whose court he had engaged in theological disputes about Judaism and Islam. The author of the Nestorian Chronicle must have been familiar with the Life of Cyril (he borrows from it once), and he may have derived from it the idea of the comparison of religions.

The comparison of the religions in the Nestorian Chronicle is very superficial. Theological issues are not touched upon, just a few external features. The procedure seems to be merely a stylistic device enabling the author to recommend Greek Christianity as the most important religion. An elaborate explanation of its faith and creed is given. In that sense the method shows a resemblance to another remarkable comparison of faiths which is also connected with the Khazars, namely the book *Kitab Al Khazari* by the Spanish Jew Judah Hallevi.[15] This book was written in 1140, a few decades after the Russian conversion story, at a totally different place in the world, but it applies a similar formal comparison of faith between Christianity, Islam and the non-religious philosophical world-view, after which it discusses at great length the Jewish faith as the true one. It is put in the form of a dialogue between a rabbi and the Khazar king and is a serious, theological defence of Judaism. In its intellectual depth and textual dimension Hallevi's work differs essentially from the narrative in the Nestorian Chronicle, but in both cases the introduction of the competing religions serves as a literary-stylistic prelude to an apologia for the true religion, Judaism or Christianity.

The Khazar king may have been an intellectual, but the Russian king certainly was not. And his choice in favour of Christianity was less theological than would appear from the examination of the faiths. The specific occasion for Vladimir's baptism is found in the story described under the year 988.

When a year was past, in the year 6496 (= 988), Vladimir went with his army to Korsun, a Greek city, and the inhabitants of Korsun ensconced themselves in the city. And Vladimir encamped over against the city, by the harbour, a bowshot from the city, and there was brave fighting from the city. However, Vladimir besieged the city. When the people in the city were exhausted, Vladimir said to the citizens: 'If you do not surrender, then I will remain here for three years.' But they did not listen to him. Vladimir drew up his troops and commanded that an earth wall should be built round the city. While they were building it, the inhabitants of Korsun digged a hole in their city wall and stole the earth that had been thrown up. The warriors threw up yet more earth and Vladimir held firm. And behold, a man from Korsun named Anastasios shot an arrow on which he had written: 'There are springs behind you on the east side, from which water flows along a pipe. Dig through this and cut off the water supply.' When Vladimir heard this he looked to heaven and said: 'If this comes to pass I shall have myself baptized.' And immediately he had the pipes dug through and cut off the water supply. The people became weak from thirst and surrendered. Vladimir entered the city with his following and sent a messenger to the emperors Basil and Constantine to say: 'Behold, I have captured your famous city. I hear that you have a sister who is a virgin. Unless you give her to me as wife then I will do to your city what I have done to this city.' When the emperors heard this, they became sorrowful and sent the

following report: 'It is not fitting for Christians to give women
to pagans in marriage. If you have yourself baptized, you shall
have her. If you do not, then we cannot give our sister to
you in marriage.' When Vladimir heard this, he said to the
emperors' ambassadors: 'Say the following to your emperors:
I shall have myself baptized, for I have already investigated
your law, and your faith and worship, about which the men I
sent formerly have told me, please me.' When the emperors
heard that, they were delighted, and they summoned their
sister, who was called Anna, and sent a report to Vladimir
with the words: 'Be baptized, then we shall send our sister to
you.' But Vladimir replied: 'You must come with your sister
and baptize me.' And the emperors obeyed and sent their
sister, some dignitaries and priests. But she said, 'It is as if I am
going into captivity; I would rather die here.' But her brothers
said to her: 'Through you God may perhaps lead the Russian
land to repent and you will preserve the Greek land from a
bloody war. Do you see how much evil the Russians have done
to the Greeks? If you do not go, they will do the same thing to
us.' And they had almost to force her to go. After she had
taken leave of her kinsfolk with tears, she boarded the ship and
crossed the sea. She came to Korsun, and the inhabitants of
Korsun ran out and greeted her, escorted her into the city and
brought her to the palace.

At the same time, by divine providence Vladimir had an
ailment of his eyes and could see nothing. He became very
depressed and did not know what to do. And the emperors'
sister sent him a message and said: 'If you want to be rid of this
sickness, then immediately be baptized, otherwise you will not
get rid of this evil.' When Vladimir heard that, he said: 'If that
really happens, then the God of the Christians is truly great.'
And he gave orders that he should be baptized. The bishop
of Korsun together with the priests of the emperors' sister
baptized Vladimir after giving him instruction. And when he
laid hands on him he could see again. When Vladimir saw his
sudden healing, he praised God, saying: 'Now I have learned
to know the true God.' When his following saw this, many had

themselves baptized. He was baptized in the church of St Basil, and this church stands in the city of Korsun in the middle of the city square where the inhabitants of Korsun hold their market. To the present day Vladimir's palace stands next to the church, and the palace of the emperors' sister behind the altar. After the baptism the emperors' sister was brought for the solemnization of the marriage. Those who do not know say that he was baptized in Kiev; others say in Vasilev and yet others assert that it was in yet another place.

We also know about the political event discussed in the text from two Arabic sources and an Armenian one. The most elaborate is that of Jahja of Antioch: he reports how the Byzantine emperor Basil II was forced to ask the prince of the Russians for military aid, 'although they were his enemies'. The latter stipulates as a condition a marriage with the sister of the emperor, who in his turn stipulates as a condition that the king of the Russians will have himself baptized along with his entire people. Thus the matter was settled, and the Byzantine emperor quelled the revolt with the help of Russian troops. Jahja continues:

> And afterwards emperor Basil sent him metropolitans and bishops, and they baptized the grand prince and all those who lived in his territory. And he sent his sister to him and she built many churches in the land of the Russians.[16]

In this account there is a direct relation between military aid on the one hand and marriage and Christianization on the other. This relation becomes even clearer in the corresponding narrative in the Nestorian Chronicle. Apparently the emperor had still hesitated to send his sister and Vladimir had to enforce the marriage by military means. Vladimir conquered the Byzantine town of Cherson (Korsun) in the Crimea, threatening that he would also conquer Constantinople if the emperor did not give his sister to him as his wife. And when Anna 'had come to the Russian prince, she still had to persuade him actually to be baptized.

So all in all, things did not pass off as smoothly and certainly not in such a theologically reasoned manner as is described in the narrative of the 'investigation of the faiths'. Nestor very briefly relativizes the pragmatic aspect of the political deal between the Russians and the Byzantines by having Vladimir say to the envoys of the emperors that he has 'already investigated your law' and that the Greek religion had pleased him. In this way, by means of a literary artifice, the two different conversion stories are attractively connected with each other and the earlier religious reconnaissance assumes the most important place in the history of the conversion of Russia.

After the performance of Vladimir's baptism the Chronicle continues with the theological content of the Christian faith in the form of a confession of faith. This confession, together with the earlier exposition by the Greek philosopher, sets a strong theological stamp on the entire conversion story and shows that – in the self-awareness of the Russians – their conversion is more than mere aesthetic emotion or political agreement. It leads us to the theological core of the Christian faith. It echoes the christological and trinitarian discussions of the fourth and fifth centuries. For the Russians at the moment when Nestor is writing his account they are present-day elements of faith. The repetition of doctrine in the Chronicle is not a theological routine, but a living confession of faith. Apart from being a historiographer, the chronicler is also a theologian, and so as well as religious romanticism the Chronicle also offers high theology. This is what makes it special.

The meticulous theological formulation of the Chronicle text makes one realize that it is not yet a matter of course: here is an incomprehensible but sacrosanct article of faith. We must imagine how prince Vladimir, without the intellectual baggage of centuries of theological history, indeed illiterate, must have embraced the new theology with amazement. Now that he had finally achieved his political aim, namely marriage with a member of the Byzantine imperial family, by which as the tribal head of a still uncivilized people he was received into the European circle of kings, he was confronted with theological notions which remain a mystery even to a theologian:

When Vladimir was baptized, he was given the Christian creed and told: 'Let no heretics lead you astray but always believe and speak thus: "I believe in the God, the Father, the almighty, creator of heaven and earth" and this creed to the end. And then again: "I believe in the one God, the Father, who is unbegotten, and in the only Son, who is begotten, and in one Holy Spirit who proceeds: three perfect spiritual substances, which are divided in number and substance but not in divinity; for they are separated without distinction and united without confusion. The Father, God the Father, is eternal in fatherhood, not begotten, without beginning. He is the beginning and the cause of all, and is older than the Son and the Spirit only by not being begotten; of him was the Son begotten before all times and the Holy Spirit proceeds without time and without body; he is at the same time the Father, at the same time the Son, at the same time the Holy Spirit. The Son is consubstantial with the Father and differs from the Father and the Spirit only in being begotten. The Spirit is all-holy, consubstantial with the Father and the Son, and with them everlasting. The Father possesses fatherhood, the Son sonship, and the Holy Spirit proceeds. For the Father is not transformed into the Son or the Spirit, nor the Son into the Father and the Spirit, nor the Spirit into the Son and the Father, for their attributes are invariable. Not three Gods, but one God, since there is one divinity in three Persons. Through the will of the Father and the Spirit, to save his creation, he descended from the bosom of the Father, yet without leaving it, and went as divine seed into the pure womb of a virgin most pure. He assumed flesh with soul, word and understanding, which had not been hitherto; he came as God incarnate, and was born in an ineffable way, while his mother preserved her virginity immaculate. Suffering neither confusion, nor mingling, nor alteration, he remained as he was, became what he was not, and assumed the aspect of a slave in truth, not in semblance, being like to us in every respect except in sin. Voluntarily he was born, voluntarily he suffered want, voluntarily he thirsted, voluntarily he endured, voluntarily he feared, voluntarily he died in truth and not in semblance. He experienced all natural and unfeigned human sufferings. After he had been crucified and had endured death without sin, he rose in his flesh, ascended into heaven without having seen corruption, and sat down at the right hand of the Father. And he shall come again in glory to judge the living and the dead. As he rose with his flesh, so he will descend."'

After this dogmatic exposition Vladimir is also given a piece of church history and a warning against the Latin Church. A number of minor ritual customs and external misunderstandings are given as mistakes of this church, but no matters of faith. It is also said that Rome was formerly on the right path.

> Moreover I confess one baptism through water and spirit, come to the pure sacraments and truly believe in the body and the blood. I accept the tradition of the church and revere the venerable icons, I revere the venerable wood of the cross and every cross, the holy relics and the holy vessels. I also believe in the seven councils of the holy fathers, the first of which was held in Nicaea with 318 fathers, who anathematized Arius and proclaimed the untainted and pure faith. The second council was in Constantinople with 150 holy fathers, who anathematized Macedonius, the denier of the Spirit, and proclaimed the Trinity in one substance. The third council was in Ephesus with 630 fathers against Nestorius, whom they anathematized and they proclaimed the holy Mother of God. The fourth council was in Chalcedon with 630 holy fathers against Eutyches and Dioskoros, and they anathematized the holy fathers and proclaimed our Lord Jesus Christ as perfect God and perfect man. The fifth council was in the imperial city with 165 holy fathers against the traditions of Origen and Evagrius; the holy fathers anathematized them. The sixth council was in the imperial city with 170 holy fathers against Sergius and Cyrus; the holy fathers anathematized them. The seventh council was in Nicaea with 350 holy fathers; they anathematized those who do not revere icons.

> Do not accept the doctrine of the Latins, for their doctrine is deformed. When they go into the church they do not revere

the icons by bowing but he reveres them standing, and when he has revered them he makes the sign of the cross on the ground and kisses it and when he has stood up he continues to stand on it; when he goes to lie down he kisses it, but when he has stood up he tramples it under foot. That is not what the apostles handed down. For the apostles handed down the kissing of an upright cross and they handed down the icons. For the evangelist Luke painted the first icon and sent it to Rome. As Basil says, an icon goes back to its original. Moreover they call the earth mother. But if the earth is their mother then the heaven is their father, for in the beginning God created heaven and earth. Thus one says: Our Father who art in heaven. Now if in their view the earth is the mother, why do you spit on your mother? First you kiss her and then you soil her.

The Romans did not use to do that, but they decided correctly at all the councils, when people came together from Rome and all the episcopal sees. For at the first council, which took place in Nicaea against Arius, Silvester from Rome sent bishops and priests, from Alexandria Athanasius and from the imperial city Metrophanes sent bishops. So they restored the faith. At the second council Damasus was present from Rome, Timotheos from Alexandria, Meletios from Antioch; Cyril from Jerusalem and Gregory the Theologian were also present. At the third council there were Celestinus from Rome, Cyril from Alexandria and Juvenal from Jerusalem. At the fourth council there was Leo from Rome, Anatolios from the imperial city and Juvenal from Jerusalem. At the fifth council there were Vigilius from Rome, Eutyches from the imperial city, Apollinarios from Alexandria and Domninos from Antioch. At the sixth council there were Agathon from Rome, Georgios from the imperial city, Theophanes from Antioch and the monk Peter from Alexandria. At the seventh council there were Adrian from Rome, Tarasios from the imperial city, Politianos from Alexandria, Theodoret from Antioch and Ilias from Jerusalem. And all these came with their bishops and restored the faith. But after this last council Peter the Stutterer went with others to Rome, took over the bishop's throne and corrupted the faith after turning away from the bishops' thrones of Jerusalem, Alexandria, the imperial city and Antioch. They brought the whole of Italy into confusion by disseminating their deviant teaching. Some priests who are married to one wife perform the worship but others perform the worship who have seven wives. Beware of their teaching. They forgive sins for gifts, which is worst of all. May God preserve you from them.

The warning against the Latin Church is an anachronism (the chronicle was written by the end of the eleventh century), for at the time of Vladimir's conversion a formal rupture between the Greek and the Roman Church had not yet taken place. The Russians did not reject Rome for reasons of dogma or church organization – these came later – but because of the dullness of the worship or as a result of political chance. The anti-Latin passage is a later addition to the account of the baptism. The charge of polygamy made against the Latin clergy in this passage refers to events from the time of the chronicler: the reforms of Pope Gregory VII in 1074 were directed against this, among other things. That also applies to the charge of simony. The strange accusation that the Latins practise a mother-earth cult is in fact a reference to a pagan Russian popular cult which still exists. The remarkable mention of a non-existent Peter the Stutterer probably goes back to a Greek nickname for the later successors of Peter in Rome. As a whole this primitive passage with its concern for secondary phenomena in the Latin Church contrasts strongly with the thoughtful account of the core of Christian belief which precedes it.

A multiple-choice option

The choice in favour of the Greek variant of Christianity had in the first instance already been made by princess Olga, who had adopted the Greek faith: 'and she was indeed the wisest of all people', the chronicle adds. But this choice was not yet final. Here the Russian monastic author withholds something that we know from a German episcopal author, Adalbert of Trier, namely that the 'queen of the Russians' (*regina Rugorum*) also tried to get in touch with king (and afterwards Roman emperor) Otto I of Germany, asking him for a bishop and missionaries.[17] Otto had sent Adalbert of Trier as a missionary bishop to Kiev, but on Adalbert's arrival there in 961 the Christian tide had already turned in favour of paganism through Olga's son Svjatoslav, and Adalbert returned without having anything to show for his pains. Some of his fellow missionaries had been killed on the way and he himself narrowly escaped death. In the Nestorian Chronicle there is a cryptic reference to this German episode with the answer to the 'Germans from Rome' that 'our fathers did not accept that either'.

Vladimir's choice in favour of the Greek Church settled the matter. It did not mean, however, that Vladimir had a hostile attitude towards the Latin Church. The German missionary bishop Bruno of Querfurt, arriving in Kiev fifty years after Adalbert on his way to the pagan Pecheneges, writes in a letter to King Henry II in the year 1008 how the 'Chief of the Russians' (*senior Ruzorum*) Vladimir is concerned for his safety among the Pecheneges (a Turkish tribe on the eastern border of the Kievan empire) and supports him in his missionary work.[18] At the time of Vladimir there was still a sense of the unity of the Christian world.

A colleague of Bruno, however, Bishop Thietmar of Merseburg, is considerably less friendly about Vladimir. In his chronicle from the year 1012 he gives a negative picture of the *rex Ruscorum Wlodemirus*, although this has nothing to do with ecclesiastical considerations, but only political ones.[19] Vladimir's marriage with Anna had caused bad blood in German court circles, for Otto II, himself married to the Byzantine princess Theofano, had intended that this same Anna Porphyrogenneta ('born in purple', i.e. of imperial descent) should become the wife of his son Otto III. That plan – according to Thietmar, Anna had already been betrothed to Otto II – was thwarted by Vladimir's marriage, which was an affront to the Germans. Thietmar calls Vladimir a *fornicatur immensus et crudelis*.

Probably there is some justification for attributing this reputation to Vladimir, for, also according to the Russian chronicle, before his conversion Vladimir was 'obsessed by lust' and, besides five wives, also had '300 concubines in Vyšgorod, 300 in Belgorod, 200 in Berestovo . . . and he was insatiable in that respect'.[20] But these fantastic details were perhaps added to make a contrast with Vladimir's pious conduct in life after his baptism: a hagiographic stylistic device, which occurs frequently.

Thietmar also has few good words for Vladimir and his empire. Instead of being delighted at Russia joining the Christian world, he gives a very unfavourable picture of the Russian ruler and his land, for which Christendom can only pray:

> He brought from Greece his consort, named Helena (the baptismal name of Anna) . . . At her urging he accepted the faith of holy Christianity, which faith he did not honour with works of righteousness. For he was an unbridled and cruel fornicator and did much violence to Greek women . . . The king's name incorrectly means 'power of peace', for what the godless do to one another and what the inhabitants of this world possess is not true peace.. The whole of Christianity must therefore pray that God will turn his judgment from these lands.

Despite this early negative judgment, there were actually still contacts between Russia and Europe, even after the schism between the Eastern and Western churches, and in a way that was not to occur again afterwards in Muscovite Russia: Vladimir's son Jaroslav the Wise and his children married partners who belonged to the Latin Church, partners from Swedish, German, Polish, Hungarian, Norwegian and French dynasties. His son and heir Vsevolod was the only one to marry a Byzantine princess from the Monomachos imperial dynasty, of whom the last great ruler of Kievan Russia, Vladimir Monomach, was born. He himself in turn married an English princess. These are far from major historical facts, but they are all symbols of a 'European' interrelatedness. After this, Russia disappears behind the European horizon for a period of three centuries.

Vladimir's baptism gained a historical significance far exceeding the pragmatic aspect of being a necessary condition for his marriage with princess Anna. It has become the decisive turning point in Russian history and therefore one of the turning points in the history of Europe. For what would present-day Europe have looked like, had the Russian ruler opted for Latin Christianity, or for Islam? Here one is inclined, or perhaps tempted, to lose oneself in historical speculations that may be useless, but, anyway not pointless. Vladimir's choice has been as determinative for the history of half of Europe as was the legitimization of Christianity by Constantine the Great for the whole history after him. Of course believers see the hand of God in universal history, which is also salvation history, but humanly speaking things might also have turned out otherwise.

The theoretical multiple-choice option for the Russian prince is known to us from the Russian narrative of the examination of the faiths, but we know from German and Arabic sources that the choices were also real historical options.

There was already an option for Rome as far as Olga was concerned. Had it actually opted for Rome, the Russian world would have participated in mediaeval Latin civilization, with its Renaissance and humanism, and Russia's political culture would have evolved together with that of the West. In that case present-day Europe would be far more politically and culturally united than is now the case. The only 'ideological' dividing line in present-day post-Communist Europe runs along the old religious line of the rupture between Orthodoxy and Catholicism.

That yet another choice, namely in favour of Islam, was at one time a historical possibility may be concluded from an eleventh-century Arabic source, the chronicler Marwazi. He relates that the belligerent Russians, having adopted Christianity, felt restricted in their marauding and waging of wars and therefore in their means of subsistence, whereas Islam offered the possibility of holy war.

Then they had a desire for Islam so that they would be allowed foray and holy war . . . Then they sent emissaries to the ruler of

Hwarizm, and these were four relatives of their grand prince Vladimir . . . Then the Hwarizm shah was glad that they had a desire for Islam. Then he sent somebody to them who instructed them in the law of Islam. Then they became Muslims.[21]

It is clear that Marwazi was too rash in interpreting the interest in Islam shown by the Russians as a conversion; furthermore he gives a wrong date for the earlier Russian adoption of Christianity. On the other hand, this Arabic source does provide unique confirmation outside the Nestorian Chronicle of the inquiry into the Islamic faith by a Russian delegation.

If Kievan Russia had indeed preferred Islam, a great Islamic power would have come into existence in Eastern Europe, and who knows what this power, in combination with an Ottoman ally, who was now beaten in Vienna, would not have been able to achieve? Applying a *reductio at absurdum* and mocking divine providence, one might say that, if the Russians had not been deterred by the ban in Islam on the use of alcohol, Christian history would have taken on a totally different aspect. But this kind of hypothetical rewriting of history may of course be applied at countless moments in history: if Clovis, king of the Franks, had not been converted, if Charles Martel had not beaten the Saracens, there would not have been a Frankish empire, nor a Holy German empire, nor a Christian Europe, etc., etc.

The only philosophical piece of wisdom to be derived from this gratuitous contemplation of history is an awareness of its fragility. There was no historical inevitability in the origin of a Christian Europe. And when pious historiographers detect the hand of providence in it, then cynics may point, if not to the drinking habits of the Russians, then to Vladimir's eagerness to marry as a decisive factor. If, however, the person of Anna Porphyrogenneta was the decisive factor, then she may rightly, in a theological sense, be regarded as a human instrument whereby God's plan in history is accomplished. God works only through people. And often through women, for princess Anna is not the only person through whom a royal husband and thereby a whole people came to adopt Christianity. The wife of King Clovis, Chrodichilde, also played a decisive role in the process of the conversion of her initially reluctant husband, as appears from Gregory of Tours' *History of the Franks*.[22] The formulation, 'The queen, however, did not stop preaching, so that he might get to know the true God', evokes the same picture as Thietmar of Merseburg's formulation with respect to Anna: 'And as a result of her persistence he adopted the faith of holy Christianity.' And the same is the case in the conversion of the English king Edwin, in which his wife Ethelburh played an important role, as is related at length by Bede in his *Ecclesiastical History of the English People*.[23]

Anna's role in the conversion of the Russians has been duly recognized by Russia's first national historiographer. Nikolaj Karamzin. He says of her: 'She was an instrument of divine grace, which drew Russia out of the darkness of idolatry'.[24] Before Anna, Olga had tried to do the same with her son Svjatoslav, though in that case without any result. So things may also go wrong! And that is the only other theological conclusion to be drawn from history, that God is playing a hazardous game in the conversion of humanity. Whole areas may be lost again for Christianity, which is what happened in the case of Asia Minor, the scene of the seven ecumenical councils and the theological cradle of the Christianity.

Christianity and civilization

Let us go back to the facts. After his wedding and baptism Vladimir went to Kiev, had the idols destroyed and ordered the entire population of the city to have themselves baptized in the river Dniepr. The conversion of the Russian people begins with a mass baptism.

> After this Vladimir took the emperor's sister and Anastasios and the priests of Korsun with the relics of St Clement and his disciple Phoebos; he also took the church vessels and icons for his blessing. He also built a church in Korsun on the hill which

people had thrown up in the middle of the city by stealing the sand, and the church stands there to this day. On his departure he also took two bronze idols and four bronze horses which also still stand behind the church of the holy Mother of God and which the ignorant think to be of marble. However, he returned Korsun to the Greeks as a dowry for the emperor's sister and he himself went to Kiev. When he arrived there he gave orders to cast afar the idols, to smash some and burn others. He ordered Perun to be bound to the tail of a horse and to be dragged from the hill over the Borichov to the stream and he appointed twelve men to strike him with rods. This was not because the wood would feel it, but to mock the devil, who had misled people through this image, because he got his reward from people. 'Great Thou art and marvellous are Thy works.' Yesterday he was still worshipped and today we are mocking him. When Perun had been dragged over the stream into the Dniepr, the unbelievers bewailed him, for they had not yet received holy baptism. And Vladimir set men there and said: 'If he washes up anywhere, then push him from the bank. And when he gets to the mouth of the river, then leave him.' They did what they were commanded. And when they let him go he drifted past the mouth of the river and the wind cast him on a sandbank, and since then tis place has been known as the Perun sandbank, as it is called to the present day.

After this, Vladimir sent messengers all through the city who proclaimed: 'If anyone does not come to the river tomorrow, be he rich or poor, beggar or workman, he will be an enemy to me.' When the people heard this they went with joy and rejoicing, saying: 'If this were not good, then our ruler and the boyars would not have accepted it.' The next morning, Vladimir went to the Dniepr with the priests of the emperor's sister and those from Korsun, and countless people were assembled there. They went down into the water and some stood in it up to their necks, others to their chests, the young ones near the bank up to their chests; some held tight to small children, and the adults waded further; and the priests said the prayers standing. And joy was visible in heaven and on earth because of so many saved souls. But the devil said with a groan: 'Woe is me! They have driven me from here. I had thought that I had found a dwelling place here, for here there was no apostolic teaching, there were no people who knew God, and I rejoiced over the service that they performed for me. But behold, I am already overcome by the ignorant and not by apostles or by martyrs. I shall never again rule in these lands.' After the people had been baptized they went to their homes. And Prince Vladimir himself rejoiced because he himself and his people had come to know God; he looked to heaven and said: 'Christ, God, who hast made heaven and earth, look upon these new people and let them, Lord, acknowledge Thee, the true God, as the Christian nations have acknowledged Thee. Confirm in them the true and unshakeable faith and help me, Lord, against the enemy who opposes us, so that I, trusting in Thee and Thy rule, may overcome his wiles.'

When he had said that, he commanded the people to make churches of wood and to put them in those places where the idols had formerly stood. And he put a church in honour of St Basil on the hill where the idol of Perun and others had stood and where the ruler and the people had offered sacrifices. And he began to erect churches in other cities and to appoint priests and bring people to baptism in all the towns and villages. He sent messengers and began to summon children from the families of the nobility to devote themselves to the study of books. But the mothers of these children wept for them, for they were not yet established in the faith, and they wept for them as though they were dead.

Thus the baptism was an order, but according to the account by the chronicler people did not feel it as compulsion since they accepted the command 'with joy and rejoicing'. The chronicle strongly emphasizes the joyful aspect or the event: 'Joy was visible in heaven and on earth because of so many saved souls.' Prince Vladimir himself also 'rejoiced because he himself and his people had come to know God'.

Vladimir's prayer to Christ is very significant: 'Look upon these new people and let them, Lord, acknowledge Thee, the true God, as the Christian nations have acknowledged Thee.' The mention of other 'Christian nations' shows that for the Russian ruler the Christianization of the land signified an entry into the contemporary civilized world.

And for the Russians Christianity indeed meant the beginning of civilization: they were given an alphabet, they learnt how to read and write, the art of painting, and architecture. These tasks are directly connected with founding churches and appointing priests. Thus the most direct consequence of the Christianization is the art of reading and writing, i.e. literature. The text talks of 'the study of books', not of holy books, although that may well be meant. Jaroslav the Wise, Vladimir's successor, was already a bibliophile, 'often reading day and night': he had a lot of books translated from the Greek and established a library in the Sophia Cathedral in Kiev.[25] In the chronicle this statement is followed by a eulogy on 'the great advantage of knowledge from books . . . which are rivers with which the world quenches its thirst, and sources of wisdom'. That is a notable statement, given that later the Russian experience of theology was not particularly focussed on study.

And the Russians learned quickly. Russian historians report with pride that when Jaroslav's daughter, Anna, married the French King Henry I in 1051, Anna was able to put her name under the marriage certificate in Cyrillic and in Latin letters, while the French king could only put a little cross.

The Slavonic script is very closely connected with the preaching of Christianity and therefore acquired an important position in Russia's national religious consciousness. Whereas Europe was already familiar with an alphabet in the pre-Christian period of the Roman Empire, the explicit combination of Christianization and literary civilization is a typical characteristic of the South- and East-Slavic peoples. The Bulgarians, Serbs and Russians/Ukrainians are particularly proud of their Cyrillic script, which they received with the Christian faith. This is indeed a fine national and religious fact, but, objectively, it has also to be stated that this combination of Christianization and literacy yielded little theological advantage for the Orthodox churches in those countries. The use of their own language made the Russian clergy as it were intellectually passive. With the exception of the translators and copyists of religious texts, Russian monks did not learn Greek. with the result that for centuries the whole of classical Greek literature remained inaccessible to Russia. And, eventually, even the Greek originals of the liturgical books became unintelligible to the Russians.

In nationalist circles of the present-day Russian Orthodox Church, Church Slavonic plays an important part in church conservatism. It has acquired an almost dogmatic status that stands in the way of any liturgical innovation. This attitude means that the present episcopal opponents of the use of modern Russian in liturgy in the Russian Orthodox Church are, theologically speaking, as narrow-minded as the Bavarian bishops in the ninth century in their resistance to the use of Slavonic in neighbouring Moravia.

The Slavonic script is connected with the work of the Greek missionaries Cyril and Methodius. The origin of the script created by them and the ensuing struggle over church language with Latin bishops is described in the *Life of Constantine the Philosopher* and the *Life of Methodius*.[26] These ninth-century Lives are the two oldest documents of Slav culture and at the same time two of the most interesting saints' lives from the early Middle Ages: no pious talk, no miracle stories, but informative biographies in a smooth style.

In 865 Constantine and his brother Methodius, who knew Slavonic from the Bulgarians in the neighbourhood of their native town of Thessaloniki, were sent by the Byzantine emperor to Greater Moravia at the invitation of the ruler of the this Western Slav empire, Rostislav. Shortly before, Rostislav had been converted to Christianity by Latin missionaries, but he was looking for priests who might instruct the people in the faith in understandable language. (Quite recently, in 1994, Rostislav was canonized for this by the Czech Orthodox Church.)

Cyril designed the so-called Glagolitic script, and the two

brothers translated the New Testament and the liturgical books into Slavonic. They provoked the hostility of the Latin clergy who were also active in that field, and Cyril and Methodius decided to go to Rome to ask official approval from the Pope for their work. In the Life of Constantine we read how on the way, in Venice, Cyril defended the use of Slavonic to Latin clergy. The latter objected that the apostles and the church fathers did not know any Slavonic, and, furthermore, that only the use of Hebrew, Greek and Latin was justified, because Pilate had had an inscription written on the cross in these three languages: this was the doctrine of the three languages. Cyril answered with the democratic argument that all nations are equal ('Does not the rain from God come equally upon all, does not the sun shine for all nations?'); with the historical argument that a great many other nations were already celebrating the liturgy in their own language (Armenians, Georgians, Persians, Syrians, Egyptians, Goths); and with the theological argument that one should understand what one is praying ('praying with the mind'). In Rome the two Greeks gained the approval of Pope Hadrian II, who laid the Slavonic books solemnly on the altar in the main Roman churches, and consecrated Methodius the first bishop of the Slavs. Ten years later, in 880, John VIII reconfirmed the right to celebrate the Byzantine liturgy in *litteras Sclaviniscas* in a letter to the Moravian prince Sventopulk and defended Methodius against the slanders of German-Frankish clergy.[27]

The work of Cyril and Methodius in Moravia and the struggle over religious language are also mentioned in the Russian Chronicle.[28]

When the Pope at Rome heard of this [the doctrine of three languages], he rebuked those who murmured against the Slavonic books, saying, 'Let the word of the Scripture be fulfilled that "all nations shall praise God" and likewise "Let all nations declare the majesty of God according as the Holy Spirit shall grant them to speak". Whoever condemns the Slavonic writing shall be excluded from the church until he mend his ways. For such men are not sheep but wolves.'[29]

Unfortunately, the bishops of Passau and Salzburg, who wished to lead Moravia back into their own sphere of influence, were to turn a deaf ear to this papal approval of Slavonic and won Stephen V, John VIII's successor, over to their side. After Methodius' death in 885, when the theological dispute between Rome and Constantinople over the question of the *filioque* was at its height, Stephen V banned Slavonic as a liturgical language.[30] This was a tragic reversal of the situation, which encouraged the later distancing of the Orthodox Slav peoples from the rest of Europe.

Methodius' disciples fled to Bulgaria, which was a great empire on the Balkans at the time and had gone over to Greek Christianity fifteen years before. There the Slavonic script was further developed into its present form: the laborious Glagoitic letters of Constantine/Cyril were replaced by the 'Cyrillic' alphabet based on Greek, and in this form Slavonic replaced Greek as the liturgical language in Bulgaria. However, this process met with opposition from the Greek bishops, who were therefore as narrow-minded as the Latin bishops in matter of church power.

The church in Central Europe was an element in the struggle over the spheres of influence between the Byzantine empire and the Frankish empire, a struggle which was fought out in the newly converted Slavonic territories of the Czechs and the Bulgarians. The allegiance of the two nations to the Byzantine or Latin rite was determined by political factors. In the 860s both the Moravian ruler Rostislav and the Bulgarian ruler Boris steered a middle course between Rome and Constantinople in their attempts to gain as much church autonomy as possible. A century later we see a similar weighing of pros and cons between East and West in Kievan Russia, when princess Olga, having been received into the Greek Church, still turned to the German king. In short, it was a close thing in Eastern Europe in the ninth and tenth centuries.

Be that as it may, Cyril and Methodius are the last common saints of the Catholic and Orthodox churches. They also managed to preserve church unity in their missionary activities: although sent by the emperor of Constantinople. they asked the pope of Rome's approval for their translation work. In 1985, in his encyclical *Slavorum Apostoli,* Pope John Paul II proclaimed Cyril and Methodius patrons of Europe and bridge-builders between East and West, thereby making good the wrong which had been done to the two Greeks from the side of Rome 1100 years previously, if not its consequences.

To return to Kievan Russia. In 988, as has been said, as a result of their Christianization the Russians felt accepted among 'the Christian nations'. And not only that. The Nestorian Chronicle ends the conversion narrative with a theological interpretation of history: as a result of its Christianization Russia was admitted not only to the civilized world but also to God's plan of salvation. The Chronicle gives the conversion of Russia a biblical conclusion.

> When they were assigned for study, there was fulfilled in the land of Rus' the prophecy which says: 'In those days the deaf shall hear the words of the Scripture, and the voice of the stammerers shall be made plain.' For these persons had not heard the words of scripture before this, but by divine providence and through his mercy the Lord took pity upon them, as the prophet said: 'I will be gracious to whom I will be gracious.' For he had mercy upon us in the baptism of rebirth and the renewal of the spirit, following the will of God and not according to our deeds. Blessed the Lord Jesus Christ, who has loved his new people, the land of Rus', and illumined them with holy baptism.

Not according to our deeds! It is true that accepting Christianity was Russia's own choice, but from the perspective of faith in the end it was God's own initiative. Here Russia's self-conversion is given an explanation which puts it in the right theological context. This removes the semblance of religious self-achievement. And the conversion narrative indeed ends with a eulogy on 'the Lord Jesus Christ, who has loved his new people, the land of Rus'.'

God has acquired a new people, the Russians have been admitted by God to his plan of salvation: this thought became the basis of the Russian religious consciousness, developed in the eleventh century. Trivial though the occasion for Russia's Christianization may be from an empirical-historical point of view, there is grandeur in the divine goal achieved by it.

Amidst all the stylistic embellishment of the Christianization of Russia in the Nestorian Chronicle, one thing is certain, and constitutes the specific characteristic of the transition of Russia to Christianity. That is the fact that the Christianization was not the result of the conquest of Russian territory by a foreign political power, or of the subjugation of other Christian peoples by Russia itself. Nor did it result directly from missionary activities of the Christian church. Even Byzantium does not claim the honour of the conversion of its northern neighbour.

The Greek silence

It is striking that contemporary Byzantine chronicles are silent about Vladimir's conversion and his marrying Anna. They do mention the military aid given by the Russians to the Byzantine emperor. They probably felt embarrassed by the marriage of an imperial princess to one who in the eyes of Byzantium had until now been the commander of a barbarian army. Or by the fact that Anna was, against her will, used in exchange for six thousand Russian warriors.

So this decisive moment in Orthodox church history, about which the Greeks should have been very glad, is suppressed in the Greek sources. Glad, not only because of religious considerations, but also because of political ones. For the land of the Russians had been a military threat to Constantinople for 130 years. The earliest Greek mention of the Russians dates from 860 when, together with Vikings, they launched a surprise attack on Constantinople on 200 boats. Patriarch Photios devoted two sermons to this event, which made a traumatic impression on the Byzantines. One was delivered during the attack of 'the savage and wild tribe from the north' and one after the miraculous deliverance of the city by Mary, the Mother of God. In the sermons Photios gives a graphic description of the terrible manner in which the Russians raised hell in the city and of the great humiliation of the Byzantines at the hands of 'that obscure and insignificant people which was even unknown until their raid on our city'.[31] Constantinople was saved because the population carried the garment of the Mother of God, an important relic of the city, in procession along the whole length of the city walls.[32] Six years later Photios writes in an encyclical letter to the other Eastern patriarchs that 'a nation which used to surpass all in cruelty and which is called *to Rhos* (the Rus')' has asked for a bishop and has accepted the Christian religion.[33] This report does not provide any other clear information. Possibly it relates to a Russian settlement along the north-east coast of the Black Sea, or near Cherson in the Crimea, where Cyril and Methodius had preached some years before.

The Russians must indeed have made a fearful impression on the civilized Byzantines with their refined court culture. And not only on them, but also on the Arabs. In the Arabic sources quoted above it is frequently stressed how belligerent and fearless the Russians are. From an other Arabic document, the travel account of Ibn Fadlan, who went to the Kievan empire and the Volga area in 922, a world emerges 'which belongs to a barbarian age and towers up into the world of the Byzantine and Arab culture of the age of the emperors and caliphs like an erratic block from sunken periods of human history'.[34] And it is therefore understandable that the Byzantines did not like to be reminded of 'how the Russians became Christians or that the princeling of this people was given an imperial princess, truly born to the purple, as consort'.

What a difference from a century later, when the German chronicler Adam of Bremen speaks of the capital *Chue* (Kiev) of the then Christian *Ruzzia* as 'the rival of the sceptre-city Constantinople, the finest ornament of Greece'.[35] And how could the Byzantines ever imagine Russia at one time becoming the protector of Orthodoxy after the downfall of their own powerful Byzantine empire?

But things had not yet got that far. For the time being, Byzantium was silent about traces of Christianity in the land of

Russia. Nor does Emperor Constantine VII Porphyrogennetos, who in his *De Administrando Imperio* devotes a chapter to the *Rhos* and *Rhosia,* with the capital *Kioaba* (Kiev), mention that there were any Christians, although there in fact were, as appears from the account in the Russian chronicle of the commercial treaty with Byzantium in 945.[36]

The silence of the Byzantine sources about Russian progress on the Christian path is certainly most striking in the case of the prominent convert princess Olga. It is all the more striking, because her state visit to Constantinople in 957 is elaborately described in the journal of Emperor Constantine VII, *De Cerimoniis Aulae Byzantinae.*[37] Olga was already a Christian then, for it is said of the *archontissa Rhosias* in the emperor's account that there was a Greek priest among her attendants. And the fact that such personal privileges were accorded to her at the imperial court, which would be unthinkable in the case of a non-Christian ruler, also illustrates that Byzantium maintained a special relationship with her.[38] Perhaps Olga was even baptized on the occasion of that visit. This, at any rate, is what is maintained in the Nestorian Chronicle, which also says that the emperor acted as godfather on that occasion.[39] Then, however, the Russian chronicler's imagination loses touch with reality, when he adds that the emperor 'on seeing her extraordinarily pretty face and her good sense' wanted to marry her. The emperor was already married and his wife was present at the reception of Olga.

All in all, it remains strange that definitive adherence to the Greek church of the land of the Russians under Vladimir and the political peace with the old enemy from the North is known to us only from Russian, German, Arabic and Armenian sources. For that matter, Byzantine silence about the supreme moment of Russian church history did not prevent Kiev from becoming a metropolitan see of Constantinople, and for centuries the head of the Russian church was to be a Greek. The first official mention of the Russian church in Greek documents dates from 1039: a list of metropolises of the patriarchate of Constantinople mentions *Rhosia* as the sixty-second metropolis.[40]

But relations between the land of the Russians and Byzantium never became idyllic. Once more, in 1043, the Russians and the Greeks fought one another in a cruel war which the Russians lost. The Byzantine Michael Psellos, who describes the war in his *Chronographia,* trots out old Greek clichés with reference to the Russians, 'that barbaric nation', consistently using the adjective *barbaros* for 'Russian'.[41] Of course it primarily means 'foreign', but the connotation of 'cruel' will not have been alien to the Greeks, in view of former military confrontations with their northern neighbours. Actually, the qualification is a perverse one, since the Byzantines were no less barbaric towards their fellow-believers: great numbers of the defeated Russians had their right hands cut off and eight hundred prisoners had their eyes gouged out.[42]

This development, however, does not detract from the fact that the new church province of the patriarchate of Constantinople was neither a colony nor a missionary province of Byzantium. This preserves the specific character of Russia's adoption of Christianity: it was based on the country's own decision and, at least in retrospect, was theologically well-considered. This fact has become an essential part of the Russian religious self-consciousness. Centuries later, this self-consciousness would be elaborated into a national ideology, in the time of building of the Russian state by the Moscow rulers and, still later, in the nineteenth century by Slavophiles and Panslavists. In Kiev, however, there was no question of any ideological exploitation of its conversion story. On the contrary, the new religious sense of identity was the source of a feeling of being a part of universal Christianity, of being the last among the workers called to labour in the Christian vineyard and yet of being equal to the others. This awareness will become explicit in that other classical document of the Christianization of Russia, the *Oration on the Law and the Grace* by Ilarion, metropolitan of Kiev.

2

A Moment of Christian Unity
in Europe

Although Kievan Russia had opted for Greek Christianity, it did have links with the other Christian lands in Europe. Only about fifty years after the introduction of Christianity in Kiev, there was a split in the world church, the schism of 1054. At that time Christianity was divided by church-political rivalry between Rome and Constantinople into a Latin Catholic and a Greek Orthodox Church. However, in the old Russia the division was not immediately perceptible, and certainly not absolute. Only one hundred and fifty years later, after the plundering of Constantinople by Western Crusaders, did the division psychologically become a reality in the minds of the population. And in Russia it was to be even later, in the rising Muscovite empire, that the schism became politically and ideologically final. But in the eleventh century that was not yet the case, and both the Orthodox and the Catholics in both present-day Ukraine and in Russia could derive their origin from the church of Kiev. Moreover in the eleventh century the two territories which later developed, Russia and Ukraine, still formed a political unity under the common name 'the Russian land' (*russkaja zemlja*) or the land of *Rus'*.

Metropolitan Ilarion of Kiev can be considered a symbol of Christian unity in Kievan Russia. He was the last head of the church in Kiev before the schism between the East and the West and as a Russian bishop of the still undivided world church he has a special place in church history.

Ilarion of Kiev holds this special place not only because of his accidental position on the eve of the church schism of 1054; he has also earned it with the legacy of a unique theological work: The Oration (or Sermon) on the Law and the Grace (*Slovo o Zakone i Blagodati*). In retrospect, this work gained an added significance as a result of its being situated on the eve of the loss of church unity in Europe.

Ilarion of Kiev

Little is known about Ilarion's life. He was an erudite monk, priest at the Apostles' Church in the residence of the Kievan grand prince Jaroslav the Wise, and he was head of the church in Rus' from 1051 to 1054. He was the first metropolitan of Russian descent after some Greek predecessors, and was elected to that function by the Russian bishops on Jaroslav's recommendation.[43] Whether Jaroslav was prompted in this by an aspiration to church independence from the patriarch of Constantinople is a point of controversy among historians, and is in any case not clear from the chronicles. It is certainly a fact that after Jaroslav's death another Greek was appointed head of the Russian church, and this was to remain the case, with only one exception, until the fourteenth century. If the Kievan prince was at all prompted by anti-Byzantine political motives then he was certainly not opposed to the ecclesiastical cultural influence from Byzantium, since Jaroslav's art-and-culture policy was aimed at promoting this influence. Ilarion, too, was well versed in Greek patristics and Byzantine rhetoric, and in his Oration he explicitly praises 'the devout Greek land, its love of Christ and strong faith'.

The *Slovo* was pronounced by Ilarion a few years before he became metropolitan, in the Church of the Mother of God, which contained the tomb of prince Vladimir, or possibly in the newly completed Sophia Cathedral in Kiev. Given the fundamental theme, it must have been pronounced on a solemn occasion or feast, perhaps on the anniversary of Vladimir's death. It took place, as appears from the text, in the presence of the royal family and the other elite of the city, for Ilarion calls his audience 'not the ignorant, but those who have feasted to fulfilment on the sweetness of books'. In any case it is the second generation of Russian Christians, and the first which may have received coherent religious instruction.

Next to the Chronicle *Povest' vremennych let* (The Narrative of Bygone Years), about the investigation of the faiths and the baptism of Vladimir, Ilarion's Oration is the second 'charter' of the Christianization of the Russian people. Both documents are an original Russian development of the Byzantine heritage. Just as the *Povest'* is a creative adaptation of Byzantine historiography, so the *Slovo* is a quite distinctive continuation of Byzantine homiletics; and while the Chronicle strikes one through its naive beauty, the aesthetic value of Ilarion's Oration lies in a well-considered application of a range of rhetorical figures of speech: antitheses, metaphors, anaphorae (repetitions of the same words at the beginning of successive sentences), syntactic parallelisms and rhythmic sentence dynamics.

As the showpiece of Old Russian literature, Ilarion's Oration is well-known to every Slavist, but unknown among theologians and church historians in the West. And that is a pity, for it contains an important theological message. The author fills the Chronicle with it. Whereas the Chronicle narrative is a historical or historicizing description of the Christianization of the Russian land, the Oration is a salvation-historical account of it. It is an evocative expression of the religious self-awareness of the newly converted Russians. The theological arguments and the more than one hundred Bible quotations are aimed at defining the position of the Russian nation in the whole history of redemption. The relation between Christian universalism and Russian religious self-awareness is the underlying idea of the exposition. So, contrary to what the title leads one to expect, the Oration is not a theological treatise on justification through grace in the Pauline sense, but a religious-historical exposition of the expansion of Christianity.

The Oration is generally considered as a plea for the canonization of prince Vladimir. This is highly probable, but the significance of the Oration goes beyond this practical intention of

Ilarion. Just as important, and indeed more important in terms of intellectual history, is the theme of the universalistic context within which the young Russian church is placed. That is what I want to make clear in my interpretation. What makes the Oration theologically unique in Russian history is the balance between an awareness of Christian 'ecumenicity', in the original sense of *oikumene,* and Russian religious-patriotic self-awareness. After Ilarion there was no other church leader in Russia/Ukraine with the same sense of involvement in the world church.

It is in this spirit that I see the symbolic significance of the Oration for church unity in Europe. For all the attention paid to the distinctive place of Russia in the history of Christianization, the Russian church confesses its links with the rest of the Christian world. There is not yet anything in the nature of an East-West antithesis, of papal 'imperialism' towards Russia, and of the false mystique of 'Holy Russia' with its feeling of religious superiority over against the West.

In a political sense, too, this short period of church unity in the eleventh century coincides with a close connection between the old Russia and the rest of Europe which was to remain unique in history. I am referring to the marriages of Jaroslav himself and six of his sons and daughters with Western princely families. With a feeling for drama, for a short period of time Europe can be called one political family. Not until the thirteenth century, with Aleksandr Nevskij and the struggle against the German Order of Knights, would Russia and the rest of Europe for the first time find themselves in opposite church and ideological camps. In that century, too, the ecclesiastical rupture between Orthodoxy and Catholicism becomes reality, the last chances of unity being thrown away with the Western plundering of the capital of Orthodoxy, Constantinople, and the formation of the Latin empire.

We can look back upon the eleventh and twelfth centuries as Europe's innocent childhood. Russia and Europe shared a religious and cultural unity, even though people were not always aware of that unity. Dwelling on this period is not a matter of

nostalgic historiography, but may stimulate the awareness that
ecclesiastical separation in Europe is not something that was pre-
conditioned from the beginning, and therefore does not have to
be permanent. Ilarion of Kiev can be a guide in the search for a
restoration of the unity.

The universality of Christendom

The subject and structure of the Oration are indicated in the
extensive superscription to the text.[44]

– On the law that was given by Moses and the grace and the
truth which have come from Jesus Christ;
– and how the law passed by, but grace and truth filled the
whole earth and faith spread among all nations and also among
our Russian nation;
– and a eulogy on our King Vladimir by whom we were baptized;
– and a prayer to God from all our land.

The first two parts form a structural whole. The first part deals
with the theme – which already occurs in Paul's letter to the
Galatians and is often repeated in patristics – of a comparison of
the Old and the New Testament, the replacement of the Jewish
law with the Gospel of Christ. So here Ilarion is part of a long
exegetical tradition, but he elaborates upon the subject in an
original manner, using all the means of rhetoric. In doing so,
Ilarion shows that he does not just repeat tradition, but makes it
come alive again. The second part contains the core of the
argument: the Russian land joining the Christian world. The
third part is the most extensive in size and describes the special
way in which the Russian nation came to embrace Christianity
through prince Vladimir. The final part, the prayer, is steeped in
Christian humility, which, theologically speaking, compensates
for the religious confidence strongly emphasized in the preceding
part.

The first two parts belong to the genre of the homily, a sermon
based on Bible texts. The final parts, the eulogy (*pochvala*, the

Greek genre of the encomium) and the prayer, may originally have been separate works which were added to the homily by Ilarion later on. Thematically and structurally, the constituent parts link up with each other and in terms of the composition form a harmonious whole.

The theme of the Oration is the history of salvation: God's revelation to humankind. The revelation passes from Israel to the whole of humankind and is then narrowed down to the Russian nation. It is a thematic triptych: on the left Israel, in the middle humankind, and on the right Rus'.

The first sentence indicates the unity of Jews and Christians: God is called upon as 'God of Israel and God of the Christians', but this is immediately followed by a contrast between the 'tribe of Abraham which is justified by the Law' and 'all nations which are redeemed by the Son'. This antithesis is indicated theologically as that between the law and grace, which relate to each other as 'the shadow to the truth'. Ilarion works out the antithesis in greater detail, metaphorically, in the comparison between Hagar and Sarah, the slave girl and the free woman, Ishmael and Isaac. They symbolize the destiny of the Jews and the Christians, who eventually confront each other in the church of Jerusalem in the dispute over circumcision and baptism. That is where the separation takes place, and here Ilarion adopts an anti-Jewish tone: the Jews were cast out and dispersed among the nations, while the Christians became God's heirs.

Then the universal phase in the history of salvation begins, in which the law is followed by grace 'as moonlight by sunlight'. The bondage of the law is replaced by the freedom of grace, the justification of one people by the redemption 'which stretches to all the corners of the earth'. Ilarion conveys the message of the geographical universality of salvation by the frequent use, more than forty times, of the following expressions – in Bible quotations or otherwise: the whole earth, the ends of the earth, the corners of the earth, the whole of creation, the whole world, humankind, all nations, new nations, every nation, East and West, all tribes and languages, all flesh, every knee, the kings, princes and judges of the earth, men and women, young and old.

Through this accumulation of synonyms Ilarion bears unequivo-
cal witness to his faith in the universality of redemption, of
Christendom.

The reverse side of emphasizing the universality of salvation is,
in Ilarion's view, the theological rejection of Judaism, which continues to keep to the law. The Oration contains harsh statements
about the Jews, who rejected Christ, whereas he had also come
for them, as Ilarion shows by means of Bible quotations from
Matt. 15.24 ('to save the lost sheep of the house of Israel'), Matt.
5.17 ('not to abolish the law but to fulfil it'), and Matt. 23.37 ('O
Jerusalem, Jerusalem, that murders the prophets sent to you').

What we have here is a theological anti-Judaism. Anyone who
thinks that here we have the roots of the Russian antisemitism of
a later date is wrong. This theological attitude was already
adopted by the church fathers, and one cannot disqualify Ilarion
theologically for this reason, any more than one can reject John
Chrysostom as a church father for his anti-Jewish remarks. In the
eleventh century – and for centuries afterwards – the whole of
Christianity shared Ilarion's view about the Jews. Moreover in
Ilarion's time there was still no actual antisemitism in Kiev,
despite the presence of a Khazar-Jewish colony in the city.[45]

Still, according to Georgi Fedotov there is a specific explanation for the Russian preoccupation with the Jews. In contrast to
the abstract, logical thinking in theology among the Greeks, the
Russian approach to theology is chiefly of a concrete historical
kind. People in ancient Russia, however, had only a slight
historical knowledge of the past: they lacked the classical Greek-
Roman heritage in this respect and were familiar only with the
sacred history of the Old Testament. That is why the Russian
church in its theological-historical self-image immediately finds
itself in a confrontation with Judaism.[46] It is also significant that
one of the very few non-Christian works from antiquity to be
translated into Russian, and as early as the middle of the eleventh
century,was Flavius Josephus' *The Jewish War*.

Be this as it may, for us modern readers, the unfriendliness
towards the Jews in the *Slovo* remains a serious theological false
note in an otherwise joyful theological exposition. For that is the

principal tone in Ilarion's Oration: joy in the redemption of the whole world and great joy at the participation of the Russian land in it. Thus we arrive at the point where Ilarion makes the Russian nation enter the history of salvation. He does so after mentioning Christ's command to the apostles, 'Go forth and instruct all nations', and the imagery of new wine (the gospel) which one should not pour into old bottles (the Jewish law).

(34.6–36.23)

And so it is. The grace of faith has spread over all the earth: and it has reached our nation of Rus'. The lake of the law dried up, but the stream from the gospel swelled and flowed over all the earth. And the stream flowed to us: for behold how we too, with all Christians, glorify the Holy Trinity, while Judaea is silent. Christ is glorified, and the Jews are vilified. The nations are gathered, and the Jews are scattered. As the prophet Malachi pronounced: 'I have no pleasure in the sons of Israel, and I will not accept a sacrifice at their hands. For from the east even to the west my name is glorified among the Gentiles, and in every place incense is offered to my name, for my name is great among the Gentiles.' And according to David: 'All the earth shall worship Thee, and sing unto Thee'; and: 'Lord, our Lord, how wonderful is Thy name in all the earth.'

Now we are called Christians, no longer idolaters; no longer the hopeless, but longing with hope for eternal life. No longer do we build pagan shrines, for now we construct Christ's churches. No longer do we slay one another as offerings for demons, for now Christ is ever slain and segmented for us as an offering to God and the Father. No longer do we imbibe the blood of the offering and perish, for now we are saved by drinking the pure blood of Christ.

We were saved by will of the Lord, who extended his mercy to all the nations, and thus he did not neglect us, as he brought us to the knowledge of the truth. We were thirsty: when our land was parched and desolate, when the sweltering heat of idolatry had dried it up, then suddenly the stream of the gospel flowed and slaked the thirst of all our land. As Isaiah foretold:

'Water shall burst forth for those that walk in the wilderness, and the waterless land shall become pools, and a stream shall spring in a thirsty land.'

We were blind: not knowing the true light, we strayed in the false light of idolatry. And we were deaf: deaf to the teaching of salvation. Yet God had mercy upon us, and the light of understanding shone upon us, that we might know him. As was foretold in the prophecy: 'Then shall the eyes of the blind be opened, and the ears of the deaf shall hear.'

We were lame: we stumbled in snares of perdition, pursuing the demons, not knowing the pathway to life. And we stuttered: our tongues stammered prayers to the idols and not to our God and Creator. Yet God's love for mankind came upon us: we chase after demons no longer, but plainly and clearly we glorify Christ our God. As is foretold in the prophecy: 'Then shall the lame man leap as an hart, and the tongue of the stammerers shall speak plainly.'

We were as the beasts and as the cattle, not knowing our right hand or our left hand, caring only for the things which are on earth, not caring at all for the things which are in heaven. But then God sent his commandments to us, which lead to life eternal. As Hosea foretold: 'And it shall come to pass in that day, says the Lord, that I will make for them a covenant with the birds of the air and with the beasts of the earth, and I will say to that which was not my people, "You are my people," and they shall say to me, "You are the Lord our God."'

And so we who were aliens will be called God's people, and we who had been enemies will be called his sons. And we do not mock in the way of the Jews but praise in the way of the Christians; we do not take counsel to crucify him, but we worship him as the crucified; we do not crucify the Redeemer but stretch out our hands to him; we do not pierce his side but drink from it as from the source of incorruption; we do not take thirty pieces of silver for him, but give one another and all our life to him; we do not hide the resurrection, but proclaim it in all our houses: Christ is risen from the dead! We do not say that he has been stolen, but that he is risen to where he was before; we are not unbelieving, but like Peter we say to him, 'You are Christ, the son of the living God,' and with Thomas, 'You are our Lord and God', and with the robber, 'Remember us, Lord, when you come into your kingdom.' And thus, believing in him and maintaining the tradition of the seven councils of the holy fathers, we pray to God constantly to urge us on and to lead us to the way of his commandments.

Ilarion puts the entry of his nation into the history of salvation within the context of the calling of the heathen, of the other nations. 'We, too', 'us, too' are typical turns of phrase with Ilarion. The Russians join as it were the other nations that have been called. The fulfilment of biblical prophecies about the heathen also applies to the Russian nation. And the contrast between pagan Russia and converted Russia, which Ilarion expresses in a whole series of antitheses, is the general contrast between heathen and Christians. The we-figure that Ilarion uses here goes beyond his audience to all Christians, with whom the Russians are now united, and before that applies to all pagan nations, to which the Russians belonged before their conversion. In this passage about the conversion of the Russian nation the adjective 'Russian' is only used once, in the first sentence. The contrast is therefore not between Russians and Jews, but between pagans and Jews and between Christians and Jews.

By way of concluding the passage quoted, Ilarion again evokes his biblical vision of the conversion of all nations by means of fifteen Bible quotations in succession (36.25–38.2). In doing so, he speaks about the fulfilment over 'us, the nations' (*nas jazycech*), in which the word for nation has the connotation of 'pagans'.[47] These are mainly quotations from the Psalms about the radiance of God's glory and a eulogy from the whole earth to God. It is a jubilant, cosmopolitan conclusion to this part of the Oration.

According to Ludolf Müller, this collection of texts from the Old Testament about the calling of the nations was perhaps compiled by Ilarion as an independent theological treatise which also existed apart from the Oration.[48] He thinks that putting the Bible quotations here in the Oration disturbs the balance of the composition, as it is a repetition, and the quotations would have better suited Ilarion's earlier pronouncements on the universality of salvation. Perhaps, however, we should conclude that Ilarion could not emphasize the universality of Christian redemption too strongly, and this was why he inserted this kind of Bible quotation before *and* after the passage about Russia's participation in the divine scheme of redemption, although in doing so he slightly spoils his own carefully planned structure.

Apart from the frequent use of collective nouns like 'nations', 'lands', 'the whole earth', Ilarion expresses his ecumenicity by using the terms 'Christians' and 'Christian'. The passage quoted says: 'We, too, now, with all Christians' (here, moreover, again using the phrase 'we, too'), and 'now we are called Christians'. Before that, he had already spoken of 'the Christian faith', 'the Christian church', and 'redemption of the Christians'. Ilarion calls himself and his audience 'Christian'. This is highly significant within the Russian context, because later on in Russian church history the confessional designation becomes 'Orthodox' (*pravoslavnyj*). 'Orthodox' then becomes identical with 'Christian', outside which it is no longer possible to imagine any Christianity. There is still nothing in the nature of such an identification of one's own partial church with Christianity in Kievan Russia, where there is still the awareness of being connected with 'all Christian lands', including 'the Roman land', as we shall see.

It is remarkable that later on in Russia and other Orthodox countries there is never talk of 'Christian Europe'. Then Christianity in these countries has been narrowed down to a characteristic of national (Russian, Bulgarian or Greek) identity. Then Russia has already for a long time replaced Ilarion's idea that Russia, through its conversion, joins 'the other Christian nations' with the notion of being the only true Christian land; the idea of 'we, too' by that of 'only we', or 'we, most of all'.

National elaboration

After his convincing profession of faith in the universalism of Christianity, Ilarion can proceed to the 'national' part of his Oration, without becoming open to accusations of nationalism. His nationalistic elaboration of the conversion of the nations is a particularization of the general part; Russian Christianity is a concretization of world Christianity.

The eulogy concerns the one who brings Christianity to Rus': 'King Vladimir'.[49] This part of the *Slovo* often occurs independently in the manuscripts, and is then given a disproportionately patriotic accent. However patriotic Ilarion may become here, though, we have to see this against the background of the preceding part. In the eulogy itself, however, Ilarion never loses sight of the universal context of Christianity. Here, too, he takes as his starting point the idea of putting the Russian nation on a par with the other Christian nations. He starts his eulogy by once more singing the praises of the ecumenicity of the world church in a splendid opening sentence. I shall now first give part of the text before discussing some aspects of it more closely.

(38.3–40.28)
The Roman land, with the voices of praise, praises Peter and Paul, for through Peter and Paul it came to believe in Jesus Christ, Son of God. Asia and Ephesus and Patmos praise John the Theologian. India praises Thomas, Egypt praises Mark: every land and every city and every nation honours and glorifies its teacher that taught it the Orthodox faith. Let us, too, therefore, praise to the best of our strength, with our humble praises, him whose deeds were wondrous and great, our teacher and guide, the great king of our land, Vladimir, the grandson of Igor of old, and the son of the glorious Svjatoslav, who in their years when they ruled with courage and bravery were known in many lands, and who through their conquests and power are still held in glorious memory today. For they did not rule in a small and unknown land, but in the Russian land, which is known and heard of to all the ends of the earth.

Glorious by birth from glorious ancestors, noble through noble ancestors, our king Vladimir grew up and became strong from his childhood on; indeed truly he became a man through strength, increased in might, was pre-eminent in bravery and understanding, became sole ruler of his land and subjected to himself surrounding lands, some through peace but the disobedient by the sword.

And when he thus lived in his days and preserved his land through truth, bravery and understanding, the visitation of the Most High came upon him, and the eye of the good God who has mercy upon all looked down upon him, and the light of understanding began to shine in his heart, so that he understood the vanity of the seduction of idolatry and began to seek the one God who has created all things visible and invisible. And there was more: for he often would hear about the devout land of the Greeks, their love for Christ, and the strength of their faith: how they honour and revere the one God in three Persons; how mighty are the works and the wonders and signs that are worked among them; how their churches are filled with people; how devout are their cities and villages; how, zealous in prayer, all stand before God. When he had heard all this, his soul was enkindled, and he desired in his heart that both he and his land should be Christian. And so it was: God deigned it so, in the love he bears mankind.

So our king cast off his clothing; and with his clothing he cast off the old corruption and shook off the dust of disbelief; and he entered the font of holy baptism and was born of the spirit and of the water. Then, baptized into Christ, in Christ he clothed himself, and he departed the font in the image of whiteness, a son of incorruption, a son of the resurrection. Now he was named the eternal name of Vasilij, a name which is famed from generation to generation. By this name he was written into the book of life, in the heavenly and eternal city of Jerusalem.[50]

But even when this had been done, he was not yet finished with his deeds of devotion; not only in this did he show all the love for the Lord that was in him. He achieved even more: he commanded throughout all his land that his people be baptized in the name of the Father and of the Son and of the Holy Spirit, and that the Holy Trinity be glorified loudly and clearly in all the cities, and that all should become Christians – the small and the great, the bond and the free, the young and the old, the high and the humble, the rich and the poor. And not one single person resisted this pious command. And if some were not baptized for love, then they were baptized in fear of him who had given the command, since his piety was coupled with power. And at one and the same time all our land began to glorify Christ with the Father and with the Holy Spirit.

Then the darkness of our idolatry began to clear, and the first rays of true piety dawned. The darkness of demonolatry dimmed, and the sunlight of the gospel illumined our land: pagan shrines were torn down, and churches set up; the idols were smashed, and icons of saints were installed; demons fled, and cities were graced by the cross; and bishops – shepherds of Christ's spiritual flock – brought the bloodless sacrifice before the holy altar; priests and deacons and all the clergy adorned the holy churches and clothed them in beauty; the trumpet of the apostles and the thunder of the gospel resounded throughout all the cities; incense, wafting towards God, graced the air; monasteries rose on the hills; monks appeared; men and women, small and great, and all people, filling the holy churches, sang praises, saying: 'One alone is holy, the one Lord Jesus Christ, to the glory of God the Father, amen'; 'Christ conquered, Christ overcame, Christ became king, Christ was glorified! Great art Thou, O Lord, and wondrous are Thy works! Glory to Thee, our God.'

The first sentence is a short but powerful survey of the Christian world. It is remarkable that Rome is mentioned first here: this is possible, because a schism between East and West has not yet taken place. Syntactically, Ilarion acknowledges the hierarchical primacy of Rome among the Christian lands. This is the first and at the same time the last time that a Russian church leader refers to Rome in neutral-positive terms. Shortly after him this has already ceased to be possible. The Nestorian Chronicle, a few decades later, already contains anti-Roman thrusts ('there is no joy in their churches', 'nor did Olga accept their faith') and an elaborate warning to Vladimir against the 'doctrine of the Latins'. And a very anti-Latin piece of writing is attributed to Feodosi Pecerskij, a contemporary of Ilarion.[51] Ilarion, however, counts Rome among 'all the lands and cities and nations each of which glorifies its teacher that taught it the Orthodox faith (*pravoslavnaja vera*)'. So the term 'Orthodox' does occur in the Oration once alongside the term 'Christian' (*christianskaja*), but then it also refers to the Latin church, to the whole of Christianity.[52]

This ecumenical approach is again followed by the characteristic and modest 'we, too', in which Ilarion has the Russian people joining the others. After this, however, Ilarion lapses into strong patriotic exaggeration with regard to Vladimir and his ancestors. Of course this suits the rhetorical style of his exposition and is certainly addressed to his royal audience, but it remains an uncritical account of the uncivilized, and at times cruel, rulers of Rus'. Vladimir's active pagan life is certainly prominently ignored. However, Ilarion is not writing history, but is making a plea for canonization, so raking up such a phase is not expedient. Incidentally, the observation that the Russian land is known as far as the ends of the world is not merely boasting, for at the time prince Jaroslav the Wise was connected through family relationships with seven European royal houses and with the Byzantine imperial family.

Ilarion does not describe Vladimir's conversion in historical terms but in theological terms: as an initiative on the part of God, his mercy, his love of humankind. Here, elaborate attention is also paid to 'the Greek land' (the Russian term for the Byzantine empire), which was missing in the summary in the first line. The description of the full churches in Greece is so concrete that Ilarion is perhaps speaking from his own experience.

The description of the metamorphosis of the Russian land after the Christianization is very expressive. By means of powerful antitheses Ilarion depicts an idyllic landscape of monasteries and churches, of masses of people singing and praying.

He concludes with a phrase which has become a source of interesting speculation. It is a translation of a liturgical formula from the Latin church: '*Christus vincit, Christus regnat, Christus imperat*'. It derives from the Carolingian *Laudes regiae*, and was used at the coronations of French kings, and later on also during solemn liturgical ceremonies on feast days in France. Ilarion must have heard it from Western priests, perhaps during a church service of a French delegation in Kiev which was there in 1048 for the purpose of preparing the marriage of Jaroslav's daughter Anna with the French King Henry I. It is sometimes also assumed that Ilarion heard the formula himself in France, when he accompanied Anna on her journey there.[53]

It would, of course, support beautifully Ilarion's symbolic place in European history if Ilarion had visited Western Europe, but this hypothetical support is not necessary. More significant for his symbolic function is the fact that Ilarion uses a Latin liturgical formula in his sermon, especially when he does so together with a formula from the Liturgy of St Chrysostom: 'One is holy, one is the Lord, Jesus Christ, for the glory of God the Father.' Eastern and Western liturgy thus become one common eulogy of Christ. This, too, bears witness to an uncomplicated sense of church unity.

Vladimir's role in the Christianization

We now come to the actual eulogy. From now on Ilarion no longer speaks about Vladimir, but addresses him directly, no longer calling him Vladimir, but using his baptismal name Vasilij. Besides, in doing so, he uses the adjunct 'blessed one' (*blažennyj*), in anticipation of his canonization. Ilarion apostrophizes the dead prince in front of whose tomb he is probably standing. He does so at least a hundred times, either by means of the verbal form, or by means of a personal or possessive pronoun.

The eulogy now changes its theme. In the preceding passage

Ilarion has described the pagan Vladimir and his ancestors with stereotyped attributes, and now, once again, he also begins with a litany of decorative epithets. This is one of the characteristics of the genre. After this, however, Ilarion strikes a completely new note with his questions about the manner of Vladimir's conversion. He has ceased to be the court preacher, and is now a theologian who expresses his sincere admiration, even astonishment, about Vladimir's conversion. He no longer praises him to the skies, rather the contrary: the suggestive power of the thirteenfold question about his conversion and the accumulation of evocations make it seem as if the deceased is about to descend from heaven in order to answer!

Ilarion wishes to make it clear to Vladimir that the latter's work has borne fruit. In lyrical terms he describes to him the results of his work: a Kiev full of splendid churches. He mentions and eulogizes three churches in particular: the Mother of God Church, built by Vladimir himself and where he now lies buried; the Annunciation Church at the city gate; and the Sophia Church, built by Jaroslav and just completed (1045) at the time when Ilarion delivers his oration. Especially this church of Holy Wisdom (Sophia) is praised as one 'that is unequalled in the North of the earth, from the East to the West'. In saying this, Ilarion remains modest, for the fact that he excludes the South (the Byzantine empire) means that he knows that the Sophia Church of Constantinople, and possibly other churches which he has seen in Greece, are even more beautiful.[54] That Ilarion is not exaggerating here is confirmed by testimonies of Western chroniclers, Adam of Bremen and Thietmar of Merseburg, who were amazed at the many churches in Kiev and the splendour of the city.

Ilarion's capacity for rhetoric reaches its climax in this part. The religious message, however, remains central: the subject is not Vladimir's earthly deeds, but his role in the conversion of his nation. The deeds performed by Vladimir which Ilarion now mentions are the works of mercy with which Vladimir gives shape to his faith (42.17–43.13 and 47.15–47.21) and his activities for the Christianization. The great love of neighbour and care of the poor displayed by Vladimir after his conversion are also recorded in the Nestorian Chronicle (under the year 996), and even the critical Thietmar of Merseburg mentions them in his *Chronicon*, so there will certainly be an element of truth in this fact. Moreover, Ilarion here indirectly alludes to Vladimir's sins prior to his conversion. Underlining the importance of works of mercy also continued to be a 'royal' theme in Kievan culture after Ilarion, as appears from the work *Poučenije* (Instruction, 1117) by Vladimir's great-grandson, Prince Vladimir Monomach.

But the central position in the *laudatio* is taken by Vladimir's work of conversion. Vladimir performed the work of an apostle in this field: in contrast to many other Christian countries, Russia never had a real apostle to bring the faith. It was in fact Vladimir who fulfilled that role. Ilarion therefore once calls him 'apostle among the rulers'. This is metaphorical language: among the rulers he was like an apostle. It is not yet the more pretentious title Vladimir is to receive in the Russian church later on: 'apostolic' (*ravnoapostol'nij*). That qualification is also given to his grandmother Olga, who had been the first to introduce Christianity in Kiev as regent, and to the 'teachers of the Slavs', the saints Cyril and Methodius.

On the one hand, the fact that the Russian land never had a real apostle is seen as a negative point compared to other countries; on the other hand this is precisely what constitutes the special, the 'miraculous', character of Russia's conversion. It is the latter aspect that Ilarion wishes to emphasize. He therefore does not opt for the mythical solution that is given by the Nestorian Chronicle to compensate for the lack of a real apostle, the so-called Andrew legend. According to this legend, the apostle Andrew travelled to the north by way of the river Dniepr, after which he went to Rome after making an enormous detour. During that journey, Andrew is said to have predicted the coming of Christianity to that region, while glancing at the hills along the Dniepr. However, this is a legend which books of Russian church history nowadays are only too happy too relate.

As the founder of Christianity in his kingdom, Vladimir is

given by Ilarion the titles 'teacher' and 'guide in devotion', desig-
nations which were also used in the case of Byzantine emperors.
And Ilarion also explicitly compares Vladimir with Constantine
the Great. This, however, is not a political upgrading of
Vladimir, but a church-historical one. Just as Constantine introduced Christianity into his empire, so did Vladimir, and just as
the former convoked the first councils, so the latter conferred
with his bishops. There is not yet any trace of caesaropapism
here, for Vladimir is not designated head of the church, but as
sitting in conference with the bishops 'in great humility'.

The religious aspect of the comparison also appears from the
roles played by Helena and Olga in the Christianization: as
Constantine and his mother brought the cross from Jerusalem to
Constantinople, so Vladimir and his grandmother brought it
from Constantinople to Kiev. Thus Ilarion mentions Olga here,
but, strangely enough, he does not say anything about her
independent action in the first, premature, attempt at the
Christianization of her land.

After Ilarion, the comparison between Vladimir and Constantine was continued in historiography and hagiography. The
Nestorian Chronicle, as well as the Life of Boris and Gleb, draws
this comparison when mention is made of Vladimir's death. It is
applied in great detail in the later *Memoir and Eulogy of the
Russian Prince Volodimir* written by the monk Jakov.[55] This
comparison does not contain any political claims with respect to
Constantinople. Rulers who introduce Christianity into their
kingdoms are often compared with Constantine the Great. Cases
in point are the Moravian prince Rostislav in the Life of Cyril,
the Bulgarian ruler Boris in a letter written by Patriarch Photios,
and at a still earlier date the Frankish king Clovis by Gregory of
Tours in his *History of the Franks*.[56] In fact Vladimir is not
mentioned anywhere in Byzantine sources as opposed to the two
Slavic rulers mentioned here, but that is because his conversion
as such is surrounded with an enigmatic silence in the Byzantine
sources.

The comparisons of Rostislav, Boris and Vladimir with the
'apostolic' *(isoapostolos)* emperor Constantine are based on

their activity of Christianization as rulers. It is therefore essentially different from the politically motivated comparison with Constantine in the cases of Charlemagne and the later Moscow tsars, who considered themselves equal to or heirs of the Byzantine emperors. In short, in this fragment, too, where Ilarion is heightening his plea for the canonization of the ruler, there is no political panegyric. Everything turns on the term 'blessed', the designation of someone who is worthy of canonization. Ilarion uses numerous biblical arguments and references to indicate that Vladimir has deserved this designation. This biblical qualification then takes the place of the earthly 'glorious'.

(40.29–48.11)

And you, O noble and glorious among earthly rulers, how shall we praise you, most valiant Vasilij? How shall we marvel at your goodness, your strength, and your might? What thanks shall we offer you? You, through whom we came to the knowledge of God; you, through whom we were delivered from idolatrous delusion; you, by whose command Christ is glorified throughout all your land? What is the name to describe you? Lover of Christ? Friend of the Truth? Repository of Reason? Nest of Charity?

How did you come to believe? How did you blaze up with that love for Christ? How did such understanding enter into you, an understanding higher than the understanding of earthly sages: that you came to love the invisible and to strive for the heavenly things? How did you seek out Christ? How did you come to commit yourself to him? Tell us, your servants; O our teacher, tell us: whence did the savour of the Holy Spirit waft to you? Whence did you drink the sweet cup of the thought of the life to come? Whence did you taste and see that the Lord is good? You neither saw Christ, nor did you walk in his footsteps; how, then, did you come to be his disciple? Others had seen him, yet did not believe; you had not seen him, yet you believed. Surely in you our Lord Jesus' blessing to Thomas came true: 'Blessed are they that have not seen, and yet have believed!'

Thus, then, we can name you, boldly and surely, without hesitation: 'O Blessed One!' The Saviour himself thus named you: blessed are you, for you believed in him and were not offended in him. In his unerring words: 'Blessed is he who shall not be offended in me.' Those who knew the law and the prophets crucified him; but you, who had read neither the law nor the prophets, worshipped him who was crucified. How was your heart unsealed? How did the fear of God enter into you? How did you join yourself to his love? You saw no apostle visiting your land and inclining your heart to humility through his poverty and nakedness, through his hunger and thirst; you saw no demons cast out in the name of Jesus Christ, nor the sick being healed, nor the dumb given speech, nor fire made to freeze, nor the dead made to rise. Yet since you saw none of this, then how did you come to believe?

Amazing miracle! Other kings, other rulers, saw all these things, saw the holy men's deeds, yet did not believe. Indeed, they inflicted suffering and torment on the holy men. But you, O blessed one, without any of this, you came to Christ: you understood, through good sense and discernment alone, that there is one God, the creator of all things visible and invisible, the creator of all both in heaven and earth; and that he sent his beloved son into the world for its salvation. And you pondered these things; and so entered the holy font of baptism. What to others seemed foolishness, you discerned as the power of God.

And moreover, who can tell of all your alms by night and generosity by day, which you showed to the poor, the orphans and the sick, the debtors and the widows, and all who needed compassion? For you heard the word that was said to King Nebuchadnezzar by Daniel: 'May my counsel please you, King Nebuchadnezzar, and purge your sins by almsgiving and your unrighteousnesses by generosity to the poor.' When you had heard these words, O venerable one, you did not stop at hearing, but completed what you had heard in deed, by giving to those who asked, by clothing the naked, by feeding the hungry and thirsty, by giving all kind of comfort to the sick, by ransoming the debtors and freeing the slaves. For your generosity and alms are even now held in memory among men, and more still before God and his angels. Because of these alms which are well-pleasing to God, you have much boldness before him as a true servant of Christ.

He supports me who has said: 'Mercy triumphs over judgment' and: 'Alms are for a man like a signet ring which he wears.' But more certain is the word of the Lord himself: 'Blessed are the merciful, for they shall obtain mercy.' We bring you another clear and faithful witness from holy scripture, which is spoken by the apostle James: 'Whoever has converted a sinner from the errors of his way shall save his soul from death and cover a multitude of sins.' But if the one who has converted one person receives so great a reward from the one God, what salvation have you found, O Vasilij? What a burden of sins have you taken away, who have not converted a single man from the errors of idolatry nor ten nor a city, but your whole territory!

The Redeemer Christ shows himself and confirms to us of what praise and honour you are thought worthy in heaven, when he says: 'Whoever confesses me before men, him I shall also confess before my Father which is in heaven.' But if he who has only confessed this Christ before men is confessed by him before God the Father, how much more will you be praised, who have not only confessed that Christ is the Son of God but, after confessing this, have also confirmed belief in him, not at a council but throughout this land and have erected churches of Christ and appointed ministers there!

O you likeness of the great Constantine: of like wisdom, of like love for Christ, with like honour for his servants! With the blessed fathers of the Council of Nicaea, he set down the law for the people; and you, with our new fathers – the bishops – in frequent assembly and utmost humility took counsel on how to establish the law for these people new in their knowledge of God. He among the Hellenes and the Romans made the kingdom subject to God. And you, O blessed Vasilij, did likewise in Rus', so that now, both for us as for them, Christ is called king. He and his mother Helena transported the cross from Jerusalem, and transmitted its glory throughout all their world, and affirmed and confirmed the faith. And you and your grandmother Olga transported the cross from the New Jerusalem – from the city of Constantine – and established it throughout all your land, and so you affirmed and confirmed the faith. And as you were the likeness of him, so God granted you to partake with him in like honour and glory in heaven because of the devotion you showed in your life.

Your devotion is well witnessed, O blessed Vasilij, by the holy Church of Holy Mary Mother of God, founded by you on foundations of faith and now the abode of your earthly remains, which await the archangel's last trumpet.

Your devotion is well witnessed and faithfully proved by Georgij,[57] your son, whom God made heir to your rule after you; who does not demolish what you established, but rather strengthens it; who does not diminish your deeds of devotion, but rather embellishes them; who does not impair, but repairs; for he finished your unfinished works, as Solomon finished David's. For he built the great temple of God's Holy Wisdom, to sanctify and consecrate your city; and he adorned it with every adornment: with gold and silver and precious stones, and with holy vessels. This church is admired and renowned in all surrounding lands, for none such can be found within the bounds of the north of the earth, from the east to the west. And he adorned your city of Kiev in splendour, as though in a crown. And he entrusted your people and city to the holy, all-glorious Mother of God, the ready protectress of Christians. To her he built also a church on the great gate, in the name of the first of the feasts of the Lord, the feast of the Annunciation, so that the archangel's salutation to the Virgin may touch this city as well. For to her the archangel said: 'Rejoice, for joy is given thee, the Lord is with thee', thus to the city: 'Rejoice, city of faith, the Lord is with thee.'

Arise, O venerable head, arise from your sepulchre, arise and shake off your sleep! You are not dead, but you sleep until the general resurrection of all. Arise, you are not dead; it is not meet you should die, you who believed in Christ, the life of the world. Shake off your sleep, lift up your eyes to behold what honour the Lord has vouchsafed you in heaven; and on earth, through your son, he has not left you uncommemorated. Arise and behold your son Georgij! Behold your offspring! Behold him whom you loved! Behold him whom the Lord brought forth from your loins! Behold him who adorns the throne of your land, and so rejoice and be exceeding glad!

Behold, too, your devout daughter-in-law Irina![58] Behold your grandchildren and your great-grandchildren! Behold how they live, how they are sustained by the Lord, how they are maintaining the faith, as you had ordained! Behold how they frequent the holy churches! Behold how they glorify Christ, how they worship his name!

Behold also the city, shining in splendour! Behold churches blossoming! Behold Christianity growing! Behold the glittering city, illumined with icons of saints and scented with incense, resounding with praises and songs to the Lord! Behold all this! And having beheld, rejoice and be exceeding glad, and praise the good Lord, the creator of all this!

And you have beheld it, if not in body, then in spirit. The Lord shows you it all; so rejoice in it and be exceeding glad; for the sowing of faith has not been parched by the sweltering heat of faithlessness, but by the rain of the Lord's mediation it has been brought to fruition with fruits in abundance.

Rejoice, O apostle among rulers: you raised not the dead in body, but us who were dead in spirit. We were dead from the disease of idolatry, and through you we revived and came to know Christ, who is life. We were bent over by demonic delusion, and through you we stood straight and stepped forth in the way of the life. We were blind in the eyes of our hearts, blinded by demonic delusion, blinded by ignorance; and through you we saw through to the light, the three suns of the Godhead. We were dumb, and through you we found speech, so that now, great and small, we all glorify the one God in his Trinity.

Rejoice, O our teacher, our guide in devotion! You were clothed in righteousness, girded with steadfastness, shod with truth, crowned with understanding and you adorned yourself with mercy, as with a collar and golden jewel. For you, O eternal head, were clothing for the naked, you were one who fed the hungry, you were inner refreshment for the thirsty, you were a helper to widows, you were a resting place for strangers, you were a protection for the homeless, you were an advocate for the tormented, an enrichment for the poor.

You who for these good deeds receive in heaven as a reward the blessings which God has prepared for you who love him, you who are satisfied with the sweet sight of his countenance, pray for your land and people among who you ruled piously, that he may keep it in the peace and piety that you have handed on, and that the right faith may be praised among them and every heresy cursed, and that the Lord God may preserve them from any war and imprisonment, from hunger and all kinds of grief and sorrow.

But in particular pray for your son, our pious king Georgij, that in peace and health he may voyage over the sea of life and without damage moor the ship of his soul in the haven of heavenly calm, preserving the faith and a wealth of good works; and that after he has steered the people entrusted to him by God without offence, he may go to stand with you before the throne of God the Ruler of all; and that for the work of feeding his flock he may receive from him the crown of imperishable glory, with all the righteous who have worked for him.

Theological balance

This is the end of the third part of Ilarion's Oration on the Law and Grace. It may appear from what we have discussed so far that the Oration is not a glorification either of a specifically Russian form of religion or of the Russian state. The Oration is a hymn of thanksgiving for the calling of the Russian nation through God's grace and for its actual Christianization by Prince Vladimir.

Ilarion's description of Vladimir is actually quite unhistorical, as is his description of the actual process of the Christianization of the Russian nation. Ilarion omits the concrete historical context and greatly abstracts and idealizes the Christianization: it seems as if it took place without any problems, and covered the whole country. Nothing is said about the political complications involved which directly occasioned it, the far from Christian internecine struggle among the Russian princes after the Christianization, and the persistent survival of pagan customs among the people.

However, these matters are not essential for Ilarion, for he is not writing a chronicle, but giving a theological interpretation of the Christianization: the conversion took place within the context of the calling of the pagans, and God thought that the time for Russia had come. Ilarion illustrates this with a great many biblical quotations. The concrete political factors, on the other hand, are not essential from the perspective of God's grace; they are merely the occasion for, but by no means the cause of, the conversion. From a theological perspective, Christianity cannot be a political coincidence. Ilarion shows that the Christianization of his country was not the result of the political and military contacts between Kiev and Byzantium, but of God's design for mankind.

One important biblical text is not used by Ilarion, although it fully reflects his spirit: the parable of the labourers of the eleventh hour in the vineyard (Matt. 20. 1–7). These labourers are the last to be called by the owner of the vineyard and are put on a level with the labourers of the first hour. However, the appropriate comparison with the Russian nation is made in the introductory section of the *Lecture on the Life and Death of the Blessed Passion-Sufferers Boris and Gleb*, which was mentioned earlier. The comparison is made in order to emphasize the fact that there had never been any apostles in Russia, which was the reason why Christ, like the lord of vineyard, eventually called the Russians himself.[59]

Approaching the matter from an abstract, theological viewpoint, Ilarion in fact liberates the Christianization of the Russian nation from the nationalistic perspective in which 'the baptism of

Rus' (*kreščenie Rusi*), as it came to be called collectively, was to be put later on.

This does not mean that there is no room for national pride, or rather national joy, in the Oration. This is quite clearly the case, and this national joy is the second central theme of the Oration next to the theme of universalism. The great value of the Oration lies in the balance between the two themes of Christian universalism and Russian religious patriotism. Any political imagery and, occasionally, grandiloquence that is contained in the Oration is subordinate to the theological intent to express gratitude, without degenerating into religious and ideological conceit.

This is once more clearly expressed in the 'prayer to God from all our land', which Ilarion later added to the written version of his Oration. Any over-emphasis on Vladimir's initiative in the conversion or, more generally, on human complacency possibly expressed in the *laudatio* is completely neutralized in this prayer. Here, theologically speaking, the proper relation between man and God is indicated by Ilarion, who makes it clear that man, prior to his redemption, is completely dependent on God's 'mercy and loving-kindness'.

Ilarion's prayer, which is formulated in biblical terms, is imbued with a profound awareness of sin and an almost Reformation-like sense of dependence on God's mercy. It is, for the most part, an urgent plea for forgiveness and an appeal to God's compassion:[60] 'Though we may have no good deeds to our account, yet spare us on account of Thy plenteous mercy . . . Set aside Thy wrath, O Merciful One, the wrath which we deserve because of our deeds.' The converted Russian nation, which was still considered fortunate in the preceding Oration, does not prove to answer its calling: 'Though still we stray, yet do not abandon us; though still we offend against Thee, yet do not cast us aside . . . Though we are but a little flock, do not despise us . . .We have neither performed nor preserved what Thou hast commanded us.' And Ilarion shatters even more illusions, while continuing:

We repent, we beg, we pray: we repent of our evil deeds; we

beg that Thou wilt send into our hearts the fear of Thee; we pray that at the last judgment Thou wilt have mercy upon us. Spare us, look generously and indulgently upon us, visit us, pity us, have mercy upon us . . . If Thou, O Lord, shouldst mark iniquities, O Lord, who would stand? If Thou shouldst render unto each according to his deeds, who then shall be saved?

Ilarion does not make any exception: 'For we have all departed from the way, all together have become good for nothing. Not one of us strives and sets his affections on things heavenly, but all on the things of the earth.'

Although people do not live in accordance with faith, the only good thing they have is faith itself: 'For we do not spread out our hands to a strange god, nor have we followed any false prophet, nor do we hold any heretical doctrine, but upon Thee we call, upon Thee, the true God.'

The tone of utter humility and even fear of the punishment of God (and of disasters mentioned in the prayer such as war, famine, fires, floods and sudden death) contrasts sharply with the tone of joy and gladness which has characterized the Oration up to this point. The contrite attitude, however, and the existential fear in the prayer of 'all the Russian land', make it possible for all Christians to say. This, too, underlines the universal or ecumenical dimension of Ilarion's theological interpretation of the Christianization of his nation.

Narrowing of perspective

Ilarion's eulogy gave the impetus to the church's veneration of the founder of Christianity in the Russian land. But it was a long time before Vladimir was actually canonized. No precise date is known, but only at the beginning of the fourteenth century are there clear signs of a veneration of Vladimir by the church; in 1311 a church building in Novgorod was dedicated to Vladimir, and the first depictions of him on icons date from this century. This is relatively late, and around two centuries after the canonization of the first Russian saints, Vladimir's sons Boris and Gleb.[61]

After Ilarion, though, there was an even more explicit plea for the holiness of Vladimir, which builds on Ilarion's beginnings but is far from having the same literary quality. This is the *Pamjat' i pochvala knjazjyu ruskomu Volodimiruy* (Memorial and Eulogy of the Russian Prince Volodimir), written by a monk, a certain Jakov.[62]

The most important difference from the *Slovo* is that the *Pamjat'* does full justice to Olga, the first Christian ruler of Rus'. Moreover the author continues the typological parallel created by Ilarion between Vladimir and Olga and Constantine and Helena, but heightens it quite a bit. This is a clear hagiographical argument in favour of Vladimir and Olga. It is said of the 'blessed' Olga that 'she followed the life of the holy empress Helena'. In support of her holiness reference is made to the miracle of her body, which remained uncorrupted, as anyone 'who believes' can see through a window in the stone coffin. However, that is not the case with Vladimir, and here, to some degree opportunistically, the monastic author uses the argument 'that a saint is recognized by his actions and not by his wonders, for magicians and devils can also perform wonders'.

The memorial goes much further with comparisons. The 'blessed and thrice-holy Vladimir' is several times compared not only with the emperor Constantine but also with the Old Testament figures of David, Hezekiah and Josiah, and it is said that he 'imitated the hospitality of David, the trust of Jacob and the tenderness of Moses'. Moreover, in contrast to the *Slovo*, Vladimir's military conquests over nations mentioned by name are recorded. This includes his military campaign against the Greeks and the capture of Cherson. And then the whole argument, which has a religious purpose, falls apart, for almost laconically the conversion of Vladimir and his land is reduced to a political deal with God, to whom Vladimir prays: 'Lord God, give me this city and I shall take Christians and priests and bring them to my land, who shall teach the people the Christian religion.' He captures the city, plunders the church furnishings, icons and relics, and as extra booty asks the two Byzantine emperors for their sister in marriage, 'the more resolutely to come to Christianity'. Vladimir's exclamation to God when he tries to starve out the encircled city by cutting off the water supplies sounds unintentionally cynical: 'Lord God, ruler of all, if this succeeds, I shall immediately have myself baptized.'[63]

This unintentional profanation of Vladimir's work, which has previously been described in pious terms, is a consequence of the author's literary ineptitude. But it restores the salvation history to being human work, which it always is in its practical implementation.

The author is also realistic when in another prayer he has Vladimir confessing his former sinfulness to God: 'I was like a beast, I committed much evil when I was a heathen and I lived like an animal, but you tamed me and brought discipline through your grace.' Here the author is even more critical than Ilarion. Vladimir's supplication to God is attractive: 'If you will punish me and torment me for my sins, then punish me yourself, but do not deliver me over to the devils.'

The *Pamjat'* ends with a comparison between Vladimir and Moses and between Kiev and Jerusalem: 'O what a wonder! Kiev appeared as a second Jerusalem in our land, and Vladimir as a second Moses.' This comparison is developed further by a series of parallels. The mention of Kiev as 'a second Jerusalem' marks a new stage in the eastward progress of Christianity: from Jerusalem through Constantinople to Kiev, and it will later end in Moscow. Here the *Pamjat'* goes a step further than the Slovo, in which only Constantinople is called 'a second Jerusalem'.[64]

The revaluation of Ilarion in the 1980s

During the Soviet period, Ilarion was known as the founder of Russian literature, but because of its religious content his work could not be published, even for the use of literary scholars. N. Rozov published his edition of the text in 1963 in Prague, and only in 1984 could a scholarly edition of the Old Russian text appear in the old Soviet Union.[65] But Ilarion's Oration was not incorporated in the first volume of the series *Pamjatniki Literatury Drevnej Rusi* [Monuments of the Literature of Old Rus'], edited by Dmitry Lichačev in 1978. In the introduction, however, Lichačev praises the literary quality of the work. This makes the absence of the text in the edition of the sources all the more conspicuous. Lichačev also passes a very favourable judgment on its content: 'The Oration takes great pride in the results of the Christian culture in Rus'', and, curiously enough, in spite of all this it does not show any national narrow-mindedness. Ilarion does not present the Russian nation as superior to other nations, but speaks about the equality of all the nations in the world which have joined Christianity.'[66] The standard anthology of Old Russian literature for higher education by N. Gudzij, which was the standard work for decades, contains only one small fragment.[67]

A cultural re-evaluation of Ilarion's work started in the second half of the 1980s, as part of the millennial commemoration of Russian Orthodoxy, and because of the political phenomenon of *glasnost'*. In the years 1986, 1987 and 1989 three translations of Ilarion's Oration into modern Russian appeared.[68] However, these editions were specialist publications, and difficult for the general public to obtain at the time.[69]

The re-evaluation of Ilarion in the 1980s was chiefly based on cultural motives. But as a result of re-emerging Russian nationalism, at the end of the 1980s and the beginning of the 1990s a politico-ideological dimension was added to Ilarion's significance for Russian history. Ilarion is now presented as the 'ideologist' of Russian ecclesiastical and political independence. As a result of this, the theological significance of the Oration recedes further into the background than with the purely literary-cultural appreciation of the work.

An example of this political interpretation is V. Kožinov, who reduces the content of the Oration to mere concrete political and military circumstances in the eleventh-century kingdom of Kiev. He reduces the opposition between Judaism and Christianity, between Old and New Testament, to a metaphor for the victory of Kievan Rus' over the Jewish Khazars. Against this misinterpretation of the *Slovo,* M. Robinson and L. Sazonova, sharing their arguments with D. Lichačev and V. Toporov, rightly defend the theological and universalistic content of the Oration.[70]

A new political interpretation of Ilarion is given in the context of history of Russian law. Here Ilarion is seen as the first philosopher of law and his Oration as 'the first Russian political treatise'.[71]

At the beginning of the 1990s, popular editions of Ilarion's Oration appeared. In this area Derjagin's translation of the *Slovo* was twice republished, first in an anthology of nineteenth- and twentieth-century Slavophile texts, and later as a separate publication.[72] In the case of the first of these editions, the fact that the eleventh-century Ilarion is brought together with modern Slavophile thinkers already indicates the spirit in which the *Slovo* is presented, namely 'as one of the ideological sources of the doctrine of Moscow, the Third Rome, and as one of the cornerstones of the Russian idea'.[73]

The separate edition of the *Slovo* by Derjagin is published 'with the blessing of the Patriarch of Moscow and all Rus', Aleksij II', as the title page states. This, however, is less pious than it sounds. As an edition for a large audience this publication of course deserves appreciation and therefore also the blessing of the patriarch, but the commentary is a serious misinterpretation of the content of the *Slovo.* The introduction mentions the anti-Jewish elements in the Oration approvingly, and endorses them with tendentious biblical exposition in the footnotes. Moreover the later state-church relation in the Russian empire is projected on the relation between Jaroslav and Ilarion. Furthermore, the Kievan state and the Russian empire are contrasted, as Christian societies, with the European empires and the United States. Finally, the concept of the Third Rome, arising four hundred years later, is related to Ilarion, while one more ideological concept is added: 'Kiev as the third Jerusalem'.

At long last, in 1994, the *Slovo* was published in the series Monuments of the Literature of Old Rus'. That happened in the twelfth and last volume of the series, which deals with the seventeenth century.[74] Thus this respectable series was given the worthy conclusion with which it should really have opened sixteen years previously. The modern Russian translation of the Oration by deacon A. Jurčenko, with the parallel Old Russian text, is the fourth translation of the Oration and the seventh publication in eight years. This certainly makes good the omission of Ilarion's work from Russian publications throughout the whole of the twentieth century.

But Ilarion will truly be rehabilitated only when he is honoured not only as leading exponent of Russian or Ukrainian culture but also as a symbol of Christian unity. That is where his truly unique historical value lies. For as a metropolitan he was not only the first but also at the same time the last Russian link with the world church. He stands above the division between the Catholic and the Orthodox Church, and above that between the Ukrainian Orthodox Church of the Patriarchate of Constantinople and that of the Patriarchate of Kiev, which were proclaimed one-sidedly in the 1990s after the independence of Ukraine.

This symbolic function of Ilarion transcends his national and cultural significance, and through this he is paradoxically far greater than Russians and Ukrainians themselves sense in their present-day nationalistic interpretation of Ilarion's work.

3

The Christianization of Russia
in a European Context

The uniqueness of Russia's conversion story

Compared to other European nations, Russia's turn to Christianity is indeed special in a certain way: it was not the result of planned missionary strategy from outside, from either Constantinople or Rome, nor of the conquest of the land by a Christian state, far less of Russia's expansion into a Christian neighbouring country. The ruler of Kievan Russia, Vladimir, had had a decisive influence in the introduction of Christianity in 988, whatever his motives may have been. Once that decision had been taken, and Greek and Bulgarian priests began to engage in mission, church services in the Slavonic vernacular and the simultaneous introduction of writing brought about a special inculturation of Christianity in Russia.

These are historical facts, but the conclusions that were drawn from them later by Slavophile historians and writers are a religious myth, namely the myth of the Christianization of Russia by Russia itself, and the idea that the Russian nation 'by nature' had an affinity for Christianity, an 'innate capacity' for Orthodoxy, which in turn leads to the notion that in religious terms Russia differs from other nations. By the special way in which Christianity was introduced into Rus', Russia was to occupy an exceptional position in the history of the Christianization of Europe.

Here are a few examples. The first great Russian historian, Nikolaj Karamzin (1766–1826), sees a difference from the West in the peaceful spread of Christianity in Russia and through Russia in the territories of the Russian empire which were conquered later. It took place 'without the force and malice resorted to by the zealots for Christianity in Europe and America'.[75] In 1803 his contemporary Aleksandr Turgenev writes in his travel report from Germany of the violence with which Saxony was Christianized by Charlemagne and the pope and concludes:

> How different in spirit is our clergy from that of Rome! Wherever Roman missionaries preached the Christian doctrine the blood-stained sword preceded the cross! Our Greek teachers, however, never proved love of neighbour by means of persecutions and violence, and our forefathers did not resist their baptism in the rivers Dnjepr and Pocajna. There was no need for Vladimir the Great to resort to force or, like Charlemagne, to the horrors of death in order to overcome superstition and stubbornness.[76]

The writer Nikolaj Gogol sees evidence for the Christian disposition of the Russian people in the fact 'that Christ came to us without the sword and that the prepared soil of our hearts attracted his word of its own accord', and that 'the principle of Christian brotherhood is contained in our Slavonic nature'.[77] Danilevskij, the Pan-Slavist and philosopher of culture, refers in his 1869 book to

> the special character of Russia's acceptance of Christianity, not through subjection to a superior Christian nation, nor through political domination by a nation, nor through an active religious preaching, but through an inner dissatisfaction with paganism and an unhampered quest for truth.[78]

The twentieth-century Russian church historian Anton Kartašëv certainly oversteps the mark when he states that

> the Russian people absorbed the Greek faith as easily as a sponge does water . . . baptized on orders from above, the

Russian people, nevertheless, with the greatest of ease and speed became a `Christian peasant nation' (*krest'janskim-christianskim narodom*) as far as the ends of the as yet weakly organized Russian land.[79]

This last expression is an allusion to the etymological affinity between the Russian words for 'peasant' and 'Christian'. Over against this word-play stands the well-known maxim of Nikolaj Leskov, 'Rus' was baptized but not instructed' (it sounds more euphonic in Russian: *Rus' krescena no ne prosvescena*).

I think that the philosopher Vladimir Solov'ëv also understood the religious significance of Vladimir quite correctly, despite his eccentric idealization of him. He does not use the idealized Vladimir to prove the Christian character of Russia but on the contrary to show how anti-Christian the Russia of his time had become through the religion of Russian despotism and church servility. When the tsarist and ecclesiastical authorities were pompously celebrating the nine hundredth anniversary of the baptism of Vladimir, Solov'ëv wrote a sharp criticism of the misuse of this jubilee by the Russian state and pointed to the difference between the ideals of Vladimir and the policy of the later tsars.[80] These ideals were the opposite of what the church and state were now propagating: autocracy, caesaropapism, Russification and pan-Slavism. Solov'ëv develops the contrast between nineteenth-century tsarism and Kievan Rus' into the incompatibility in principle of nationalism and 'statolatry' on the one hand and Christian universalism and church catholicism on the other. The former is a relic of paganism. By lapsing into 'nationalistic egotism' the tsarist authorities are not at all like Vladimir but like his pagan father Svjatoslav, who turned against Christianity. In 1888, according to Solov'ëv, who wrote in French, the political and church authorities had *complètement méconnu et étrangement défiguré*, completely misunderstood and strangely distorted, the true significance of the baptism of Vladimir.

The genesis of Christian Europe

The historical sources of Russia's conversion, the chronicle *The Narrative of Bygone Years* (1116) and Ilarion's oration *On the Law and the Grace* (1050), are indeed unique documents in the history of the Christianization of Europe. No other rising European nation possesses such a literary stylizing and theologizing of its transition from pagan to Christianity. As far as written reflection on its adoption of Christianity is concerned, Russia thus occupies a special place in Europe. However, that does not mean that the conversion as such took place in a unique manner. It is interesting to make a comparison with the conversion stories of other European nations, or the conversion of their rulers, to see whether there are common elements in the creation of a national religious image. If we examine nations which were converted much earlier than Russia or in the same period, it will become clear that the Russian story indeed has elements in common with other stories of national baptisms, and moreover that Russia's conversion is a link in a centuries-long process of the genesis of Christian Europe.

This process took place between the sixth and eleventh centuries. During this period Europe discarded Germanic, Slav and Hungarian paganism, having exchanged the Roman and Celtic gods for Christian monotheism during the fourth and fifth centuries in the European part of the former Roman empire. The fact that all the various nations take this course one after the other makes this process, from our perspective, appear more collective and coherent. And in this perspective Russia's conversion is not exclusive, but only one out of many cases.

We shall take seven cases of Christianization. The first three are connected with the phase in which the great European peoples became nations, namely the Franks, the Anglo-Saxons and the German Saxons; the last four with peoples whose conversions took place at about the same time as that of Kievan Russia: the Danes, Norwegians, the Poles and the Hungarians.

The national conversion narratives of the first three peoples are recorded in the oldest chronicles of European history: the *Ten Books of History* by Gregory of Tours (formerly known as *History of the Franks)*, the *Ecclesiastical History of the English Nation* by the Venerable Bede, and the *History of the Saxons* by Widukind of Corvey. These chronicles were written about a century after the date of the event, but come from different times. The point at issue in the comparison of the much older Frankish, English and Saxon accounts of the baptism stories with the Russian one is not the relations between the texts, for there are none, but the content. Possible typological agreements are then all the more striking, because the Russian chronicler had no knowledge of his Western fellow-chroniclers. As with the account of the conversion of Russia in the previous chapters, we are not primarily concerned with the exact historical course of events, but with the deliberate construction of the event by the chroniclers.

The Franks. Gregory of Tours devotes only a few pages in his history to the baptism of the Frankish king Clovis in 496.[81] Although it is relatively short, the narrative contains a number of elements which also occur in the Russian chronicle; most are less developed than in the latter, but some are more so.

A first point of resemblance is the woman's role in the conversion: Chrodichilde and Vladimir's later spouse Anna. Both women, who are already Christian, act as intermediaries in the conversion of the sovereign. In the case of Vladimir the role of his spouse is mentioned but not developed further; however, this is the case with his grandmother Olga. She is as active in persuading her pagan son Svjatoslav as Chrodichilde is in persuading Clovis.

Gregory gives Chrodichilde an apologetic argument which, for all her great religious zeal, seems unrealistic. Here, therefore, we have a case of theological stylization: theological statements are put on the lips of people who could not have made them. However, this fact does give religious depth to the baptism, which also has a practical reason. And that reason is a second point of agreement with the narrative of Vladimir's baptism.

The immediate reason for the baptism is a military factor.

When Clovis is in dire straits in a war with the Alemann tribe, he calls upon the Christian God with the words:

> Jesus Christ, Chrodichilde says that you are the son of the living God, who is said to give help to those who are in distress and victory to those whose hope rests on you. I humbly beg for your glorious help: if you now grant to me the victory over these enemies of mine . . . then I shall believe in you and have myself baptized in your name. For I have called upon my own gods, but I see that they are far from capable of helping me.

This argument is as matter-of-fact as Vladimir's when he is capturing the town of Cherson from the Greeks: 'If I am successful I shall have myself baptized', or 'Lord God, master of all, give me this town and I shall take Christians and priests and bring them to my land, that they may teach the people the Christian religion.'

A third agreement is the fact that, before having himself baptized, Clovis consults with his followers, who agree with the baptism. The baptism itself also has an element that we know from the Russian chronicle: the aesthetic factor. The baptismal church is so beautifully decorated with carpets and fragrant perfumes and flickering candles that the people present thought 'that they found themselves amidst the perfumes of paradise'. Did not the Russians in the Hagia Sophia have the impression of finding themselves in heaven?

A fifth point of agreement is Clovis' designation by Gregory as the 'new Constantine'. However, this is not given any historical basis, as it is by Ilarion of Kiev with respect to Vladimir; still, in political, ideological, religious or cultural terms it is a striking point of resemblance. (Moreover, in his description of the first centuries of Christianity, Gregory has not even mentioned the baptism of Constantine himself!)

Finally, there are two further points of comparison between the narratives about the baptisms: one relating to the mass conversion of the people, who follow their sovereign to the baptismal font, and the other to the brief trinitarian statement which accompanies the baptism. The latter, together with the christologically orthodox statement at the baptism of Clovis's Arian sister, is a minimal theological comment at the actual baptism of Clovis. In the case of Vladimir, however, the baptism is accompanied by a very extensive confession of faith in the consubstantiality of the triune God and in the doctrine of the two natures of Christ. This, together with the reconnaissance of the religions, which in Vladimir's case preceded the baptism, makes the Russian baptismal story, despite the typological agreements with the Frankish one, theologically and historically far more a literary construction and evocative in content.[82]

The baptism of Clovis in the account by Gregory of Tours is presented less as a break in history than is Vladimir's baptism in the Russian chronicle. The event is put between the accounts of fighting and war. Afterwards, too, it becomes less of a central point in the French sense of identity than the baptism of Vladimir in the Russian. Yet in the commemoration of the fifteen-hundredth anniversary of the baptism of Clovis in 1996 France experienced a reaction by the church and by historians comparable to that in Russia; anf the criticism from anti-ecclesiastical quarters was just as narrow-minded as that in Soviet Russia at the millennial commemoration of the baptism of Vladimir in 1988.

The Anglo-Saxons. The Christianization of England is the subject of the earliest English historical work, the *Ecclesiastical History of the English People* by the monk Bede. This is one of the most instructive and readable of mediaeval histories. Bede describes various conversions of sovereigns in sixth- and seventh-century Britain, which was not as yet united. The first conversion, that of king Ethelbert of Kent, who was baptized in 597, is described briefly and plainly.[83] There is no agreement with the Russian narrative, except for the fact that here, too, the Christian wife of the pagan king plays an indirect role. There is just one element which is in sharp contrast with the Russian situation: the element of tolerance. Though king Ethelbert himself still does not feel any sympathy for Christianity, he gives Augustine, the missionary sent by the pope, an entirely free hand: 'We shall not hinder you in your preaching to win over whomsoever you can to your faith and religion.' And when, finally, Ethelbert himself is also fully convinced and goes over to Christianity, followed by a great many others, Bede says:

> The king, although he rejoiced in their conversion and belief, compelled no one to embrace Christianity; but nonetheless he showed greater affection to the believers, for they were his fellow-citizens in the heavenly kingdom. He had learned, however, from his instructors and leaders in the teaching of salvation that the service of Christ is voluntary and not by compulsion.

This element of voluntariness in the Christianization is therefore worth mentioning, because Russian historians of a later date, as we have seen, made the aspect of free choice the specific characteristic of Russia's Christianization as distinguished from the Christianization of the rest of Europe. That was done despite the fact that the Nestorian Chronicle says that Vladimir ordered his subjects to have themselves baptized, and 'those who did not do this out of love, did so out of fear'. In this connection it is also worth referring to Vladimir's father, Svjatoslav. This persecutor of Christians allowed people freely to become Christians, that is to say, 'he did not forbid it, but simply laughed at it'.

Another account of a baptism in Bede provides more material for comparison with the Russian one. It concerns the conversion of king Edwin of Northumbria in 627.[84] The immediate cause for his conversion was once again a woman, Ethelburh, the daughter of Ethelbert, who has been mentioned above. When Edwin asked her brother, who had succeeded his father as king, for her hand in marriage, the answer he received was almost word for word the same as that of the Byzantine emperor to Vladimir about Anna at a later date: 'It is not permitted to give a Christian woman in marriage to a pagan.' Edwin reacted to this by promising that his future wife and her retinue would be given every liberty to profess their faith and to celebrate Christian worship, and that he did 'not rule out the possibility that he himself would also embrace that religion, if, after an examination by his wise men, it should appear that it is holier and more worthy of God'. And just as Anna went to Vladimir accompanied by priests, so Ethelburh went to Edwin in the company of a bishop.

After this, Bede relates the story of a failed attempt to murder Edwin perpetrated by a hostile West-Saxon king, one year later. Edwin then used the same pragmatic argument from faith that we saw in the cases of Clovis and Vladimir: 'If God should grant him life and victory over the king by whom the assassin had been sent and who had wounded him, then he would abjure his idols and serve Christ.' And as a pledge that he would perform his promise he had his new-born daughter baptized immediately. After the victory over his enemy, however, Edwin still hesitated, for he first wanted, with the help of his wife's bishop, Paulinus,

> to examine the faith systematically (*rationem fidei ediscere*) and, after that, to consider with the wisest of his advisers what they thought he should do. For he himself, being a very sagacious man by nature, often sat alone by himself in silence for a long time, but he deliberated much in his heart of hearts what he should do and which religion he should serve.

This is an important agreement with the Vladimir story: the fact that Edwin, too, wanted to study the faith more closely, and after that to confer with his advisers. Edwin was given a more detailed exposition of the faith by bishop Paulinus as well as by pope Boniface, who sent the English king a pastoral letter. The function of this letter can be compared with the theological argument of the Greek philosopher in the case of Vladimir's conversion. But the difference between the pope's letter and the address of the Greek philosopher is that the former is historical. It is part of the deliberate efforts on the part of the pope to make the Angles embrace the Christian faith. And that is another difference from the Russian situation: in the latter there is no mention of a deliberate strategy for the conversion of the Russians on the part of Constantinople. The initiative lay with the Russian ruler. Nor are any Greek documents known which indicate an active (or reactive) aim on the part of the Patriarch of Constantinople in the Christianizing of the kingdom of Kiev.

The pope also sent a letter to Edwin's wife in which he urged her to continue her efforts to make Edwin accept Christian doctrine. This once again emphasizes the woman's role in the English process of Christianization; moreover the pope gives the woman's role a biblical basis by quoting I Cor. 7,14: 'The unbelieving husband is consecrated through the believing wife.'[85]

But despite the pope's instruction in the faith, Edwin continued to hesitate, just as Vladimir still had his doubts after the address by the Greek philosopher-theologian. In a story which does not follow on very well, Bede goes on to add another long passage about an earlier vision that Edwin had had about a miraculous rescue from a confrontation with a rival ruler. The memory of this vision is the decisive factor for the English king to make up his mind about his conversion. From a compositional point of view we may perhaps have an example here of a fusion of two different conversion stories.

But that still leaves the consultation with his advisers, which has already been introduced. This consultation is the last stage in the process of conversion. It is comparable to Vladimir's meeting with his noblemen, the boyars, which also results in a shared decision for baptism.

Edwin's consultation with his followers is a moving story in Bede's historiography. Here we should note that the pagan high priest himself demonstrates the inferiority of his gods and advises that,

> if upon examination it appears that these new things which are now preached to us are better and more efficacious, let us then accept them without any delay.

Another speaker shows, in a comparison which has become famous, how little we human beings actually know about things eternal: life lasts only a fraction of a time, in which we see no more than does a little bird which comes flying from the dark into an illuminated room and out again through the other window. Of what went before, however, and what is to follow after this short life, we are utterly ignorant. And the speaker concludes: 'If this new doctrine offers us something more certain, it seems justly to deserve to be followed by us.' Whereupon the pagan high priest resumes his attack on his own religion by stating that no truth whatsoever is to be found in it:

> The more diligently I sought after truth in our worship, the less I found it. Now I freely confess that the truth evidently appears in this (new) preaching, which can give us the gift of life, redemption and eternal bliss.

So the whole assembly decides to accept the Christian religion. The argument with which Edwin and his kin eventually accept the new religion sounds rational. The aesthetic rapture which is so important for the Russians plays no such role at all with the English. Nowhere in the whole story is there any mention of impressive liturgical ceremonies or outward beauty.

Once the die is cast for the church, the pagan high priest himself offers to set fire to the temples and idols. And a curious detail is that the place where that happened is given with as specific a topographical detail as the place where the Russians destroyed their idols is indicated in the Nestorian Chronicle.

The final part of the history of Edwin's conversion contains just the same apotheosis as in the case of Vladimir: the whole of his nobility and masses of people follow the example of their sovereign and have themselves baptized. For thirty-six days, from morning to night, Bishop Paulinus is engaged in teaching the faith to people who are coming from town and country, baptizing them in the river Glen. And Edwin himself built the first stone church in York, as Vladimir did in Kiev. This, however, is where the resemblance between the two kings ends. Bede's account does not contain any further hagiographical details about Edwin, nor does it elaborate on his further activities on behalf of the church. This, however, is what we do find in the Nestorian Chronicle and in Ilarion's oration on Vladimir. All in all it is an informative account, with colourful details.

The Saxons. The narrative of the Christianization of the German Saxons is quite a different matter. It was recorded by Widukind of Corvey in his *History of the Saxons*.[86] Although the monk Widukind is writing a tribal history with a sense of national pride, he has little to tell of the conversion of his people.

It is a well-known fact that the Saxons were converted to Christianity by Charlemagne in the year 785, after a war. The violence which went with this conversion has often been cited to demonstrate the violent nature of Christianization in the Middle Ages, but in fact this is not a typical case and the generalization is unfair. However, it is impossible to write romantically about it either. Widukind is therefore remarkably brief in his account, in which on the one hand he does not conceal the violence, but on the other hand he stylizes it. Here is the whole of the short fragment:

> Charlemagne, however, who surpassed all kings in bravery, no less distinguished himself in wisdom. For he who was wiser than all other mortals of his age thought that his noble neighbouring people should not be allowed to remain imprisoned in its useless heresy, and he made every kind of effort in order to lead it to the path of truth. And partly through mild persuasion, partly through force of wars, he imposed his will, and in the thirtieth year of his emperorship – he was chosen emperor having been king before – he finally achieved what he had aspired to for such a long time. As a result of this, those who at one time had been allies and friends of the Franks now became brothers, so that as it were one nation emerged through the Christian faith, as we see now.

No lies, but attractively put! The eleventh-century forgery of the charter of the foundation of the Saxon bishoprics by Charlemagne, in the *Episcopal History of the Hamburg Church* by Adam of Bremen, also mentions the use of force.[87] The Saxons were conquered 'through both arms and faith' (*et armis et fide*). Charlemagne here leaves the honour of the victory to God, 'the Lord of hosts':

> Against God and ourselves they offered resistance until through his and by no means our power we conquered them in wars and led them to the grace of baptism with God's help.

The force used in the conversion of the Saxons at any rate did not lead to feelings of resentment towards Christianity on the part of the Saxons. It was indeed not primarily a war of conversion, but a war for the purpose of expanding the power of the Franks, one of several wars waged by Charlemagne. And centuries afterwards, in fact, Christian peoples waged more cruel wars among themselves for non-religious reasons than this one between the Franks and the Saxons. It is not a typically Christian phenomenon that Christianization did not always take place peacefully. Nothing took place peacefully in the Middle Ages: whether it was the formation of states, the formation of towns, economic growth, everything was attended with the use of force. The Christianization was part of the political culture of the Middle Ages, which was not yet a later twentieth-century culture of consultation.

Vladimir's European contemporaries

The extent to which Christianization was often part of a power struggle between different peoples or between rival princes within one people which transcended the purpose of Christianization, but in the end was always the sovereign's own decision, for whatever reason, appears from the following three conversion stories. These are the conversions of Vladimir's fellow kings of Denmark, Norway, Hungary and Poland. With these sovereigns we are also geographically close to Russia. The royal houses in these countries (except the Danish) had dynastic relations with the Russian kings Vladimir and his successor Jaroslav the Wise.[88]

The Scandinavians, Poles, Hungarians and Russians together as it were constitute a 'wave of conversion' in Europe which took place at the end of the tenth century. As a result of this, the Northern and Eastern European regions joined Christian Europe as it was being formed. These national conversions were practically the last to follow the pattern of the kings attaching their peoples to the Christian world. In this way, during the previous century, Slav tribes in the frontier area between the German and the Byzantine empires had embraced Christianity: the Czechs, the Croats, the Bulgarians and the Serbs. The last conversion of a whole people by way of the conversion of the sovereign took place in 1385, when the last pagan ruler in Europe, Jagiello of Lithuania, became a Christian.

The laborious history of the Christianization of Denmark is reported at length by the national historian Saxo Grammaticus, who here bases himself on the historian of the bishopric of Hamburg, Adam of Bremen. The earliest Danish chronicle, the Roskilde Chronicle from 1140, also mentions the baptism of the king, but very briefly.[89] Still, seldom has a chronicle begun the national history so precisely and so abruptly with the acceptance of Christianity by its king. The first sentence runs:

> In the year of the Lord 826, Harald the king of the Danes was baptized in Mainz by Archbishop Otgarus and he became god-son of emperor Ludwig, in the sixth year of his reign. At the same time his brother Erik and the king's wife and a great many Danes were bound with him to the Christian faith.

After that the chronicle mentions that St Anskar went to Denmark with the company, where over four years he brought many to the faith and later as bishop of Hamburg converted 'a countless multitude both of Danes and of inhabitants from over the Elbe'. That is all about the Christianization. The chronicle does not idealize Danish Christianity, for after this we are given a bird's-eye view of the un-Christian deeds of the Danish Norsemen: their devastations in England, Normandy, Friesland and along the Rhine in Germany, in which they regularly burned down churches, killed clergy and exterminated the populations of cities. The manifold lapses into paganism on the part of various Danish kings are also mentioned in telegraphic style.

The mention of the baptism of Harald I as the beginning of the nation's Christianization is premature. The lapse after this was so serious that around a century later it was really necessary to begin all over again, in 960, with Harald II. We find that described better in the *Gesta Danorum* of Saxo Grammaticus (1216).[90] He begins by starting that his people 'only late was initiated into the holy things and that it still opposes the religion and the Latin language'. From this it is already clear that Saxo is not going to give an idealized picture of the Christianization.[91] And indeed his narrative is one of the ups and downs of Christianity.

Saxo has a quite practical explanation for the conversion of Harald in 826. Harald, hard pressed by a rival, sought military support from emperor Ludwig the Pious, who made it a condition of his support that Harald should accept baptism.[92] This is a convergence of factors which we also know from the baptism of Vladimir. Equally familiar in the depiction of a converted king is Saxo's description of Harald's zeal in the faith:

> After he had accepted the pious pattern of life after the practice of Rome, he dishonoured pagan idolatry, destroyed its temples, forbade the assemblies for sacrifice and abolished the pagan priesthood. Thus he was the first to bring the Christian rites to an uncivilized land, and by exterminating devil worship he furthered true belief. He paid close attention to everything that could help to maintain this religion.

But it was in vain. Neither the military support nor the zeal were to any avail, or, as Saxo says, 'Harald began his work with more holiness than success.' For his rival, Regner, cropped up, reversed all this and restored paganism. There was thus the same backlash against Christianity that we saw in the case of the Christianization of Russia, where after the first introduction of Christianity by Olga, her successors Svjatoslav and initially even Vladimir restored the pagan cult.

And Harald was driven to flee. But then something happened which we do not encounter in any conversion narrative: Harald apostasizes from Christianity. 'Just as he had been the guiding patron of the new faith, so he became the first to turn from it; from a glorious promoter of this faith he became a notorious apostate.' Here, then, was an anti-climax. But this apostasy of Harald I is not confirmed in other sources, so that historians doubt whether it was correct.

The opposite course was followed by Regner's grandson, Erik. Having at first persecuted the Christians in his land, on the urging of Anskar of Hamburg, the missionary bishop of the

northern territories, 'he devoted as much energy to the furthering
of Christianity as he had previously devoted to challenging it'.

After him, things again went wrong under king Gorm, who
'despised the Christians as if they were the most loathsome of all
men'. He devastated the churches and restored pagan worship.
This happened despite his Christian, English wife. The female
factor plays no role in the case of Denmark. Saxo certainly
mentions that 'others think that she [Gorm's wife], rejected the
tenderness of the marriage bed in order to win her bridegroom
for Christianity through continence', but he gives another, more
calculating, political explanation of this.

Harald II Bluetooth, the son of Gorm, brought a complete
reversal in Danish history around 960.[93] His baptism, too, took
place in a military context, namely after a war with the German
emperor Otto. Saxo notes briefly and pertinently: 'Harald came
to an agreement with the emperor: he embraced the community
of the Catholic religion (*consortium catholicae religionis*) and
gave his kingdom a divine and human peace.'

But the majority of the people did not go along with this reversal on the part of their king, and under the leadership of his son
Sven I (988–1014) rebelled against Harald. He fled the land, and
Sven earned the support of the people by 'restoring the broken
power of paganism and zealous application to the destruction of
the true religion'. In an attempt to restore his authority, Harald
was killed, but he was given a scrupulously ritual Christian
burial in his own land, 'for his land began too late to appreciate
what this most pious ruler had achieved'. However, son Sven
went on with the 'extermination of the whole tree of faith'. And
'the Danes thought a great deal of him because of his opposition
to the faith'. But despite this support from the pagan people, the
political tide turned against Sven and he was driven out. After
years of exile in various neighbouring lands and in England he
again returned to power, now purged by the setbacks and a convinced adherent of Christianity.

Now he followed in the footsteps of his murdered father and
reintroduced Christianity. But a large part of the people were still
not favourably inclined to Christianity, and therefore initially

Sven made his conversion known only to a small circle. Saxo gives a vivid description of the personal steadfastness of Sven in the faith and his clumsy attempts to convert the stubborn pagan people:

> He spoke in private to his most important subjects and tried to make them accept holy baptism by secret urgings. He practised missionary work by producing from his rough, unpolished imagination what he could not get from books and study. In his zeal to establish the religion, he himself played the teacher, although he was hardly fit for this in either understanding or life-style.

But it was all to no avail. And then 'God added a helper to the good work of the zealous but ineffective preacher of religion', a scholar by the name of Poppo. He summoned a gathering of the Danes and explained the faith. But the Danes still would not be convinced. Then Poppo struck with a divine miracle: to prove that the Christian God was more powerful than the pagan god, he was ready to hold a red-hot piece of iron. When his hand remained intact, the obdurate Danes were convinced and accepted Christianity. And thus 'Poppo planted in our nation the abiding spirit of religion' and finally Sven, after the zigzag movement of Christianity in Denmark, indeed became 'the very religious ruler who disseminated the Christian religion with newly established episcopal sees and adorned it with monastic cells and churches'.

It is a bit of an anticlimax in Saxo's history when after his vivid description of the long process of conversion he concludes things with a miracle. But that is a stereotyped theme in mediaeval historiography. Miracles also play a role in the last phase in the stories of the conversions of Edwin (the vision) and Vladimir (his healing from blindness). Paradoxically enough, a good theological interpretation can be given of this miraculous element in the stories of the baptisms, namely that conversion is ultimately the result of divine intervention or grace. Thus despite all the human factors which play a role in it, the conversion is in the last instance realized *sola gratia*. Miracles and visions are a primitive theological expression of this. One cannot get by with abstract theological observations in the case of illiterate warrior rulers.

The divine ordeal undergone by Poppo is also related in the Roskilde Chronicle.[94] It is also mentioned in German chronicles, like Widukind of Corvey's *History of the Saxons*, but the latter makes the miracle take place already under Harald II.[95] Adam of Bremen also mentions the event, but he has a second miracle with fire follow to confirm the first. And according to him the gathering was convened by Harald himself. In this way the gathering in a sense corresponds with the gatherings which Edwin, Clovis and Vladimir had with their noblemen to decide on the new religion.

In fact, in his *History of the Bishoprics of Hamburg*, Adam gives an extended account of the initial period of Christianity in Denmark. He describes this from the perspective of the church of Hamburg, which engaged in an active mission among its northern Scandinavian neighbours and eastern Slav neighbours between the Elbe and the Oder, the Sorbs and the Wends. This took place in combination with the imperial military campaigns against these tribes. For in Adam we encounter clear examples of what I have called the military factor in the process of Christianization. Thus, for example, he says of Henry I:

> King Henry, who feared God from his childhood on, also caused such fear among the Bohemians, Sorbs and other Slav peoples, who had already been compelled by other kings, that the survivors – and there were very few of these – of their own accord promised tribute to the king and to God the acceptance of Christianity (*regi tributum et Deo christianitatem*).[96]

That this was no mere incident emerges from Adam's account of Otto I, who equals his father here:

> Then the mighty king Otto would also have subjected all Slav peoples to his rule. His father had already compelled them in a great defeat, but he now overcame them with such power that to save their lives and their land they voluntarily offered to the conqueror tribute and the acceptance of Christianity (*tributum et christianitatem*), and the whole people of the pagans

was baptized. Now for the first time churches were erected in the land of the Slavs.[97]

Adam himself has to recognize that this method does not always work. After the death of Otto III, the Slavs, 'who had to bear more burdens from their Christian rulers than was just', threw off Otto's yoke. They set fire to the churches, tortured the priests to death, 'and they left no trace of Christianity on that side of the Elbe'. Adam expresses his amazement at God's mysterious dispositions, which allow

> the Slavs, after worshipping Christ for seventy years in this way, to separate from the body of Christ and the church . . . With astonishment at his omnipotence we see people who first believed fall back into paganism, but others who seem to be the last convert to Christ.[98]

With their violence, the Saxon emperors of the German empire remain in the tradition of their own conversion. The Danes were also partially Christianized in this way, since Adam begins his account of the Hamburg mission in Denmark with the subjugation by Henry I of the fierce anti-Christian Danish ruler Gorm. So 'through the mercy of God and the power of King Henry (*misericordia Dei et virtute regis Heinrici*)' space and opportunity were made for the work of conversion.[99]

Adam of Bremen, who was an important source for Saxo, reports a number of points differently from Saxo. In particular he puts more emphasis on the role of Harald II Bluetooth in the consolidation of Christianity than on that of his son Sven. To the degree that it is important for our comparative approach to the conversion stories, we shall look at Adam's account. In Adam, Harald II already showed a tolerant attitude to the Christian cult before his baptism and allowed Hamburg missionaries to go their way. He had himself baptized with his wife and son Sven only after Otto I had inflicted an annihilating defeat on him. The emperor himself is said to have been present at the baptism, but that is improbable. Once he is a Christian, with Harald, too, religion and power (*religio et fortitudo*) go together. He disseminates Christianity and enlarges his kingdom. But then comes the pagan reaction of Sven, 'who looked on the attractive beginning of the divine religion with abhorrence' and organized resistance 'with those whom his father had forced into Christianity against their will'. In the subsequent dispute between father and son, Harald is defeated, 'although he abhorred war'. Then Adam gives a short eulogy on the life of Harald, which contains the elements of a hagiography:

> But our Harald, who was the first to show Christianity to the people of the Danes, who filled the whole of the North with preachers of the faith and churches, who innocently received wounds and was driven out for the sake of Christ, from whom, I hope, the martyr's palm will not be withheld . . . Remembrance of him and his spouse Gunhild will remain with us for ever.

Then Adam mentions that some people believe that Harald performed miraculous cures and that he gave good laws to Friesian and Saxon tribes at the mouth of the Elbe. So in Adam's eyes Harald deserves to be canonized, and in this potential holiness he comes close to King Olaf II of Norway, who was indeed canonized.

The Norse king

The next cases of royal conversion bring us still closer to Russia. The first Christian king of Norway, Olaf I, was on friendly terms with Vladimir, with whom he had found protection against the enemies within his own people, and the actual founder of Norwegian Christianity, Olaf II, for many years also enjoyed security in Russia and was the brother-in-law of Vladimir's son Jaroslav the Wise. The close contacts between the Norwegian and the Russian kings are not surprising, for the Russian rulers were of Norse descent. The successor of the Hungarian King Stephen, Andrew, had also taken refuge in Russia, where he married a daughter of Jaroslav the Wise, and the daughter of the

Polish king Boleslav had a marriage with a son of Vladimir and half brother of Jaroslav which was fatal for Russia.

Olaf II and Stephen are what may be called 'missionary kings' of their own country, who undertook the work of conversion systematically. In addition to this, they were given the title of 'saint', which is understandable in view of their objective services to the church, but disputable in view of the wars they waged and the harsh methods they sometimes used in their Christianization. This applies especially to Saint Olaf.

In the Christianization of Norway, two King Olafs play a part. The first, Olaf Tryggvason (995–1000), took the initiative, but as with Harald I of Denmark his subjects were not yet ripe for it. Olaf himself had been baptized in England during a Viking raid (and perhaps he also got to know Christianity during a stay in Russia, where Vladimir was then going around with plans for Christianization). After returning to Norway in 995, he tried to introduce Christianity, in parallel to his struggle for power, but he was killed in 1000 in a war with the Danes.

A generation later Olaf Haraldsson (1016–1030), the later saint, put pressure on the Danes and during his reign made a more extensive attempt to establish Christianity. Olaf II was also baptized during a Viking raid, at Rouen in Normandy. His Christianization, carried out in co-operation with the archbishop of Hamburg-Bremen, was also part of his aspiration to make Norway a unified state. In 1028 he was driven out by rebel local chieftains and the Danes. Olaf fled to Russia, from where he returned with reinforcements in 1029, and was killed in the ensuing battle. As a result of this he formally became a martyr.

There are quite special sources for the history of the Christianization of Norway: Latin Lives of saints and Old Norse sagas about both Olaf I and Olaf II. The so-called *Legendary Saga* about Olaf II is the most important of these. In spite of its historical inaccuracy, it is of course highly relevant for the formation of the Norwegian self-image. As a national saint, Olaf II occupies the same prominent position in the Norwegian sense of identity as does Vladimir the Saint in the Russian one. I shall use the

Legendary Saga, which is the oldest (twelfth century) and best preserved Life of Olaf II. [100]

First, however, a remark about the description of the Olafs in Adam of Bremen.[101] Out of partiality for his own diocese, Adam denies the merits of Olaf I, because of the latter's preference for English (and not Hamburg) priests. But in the case of Olaf the Saint, Adam is objective despite his Danish informant (King Sven II), who is biassed against the Norwegians. In the ongoing wars between Denmark and Norway in which the Christianization of Norway took place, he believed that Olaf had more justification than the Danish king, and that Olaf did not wage war of his own free will. Of his method of conversion Adam says that the *beatissimus rex* Olaf decided to eradicate the widely prevailing witchcraft, superstition and magic, and to persecute the practitioners of these things. He waged 'a war against the idolaters'. In contrast to this, though without presenting it as a contrast, Adam mentions the method applied by Olaf's father-in-law, *Christianissimus rex* Olaf Eriksson of Sweden. Olaf Eriksson made an agreement with his pagan subjects according to which he was allowed to build churches in the country, but 'was not allowed to make any of the people abjure the cult of the gods by force, unless they should be prepared to be converted to Christ of their own free will'.

In the Norwegian saga the stylization of Olaf's life is not as smooth as in a church Life. The saga does confer hagiographical characteristics upon Olaf, but does not mince matters over his martial mode of action during his Viking raids and in the attainment of power ('he killed many people in the fight', it frequently says). It is also interesting that in the description of his character, first all good Christian, administrative and other qualities are mentioned (just, charitable, friendly, forgiving). After that, however, we are given the opinion of opponents, who think Olaf tyrannical, haughty, greedy and vengeful. In the description of his work of Christianization his zealous methods are recorded without reservation.

As soon as Olaf had gained sole rule over the whole of

Norway, first of all he set himself the task of promoting Christianity in the country, for since Olaf Tryggvason had proclaimed Christianity in Norway, until the time when Olaf Haraldsson came into the country, the Christian faith had decayed very much . . . King Olaf attached such importance to maintaining the Christian faith that everybody in Norway was forced to adhere to the right faith or else to suffer death. So it was throughout the country, where so far a comprehensive restoration of the Christian faith had been lacking.[102]

And then several times in the saga mention is made of specific cases of people being forced to choose between baptism and death or flight. A great many earls and farmers offered resistance, but they usually consented 'and they became good Christians'. Olaf was not satisfied with mere political loyalty, but insisted on Christian subjects. Even when warriors came to enlist in the army in order to support him in the continuous struggle for power, Olaf refused them, unless they first had themselves baptized. Nonetheless he left the choice to the warriors: those who did not want to be baptized were free to leave. And so at one time he let six hundred potential soldiers go. But the king ordered his baptized army to make their confession before the start of a fight and to attend mass.

Still, in Olaf's eyes force does not always seem the right method. The saga relates how one Valgard, confronting Olaf, refuses to submit to the latter's order to be baptized and how Olaf no longer insists, knowing that 'he certainly has the power to force him into it, but he does not want to. The best thing is to serve God without being forced.' And he allows Valgard to go, while the latter still becomes a Christian on his deathbed in Olaf's presence.

In spite of the frequent use of force, the saga also contains an episode which we have come across in other conversion stories, namely a gathering, a religious debate about the power of the gods.[103] Not an intellectual debate, but one using visual aids, with the only arguments that counted at the time, namely those demonstrating the strength of a god. When the landowner

Gudbrand resists the king's order to abandon the idols, he collects an army of all those who want to remain pagan. After losing a first battle with Olaf, Gudbrand suggests holding a gathering of the people (*thing*) with the king: 'We want to know what kind of religion he proclaims and to see what is most favourable. First we want to investigate what proof of truth this man has got.' The king agrees, and at the meeting he calls upon those present to destroy the idols and to believe in the one God, 'so that we may all be of one mind and believe in Jesus Christ who has created all things'. Gudbrand's reaction to this is: 'We do not know who you are talking about. It strikes me, however, that you call someone god whom neither you nor anyone else can see, but we have a god whom we can see every day.' And then he challenges Olaf to have his God make the sky cloud over the next day as evidence of the latter's power. The next day, of course, the sky is cloudy and the meeting is continued. Now Olaf's court bishop speaks and delivers an 'extraordinarily good' sermon about the Christian faith. The opponents then ask for a new sign, namely that the Christian god will provide sunny weather the next day, and then 'we shall decide whether we shall become one or fight with one another'. Olaf spends the night in prayer and the next morning towards sunrise the farmers led by Gudbrand arrive with an enormous statue of the thunder god Thor, shining with gold and silver. Then Gudbrand challenges the king:

> Where is your god now, Olaf? I assume that he has now hung his head and it also seems to me that your boasting has grown rather less than yesterday, yours and that of this man with the mitre, whom you call your bishop and who sits next to you. For now our god has arrived who can cause such a thunderstorm that your god cannot come to the meeting . . . Cast off your superstition and be reconciled again with our god.

Then Olaf resorts to a stratagem. He gives a speech and suddenly points to the rising sun, saying: 'There now comes our God, shining brightly.' And while all the farmers were looking at the rising sun, a man who had been instructed beforehand cut the statue of Thor in two with an axe. The farmers were thus given a fright and took flight, but their boats had been holed beforehand. Olaf called them back and gave them the choice: 'Either you will accept Christianity, or you will fight me this very day.' Then their leader Gudbrand said that they were convinced of the impotence of their own god and 'all were baptized who were still un-baptized, and those who had already been baptized in the past returned to Christianity'.

Here was a religious debate at what was then the highest possible level; however simplistic it may be, it does indicate that it was not only by force that the Norwegians exchanged paganism for Christianity. The miracle was a sham, but it convincingly showed the sham power of the Germanic thunder god Thor. Although the debate between the king and his pagan subjects resembles the one which Bede relates about the English king Edwin with his pagan advisers, in the Norwegian case it strikes one that the pagans are more persistent: in England it was the pagan high priest himself who made the proposal for conver-sion. In that respect it is more like the proof that the Danish king Harald had to give through Poppo's authentic miracle.

From a modern point of view Saint Olaf is a controversial saint. Apparently, however, he himself also had doubts about his methods of conversion. The saga tells how, after having been driven out by the Danish king, Olaf says:

> I must confess that in many cases I did not rule this kingdom with justice, but with force and recklessness. I had punish-ments imposed every time God's law was violated. What was done to me, however, I shall humbly forgive.

Then Olaf flees to Russia, where he is given a cordial welcome by King Jaroslav and his wife Ingigerd. This episode in the saga is the only one in which Olaf takes on sympathetic features.[104] Ingigerd is Olaf's former fiancée, and she was really in love with him, but her father, the Swedish king, would not allow her to marry him. Olaf then, through the agency of Ingigerd, married her sister Astrid, who of course was also happy to see Ingigerd again. Olaf tells Jaroslav and Ingigerd about the problems in his country and 'the two comfort him'. Olaf and Jaroslav, both of them zealous promoters of Christianity in their countries, undoubtedly spent more time talking about their work for the church, in blissful ignorance of the power-political quarrel between Constantinople and Rome, which already existed at the time (1028).

The passages with Ingigerd are the only ones in the saga where women play a part. For the rest they are prominently absent in the Norwegian conversion story, in contrast to other princely conversion stories (Clovis, Edwin, Vladimir, Stephen and Mieszko). But it is enough to add a human aspect to Olaf's controversial martial holiness.

After a two-year stay in Russia Olaf returns to Norway in order to regain the throne. However, he is defeated and is killed. Wounded, he still prays for his enemies, and when he dies there is a solar eclipse 'just as when our Creator passed away from this world'. But his death is not in vain. Four years later the Norwegians go to Jaroslav, in order to make amends to Olaf's son Magnus (who had stayed in Russia), 'for what they had done to the father'. And Olaf, 'the eternal king of Norway', as he is called in the saga, assists his country 'through intercession with God . . . for he who, when he was in the world, converted many people who had been lost before, has now been elevated so much that he can do much more than we are able to understand'. Olaf's help extended further than his own land. The saga relates that he performed miracles in Constantinople, where a church was dedicated to him – given the military aid which the Norsemen had given to the army of the Byzantine emperor at that time, this is not surprising – in Novgorod and in London. Thus the 'eternal king' of Norway, as he is called in the saga, also takes on an ecumenical tint.

The Hungarian king

Of all the kings who founded Christianity in their countries, Stephen of Hungary (reigned 997–1038) is the most typical in the account of his Life. The two oldest chronicles of Hungary do not say much about Stephen's work. The first (c. 1180) covers the period up to Stephen and concludes with the announcement that 'the blessed King Stephen will preach the words of life and will baptize the Hungarians'.[105] The second, the *Gesta Hungarorum* by Simon de Kéza (end of the thirteenth century) praises Stephen, 'to whom God subjected many nations and to whom the emperor Henry gave the royal crown'. It is also related that, as a result of the premature death of his son, Stephen is anxious about the one after him who 'will be able to preserve the people that is still so new in the catholic faith', and when Stephen himself dies, the whole Hungarian people mourn their *sanctissimus rex*.[106] Of greater interest in this chronicle is the passage about Stephen's father, Geza, who was the first Hungarian sovereign to be baptized, but who was then prevented by God from carrying out his plan to Christianize the whole people:

> Since his hands were tainted with so much human blood, he was not the right person for converting such a great people to the faith. He himself and his house received the grace of baptism from Saint Adalbert, but from the heavenly throne came the word that he should dismiss the idea [of converting the whole people] from his mind, for the mercy of the Most High had predestined Saint Stephen, who was to be born from him, to do all that.[107]

The baptism of Geza and of his five-year-old son Stephen took place in 974, but it cannot have been administered by Adalbert of Prague, for the latter did not preach in Hungary until around 995. Adalbert probably administered the sacrament of confirmation to Stephen at that time. Geza, to whom it was not given to baptize the people, nevertheless did 'what he could and had to do for the conversion of his people according to the guidelines of Saint Adalbert, bishop of Prague', and saw to it that a large section of the nobility became Christian.

Simon de Kéza takes the passage about Geza from the Life of Stephen, which is older than the chronicles, and also the most important source for investigating the formation of the Hungarian religious self-image. This *Vita Sancti Stephani Regis* fulfils the same primary role in religious national self-expression as the eulogy of Vladimir by Ilarion of Kiev in his oration *On the Law and the Grace,* and it also has elements that correspond with the former.[108]

The beginning of the Legenda Major is as attractive as Ilarion's address and as powerful in its universalistic approach to the Christianization. It is an expression of gratitude for 'the best gift and the most perfect present from above, from the Father of light' (James 1.17), God's plan of salvation. Jesus' disciples, who were taught to speak all languages by the Holy Spirit,

> spread the seed of the Divine word all over the world . . . so that kingdoms with kings, principalities with princes, and provinces with prefects have been brought to the worship of the Christian religion and through the fire of the Holy Spirit all over the world the foundations have been laid of the universal church, and the capital of the entire world, Rome, itself . . . has cast off its idle errors. There is no longer any country or any people where Christ's mercy has not been accepted. Thus it happened that a rough and wandering people, unaware of being God's image, that is to say the Hungarians, a people inhabiting the land of Pannonia . . . according to God's decree was led from the road of injustice to the path of justice and to the hope of eternal reward.

The version by Hartvicus also adds in the case of the Hungarians: 'who once had been the scourge of the Christians'. The Legenda Minor at once begins with the situation of the Hungarians:

> So when the barbarian people of the Hungarians were entangled in the error of their unbelief and in the practising of the idle and sacrilegious superstitions of the heathen rites, the mercy of the saviour saw fit to put an end to their sins, so that, after the diabolical delusion had been stopped, at least the rest of this people would be saved.

These are not just attractive formulations, but also theologically significant. They witness to an awareness of the history of salvation and to a correct view of redemption: it is God's initiative which breaks through man's sinfulness and constitutes salvation for all peoples. As Ilarion first depicts the universal context of Christianity, and then emphasizes the merits of the national baptist king, so Stephen's hagiographer also prefaces the description of the Christian merits of the national royal saint with an observation, short but essential, about the universality of salvation

Here, then, we also find the passage mentioned above about Geza, who was considered to be unworthy of baptizing others. Nevertheless he brought foreign priests and monks to his kingdom in order to preach the true faith. However, the Christianization did not always proceed peacefully. That is what we read in the *Chronicon Posoniense,* from which the following passage is worth quoting:

> And when he could not convert them by exhortation, he had to suppress them by force of arms. So as to be able to do so, and since there were more of those who rejected the faith than those who adhered to it, he thought it necessary to inform Christian kings and sovereigns of his wish. As soon as these had learnt his wish, they not only sent help but also came themselves, for they had suffered much harm from the cruelty of the Hungarians.[109]

Thus the neighbouring states were only too willing to come to help in the conversion, which for them also implied the elimination of the military threat of the Hungarians. This is a combination which occurs frequently in the mediaeval history of Christianization. However, the Life of Stephen makes clear that this use of force by Geza is not God's way. In a nocturnal apparition a young man says to Geza: 'Peace be with you, elect one of Christ, I command you to give up your idea. It is not given to you to do what you consider, for your hands are tainted with human blood.' This is a unique statement in the histories of the conversions of sovereigns, which would have suited Olaf II of Norway very well. Nonetheless, under Geza 'the light that lightens all people began to shine in Hungary'.

The birth of Stephen is immediately interpreted in the light of salvation history with a reference to Jer. 1.5: 'Before he was formed in the womb the Lord knew him for his own.' Nor is Stephen's baptismal name, – before his baptism he was called Vaik – 'as we believe, alien to God's plan, for Stephen is a Greek name and in Latin means "crowned one", which is symbolic of the "crown of blessedness" that he is to receive'. In spite of the earlier criticism of Geza's use of force, force yet does not appear to be excluded from Stephen's work. For it is the devil who sets a tribe which does not want to submit to Christ against Stephen, whereupon the latter goes to battle 'as a soldier of Christ' (*miles Christi*). The Life relates how it is not until after the victory that the work of Christianization really starts. In lyrical formulations reminiscent of those in other conversion stories we are informed that priests travel through the country, bishops are appointed, foundations of church buildings are laid everywhere, monasteries are established. One thing and another, for that matter, happens in agreement with the 'Holy See of Rome'.

Here we have a typical emphasis in the Hungarian story of Christianization, namely that the Christianization is clearly a Catholic affair. Whereas other stories usually speak about 'the Christian faith' or 'the Christian religion and worship', the Life of Stephen frequently uses the expression *fides catholica*. It also uses *fides orthodoxa*, which at this time is still synonymous with the Catholic faith. Sometimes, together with 'preserving the Catholic faith' there is the addition of 'strengthening the *status ecclesiasticus*', which also points to a more church-orientated activity. Finally, repeated mention is made of Mary, the mother of God, who supports the work of conversion, which was not the case in the earlier conversion stories. According to the Life, the Hungarians even have a special devotion to Mary, and Stephen continually prays to Mary as 'his queen'.

Naturally, the fact that Stephen is given the title of king 'through God's will and with the apostolic blessing' also witnesses to a clear link with the Roman Catholic Church. As a result of this, Gisela, the sister of the 'Roman' emperor Henry II, is given to him as his wife. She does much for the maintenance of the church buildings. Stephen himself has a hospice built in Rome for the Hungarians who go on pilgrimage to the tomb of

Peter. But he does not limit his horizon to the Latin world: he also builds a monastery in Jerusalem and a church in Constantinople.

For his services to the church, Stephen 'received the name of apostle, for, even though he himself did not undertake the office of evangelization, as a leader and teacher of the preachers he supported and protected them'. Here we have a striking resemblance to Vladimir, who is also called apostle by Ilarion. In the Hartvicus Legend the title of 'apostle' is given to Stephen by the pope himself with the words that 'he is truly an apostle of Christ who through him led such a great people to be converted'.

As shepherd of his flock, however, Stephen adopts an attitude of awareness of sin. For when his country is threatened by an invasion by the German emperor Conrad II, and 'the new plantings of Christianity are in danger of being destroyed by the enemy', Stephen prays to Mary: 'If the shepherd is to blame, make him pay for what he deserves, but then I pray you for the innocent sheep.' Mary does not let things get that far, and the Germans withdraw.

This passage demonstrates that there was not always peace and quiet between the neighbouring Christian countries. However, the Life does not go more deeply into the political context in which Stephen lived and leaves out of account a good deal of violence in war in which Stephen was involved. For example, there was the war against his kinsman Cupan, who wanted to marry Stephen's mother and to kill Stephen: Stephen defeated him, had him drawn and quartered, and sent the pieces to four different cities.[110] Or the war against his uncle, who ruled over Transylvania. Stephen also defeated him and added Transylvania to Hungary; the chronicle mentions *rebellio fidei Christianae* as an explanation of the war.[111] The Life itself describes an atrocity which hardly suits a saint: 'with a view to setting an example' Stephen has the eyes of criminals gouged out and their hands cut off.[112]

So in this respect, too, the one-sided Christian creation of Stephen's image is comparable with Ilarion's idealizing representation of Vladimir's activities. However, the harsh political methods which were customary in mediaeval culture are not the specific character of the Christian kings, but the Christian benefactions and steadfastness in faith which they also show. The catalogue of virtues in the Life of Stephen and in Ilarion's eulogy of Vladimir coincide closely.

There is another point which makes both the Hungarian and Russian documents about Christianization contrast with the rest of the European baptismal stories: the formulations of faith. It is not in the Life of Stephen, but in a short work which he wrote for his son, that a trinitarian creed is to be found, as well as a warning against heresy.[113] These are not as elaborate as those which are found in the Russian chronicle at Vladimir's baptism, but they are sufficient also to add a theological aspect to the case of the conversion of Hungary which is lacking in other conversion stories. The brief document also expresses Stephen's strong ecclesiastical consciousness and his concern to preserve the church 'which in other places has existed from of old, but is preached in our monarchy as a young and new religion'. However, Stephen's son, to whom these admonitions were addressed, died young and therefore the Christianization of Hungary was again in jeopardy.

As was also the case in the Scandinavian conversion stories, after the death of the Christian king resistance against the Christian religion reappeared. Stephen's successor, Peter Orseolo, who conducted a political reign of terror, also promoted paganism. In 1046 this period of de-Christianization was ended by Andrew, who was recalled from his place of exile in Kiev, where, meanwhile, he had married a daughter of Jaroslav the Wise, Anastasia. Because Andrew 'decreed that, having abandoned the pagan rite, the whole Hungarian people should return to the faith in Christ and the law given by Stephen', he is called *rex catholicus*.[114]

In reality the process of Christianization in Hungary did not proceed differently from elsewhere in contemporary Europe: it had its ups and downs. In the chronicles of foreign contemporaries nothing is to be found, either, of a special form of

Christianization in Hungary. Thietmar of Merseburg mentions Stephen, whom he calls by his pre-Christian name Waic (Vajk), only in passing: 'By gracious consent and at the instigation of the emperor, Waic, the brother-in-law of duke Henry of Bavaria, founded episcopal sees in his kingdom and received the crown and ordination.'[115]

In Adam of Bremen's chronicle we also find a short but very interesting observation on the Christianization of Hungary. It is not found in the Hungarian sources and is specifically relevant to our comparative approach. It concerns the role of a woman. Adam writes:

> In the year of the Lord 1010 the people of Hungary was converted to the faith by the sister of the emperor, Gisela. She was married to the king of Hungary and made the king have himself and his family baptized. At the baptism he was given the name of Stephen. Afterwards he became holy as a result of his merits.[116]

A classic case! Apart from the wrong date, Adam of Bremen brings the event as it is described in Stephen's Life into line with the accounts about Edwin of England and Clovis. However, the Life itself already pointed to Gisela's care for the church buildings. So the Christianization of the Hungarian people was undoubtedly a common concern of the royal couple.

The Polish royal couple

With this addition to the Hungarian situation by Adam of Bremen we have a convenient transition to the last history of the baptism of a nation, that of Poland. This is indeed the female case *par excellence* in the history of the Christianization of European rulers, as appears from the chronicle by Thietmar of Merseburg. In his chronicle, Thietmar often pays attention to relations between rulers and women, for example, as we have seen, in his report on Vladimir of Kiev.[117] Sometimes he describes the sexual depravity and sometimes the exceptional piety of women. In the Polish case the question is one of piety, and of

deceitful piety at that. This is what Thietmar relates about the
Polish ruler Mieszko:[118]

> Mieszko had a noble spouse from Bohemia whose life truly
> answered her being. For she was called Dobrawa in Slavonic,
> which in German means 'the good one'. Seeing that her
> husband was still entangled in many pagan errors, this loyal
> follower of Christ deliberated in her simple mind and
> zealously, how she could also bind him to her in the faith.
> Deliberately she committed sins for some time, so as to be able
> to act virtuously afterwards.

Dobrawa thinks of a sin for a good cause: in Lent she allows
herself to be persuaded by her husband to eat meat, hoping that
he in his turn will allow himself to be persuaded by her afterwards. And after breaking the fast throughout Lent, 'a beautiful
fruit sprang from her pious aspiration'.

> The infinite goodness of the Creator brought the vehement
> persecutor to his senses, the constant exhortation of his
> beloved wife made him spit out the poison of innate unbelief,
> and he washed away original sin in holy baptism. And from
> now on the members of the people who had held aloof so far
> followed their beloved head and leader and, wearing their
> wedding garments, they joined the other disciples of Christ
> . . . Then the two spouses, the husband and the noble wife,
> rightly prided themselves upon their happiness, and all their
> subjects rejoiced in their marriage in Christ.

That took place in the year 966. So baptism resulted in an
ecclesiastical confirmation of the already existing marriage.
However decisive, therefore, the woman's role was, here too we
find the correct theological observation that in the end it is after
all 'the goodness of the Creator' that accomplishes the conversion.

This result, however, does not mean the end of the woman's
role in the Christianization of Poland. When Dobrawa dies after

giving birth to a son, Mieszko remarries a nun, Oda, daughter of an enemy margrave, without the permission of the church. The bishops condemn her sharply for 'forsaking the heavenly bride-groom for a warrior', but Thietmar makes it clear that in the end this was also a sin which led to the 'greater welfare of the country'. Oda 'in every respect strengthened the service of Christ and led many prisoners back to their homeland'. And, according to Thietmar, her many good and pious works will certainly compensate for her ecclesiastical lapse.

Thus on two occasions God appears to use a woman in his plan of Polish Christianization. This, however, is still not the end. In Poland, too, there is a crisis after the first Christianization. Mieszko's son from his first marriage, Boleslav, is a cruel ruler who 'ignored every worldly and ecclesiastical law'. He divorced his wife twice, but the third wife put him on the straight and narrow path again: 'she was devoted to Christ, directed her husband's wavering spirit to all that was good, and never stopped washing away the stains of sin of the two of them by boundless charity and abstinence'. Finally she bore five children, among them a daughter who married a son of the Russian king Vladimir, Svjatopolk.[119]

In Poland's own sources we find Thietmar's account of the female factor in the Christianization confirmed; however, there is a quite different evaluation of Boleslav from that in Thietmar's German view. In the oldest Polish chronicle *Cronica Galli Anonymi* (1120), Dobrawa comes to the rescue of Mieszko and Poland:

> Then he dwelt so much in the error of paganism that as a result of his way of life he kept seven wives. Eventually he asked a very Christian woman from Bohemia, called Dubrovca, to marry him. She, however, refused to be married unless he would give up that wicked way of life and promise to become Christian. When at last he agreed to abandon that pagan habit and to receive the sacraments of the Christian faith, this mistress came to Poland with a large worldly and ecclesiastical retinue, but did not yet commit herself to the conjugal bed

until he, gradually and diligently thinking about the Christian way of life and the religion of the church, abjured the heathen error and was united in the bosom of the mother church.[120]

The later *Chronica Polonorum* of Vincent of Cracow poses Dubrovca's condition of marriage even more sharply: 'she who loved the Catholic faith very much was not pleased to get married, before the whole Polish kingdom with the king himself had accepted the charter of the Christian confession'.[121]

Having recognized that there is every reason for praising Dubrovca for her influence on Mieszko's conversion, Gallus Anonymus praises the fact that 'from this blessed woman the famous Boleslav' was born. And the rest of the chronicle is one great eulogy of Boleslav I and his services to the church. It is not surprising that on this point the chronicler disagrees with Thietmar of Merseburg, for although he is anonymous, it is a well-known fact that he was chronicler at the Polish court, where Boleslav III was meanwhile ruler.

There are, however, also objective reasons for emphasizing the role of Boleslav I. He was indeed the founder of the church organization in Poland: he built churches and monasteries, established episcopal sees and was 'protector and defender of the church'. In that capacity Boleslav may be compared with Stephen of Hungary, in which case Mieszko may then be compared with Geza. The description of Boleslav's actions and virtues by Gallus Anonymus is tantamount to a hagiography: his services to the church and his work of conversion among the neighbouring pagan peoples along the Baltic Sea is enlarged upon in political as well as in religious terms. And on Boleslav's death Gallus composes a fine poem in honour of the sovereign who ruled over 'Latins and Slavs'.[122]

Boleslav's significance for Christianity is also highly praised by a contemporary of his, Bishop Bruno of Querfurt. This active missionary who, supported by Vladimir, even preached from Kiev among the Turkish-Asian Pecheneges, in a letter calls upon the German emperor Henry II to co-operate with Boleslav for the Christian cause in Prussia.[123] At that moment Henry II was at war with Boleslav. 'Is not it better to fight against pagans for the sake of Christianity than to use force against Christians for the sake of worldly renown?' Because of Boleslav's work of conversion Bruno compares him with the emperor Constantine the Great and Charlemagne. A year later (1009) Bruno himself died a martyr's death in Prussia.

Bruno's letter, in which he also reports to the emperor about his work in Russia and expresses himself in laudatory terms about Vladimir, is one of the few moments of 'Western' and Russian unanimity in the work of Christianization. Soon, however, that unanimity was to be broken by Boleslav and disrupted for good. For, in spite of his services to the church in Poland, Boleslav was not a saint. And, despite everything, Gallus is so objective that, apart from epithets like *magnus, famosus, gloriosus* and *pius,* high-sounding words easily used by a court chronicler, he does not use the adjective 'holy'. The honorific title under which Boleslav afterwards became well known in Polish history is 'the Brave' (*Chrobry*), which refers to his many wars.

In Gallus' chronicle the wars between Boleslav and his by now Christian neighbouring peoples, Bohemians, Saxons, Hungarians and, in particular, the Russians, are mentioned as if their being Christian is irrelevant. And the wars against pagan Pomeranians and Prussians are presented as missionary expeditions in which Boleslav 'either shattered those who persisted in unbelief, or strengthened those who had been converted in the faith'. Or elsewhere: 'He conquered the barbarian peoples surrounding him, not in order to have them pay financial tribute, but he subdued them for the sake of expanding the true religion.'[124] That exemption from taxation did not, however, apply to the Russians, against whom Boleslav waged a war the result of which was that 'since that time Russia has been tributary to Poland'.[125]

The war between Boleslav and Russia had important psychological consequences for the mutual relations between the two peoples. The issue here was Boleslav's political and military support for his Russian son-in-law Svjatopolk in the latter's struggle for power with Jaroslav which lasted three years. Immediately after Vladimir's death Svjatopolk had already killed two possible successors, Boris and Gleb, who became the first Russian canonized saints. In the fight against Svjatopolk, together with Stephen of Hungary and in alliance with the German emperor, Jaroslav had first undertaken a fruitless campaign against Boleslav. Later in the war, however, he was to be defeated after all by a reverse alliance of Boleslav with Stephen and the emperor. So neither the family relations between the Polish and Russian rulers nor their Christian faith led to peace between the two neighbouring peoples, as was the case with the Norwegian and Russian rulers. On the contrary, as a result of Boleslav's war against the Russians the relations between the two people were fundamentally destroyed, even before the definitive completion of the church schism between East and West.

In our context these political facts are worth mentioning for the sole reason that they serve to demonstrate that at a certain moment three of the national founders of the church, Boleslav, Stephen and Jaroslav, were at war with each other. And that means that the idyll of a Christian Europe was in fact disturbed from the very beginning. (Moreover the newly converted Scandinavian peoples were constantly at war with each other at this time.) The common faith was not able to overcome the political differences and military aspirations of the new Christian kings. Nevertheless the three Eastern European rulers, Boleslav, Stephen and Jaroslav, were all three at one time called 'Christian', 'most Christian' and some of them even 'holy', not only in their own and of course partial chronicles, but also by the 'objective' outsider Adam of Bremen. Adam mentions the war between Poland and Russia very briefly, calling Boleslav *rex Christianissimus*,[126] But a little later, on another occasion, he calls Jaroslav *rex sanctus* of Russia.[127]

Bulgaria

Christianity did not cause all those wars, but it was not able to put an end to them either. There was violence before, and there continued to be violence after the Christianization, while the Christianization itself was often also implemented with violence. Or rather, the Christianization sometimes ran parallel to wars which were being waged anyhow or was a factor in a power play without direct violence. And then it was a political factor in the rulers' calculations which made them decide to be converted: the actual Christianization of their countries was also determined by it. Thus Boleslav of Poland and Stephen of Hungary put their countries under the pope in order to be ecclesiastically independent of their powerful German neighbour and received from the pope the title of king.

We see very clearly the combination of political calculation and Christianization in the case of two peoples which we have not discussed yet, the Czechs and the Bulgarians. Their Christianization took place simultaneously and in a comparable political context. In 862 the Czech ruler of Greater Moravia, Rostislav, decided to undertake the Christianization of his people. Since, however, he wanted to remain independent of his powerful neighbour, the Roman emperor Ludwig the German, he asked the Byzantine emperor Michael III in distant Constantinople for missionaries who spoke the Slavonic language. Apart from the fact that the request was right from a linguistic point of view, Rostislav was also motivated by considerations of political expediency, while for the Byzantine emperor it was an opportunity of strengthening his influence in this border area between the Byzantine and German-Frankish empires. Michael sent Cyril and Methodius, who became the great apostles of the Slavs. Their success, with the pope's consent for that matter, in Czechia (and Croatia) was later destroyed by popes with a less open mind and under pressure from vindictive German bishops.

The introduction of Christianity in Bulgaria presents a similar case. In 864 the sovereign of Bulgaria, Boris, opted for the Christianization of his kingdom (which also included Serbia at the time). The conversion of Boris himself took place in the context of a peace treaty with the Byzantine emperor Michael III after a war that was lost by Bulgaria. Boris was baptized in the Greek church, but for the Christianization of his people he preferred Latin missionaries in order to remain more independent from the Byzantine empire. Here, then, was the same political consideration as on the part of the Czech sovereign, but the other way round. As the pope made insufficient concessions to Boris over the status of a Bulgarian archbishopric and hesitated to give Boris the title of king, Boris still opted for Greek Christianity. However, this involved frictions: the patriarch of Constantinople was no more prepared than the church of Rome had been to give the Bulgarian church too much independence by means of an archbishop of their own, let alone a patriarch, which was Boris' long-term goal. And later, when Boris replaced Greek as the liturgical language with Slavonic, the Greek clergy at first were against it, out of the same narrow-mindedness as the Latin clergy in Czechia. When, a century and half later (1018), the political balance of power turned in favour of Byzantium, the Christian emperor Basil II ('the Bulgarian-killer') deprived Bulgaria not only of its political independence, but also of the status of a patriarchate which it had acquired in the meantime.

There is no clear conversion story of Bulgaria in its own chronicles comparable to the other stories of national baptisms that we have discussed. There is, however, an attractive passage about the beginning of Bulgarian Christianity in the Greek Life of Clement of Ohrid. This Life of Clement, also called the 'Bulgarian Legend', is about the saints Cyril and Methodius, and Clement, the pupil of Methodius. Clement had fled from Moravia to Bulgaria, and became archbishop of Ohrid afterwards.[128] After it has been stated that Methodius himself baptized Boris – which, however, is improbable – and the whole people of the Bulgarians began to receive holy baptism, there is the following passage:

> And thus liberated from the Scythian error, the people of the Bulgarians acknowledged the true and unfailing road to

Christ, although they were late in entering the divine vineyard, around the eleventh or twelfth hour, through the grace of him who called them to it. The calling of this people took place in the year 6377 (= 869) since the creation of the world.

The comparison with those called last from the parable of the workers in the vineyard is a well-chosen biblical metaphor which puts the Christianization in a theological perspective. One may be surprised that it was not used in other European baptismal stories, for it is applicable to most of the national conversions we have dealt with.

The fine biblical metaphor disregards the worldly political factors that played a role in the conversion of Bulgaria. It is true that from a theological perspective these are no longer relevant, but the historical facts are certainly important enough for rejecting as unhistorical the notion that force and power politics did not play any role in the mission from Constantinople (compare the statement by Aleksandr Turgenev quoted at the beginning of this chapter). The Christianization of the developing European nations in Central Europe and the Balkans was part of the struggle for political spheres of influence by the then great powers in Europe, the German and the Byzantine empires.

The church politics of the East and the West in Christian Europe made use of the same methods and had the same secondary aims. All the conversions of rulers took place in a political context, but the political factor was never separate and all-decisive. In many cases a woman, the royal spouse, played a mediating role. And in every case there was mention of a bishop. Remigius in France, Augustine and Paulinus in England. Anskar in Denmark, Adalbert in Hungary. Methodius in Czechia, Clement in Bulgaria and the anonymous Greek bishop in Kiev are just as much the baptists of Europe as the kings who supported them.

In the eleventh century, when with the exception of the Finns and the Baltic peoples all the European peoples had adopted Christianity as their national religion, Christian Europe had formally become a historical reality. The twelfth and thirteenth centuries were then to see the addition of the Finns, the Estonians and the Latvians. This really involved the use of force: in the case of the Finns it was a crusade by the Swedish holy king Eric IX, and in the case of the Baltic peoples it was the knights of the German Order. The Lithuanians joined Christian Europe as the last to be called, in the fourteenth century. However, they came to adopt Christianity in a peaceful manner, by way of the marriage of their grand prince to the Christian Polish princess Jadwiga in 1385. Here Jadwiga was the last representative of this 'woman's way' to Christianity which was often taken, so in 1997 she was declared a saint by her compatriot Pope John Paul II.

The Christian Europe that had thus come into being was not a religious idyll, but a cultural community which functioned independently of the political differences. These continued to exist. The peoples that were converted to Christianity around the turn of the millennium, the peoples of Scandinavia and the Polish, Hungarian and Russian people, came to share a rising new, Christian, European culture, and as a first result of this they acquired literary culture. The first literary products of this are, among other things, the baptism stories discussed here. Of these, it can certainly be said after the comparison, the Russian is not only the most extensive but also the most attractive as a composition. And despite all the literary fiction, it also has the most theological content, for in none of the other accounts of the baptisms of kings is there such an extended salvation history and mention of such a precisely formulated confession of faith.

After the kings, their wives and their bishops, we have to mention the chroniclers themselves, the authors of the birth certificates of Christian Europe: Gregory of Tours, the Venerable Bede, Widukind of Corvey, Saxo Grammaticus, Adam of Bremen, Thietmar of Merseburg, Gallus Anonymus, the Norwegian and Hungarian writers of Lives, and Nestor and Ilarion of Kiev. All these monks, sometimes centuries removed from each other, and each of them in his own monastery cell or episcopal scriptorium, performed a common historiographical task. Without any knowledge of each other's existence, the monastic authors in Eastern and in Western Europe are themselves, through their work, the living proof of a common Christian culture. As a literary confirmation of this, I want to quote the Norman monk Orderic Vitalis (c.1200), who shows the same sense of history and personal modesty as the fictitious monk Pimen in Puškin's *Boris Godunov* with regard to his Russian chronicle:

> I firmly believe, following the prognostications of earlier writers, that in time someone will come with greater understanding than myself, and greater capacity for interpreting the various events taking place on earth, who will perhaps derive something from my writings and those of others like me, and will graciously insert this in his own chronicle or history for the information of future generations.[129]

Survey of 'nation conversions'

	Source
1. FRANKS	
Clovis (496)	Gregory of Tours
2. ANGLO-SAXONS	
Ethelbert (597)	The Venerable Bede
Edwin (626)	
3. GERMAN SAXONS	
(780)	Widukind of Corvey
4. DANES	
Harald I (826)	Saxo Grammaticus
Harald Bluetooth (960)	Adam of Bremen
5. NORWEGIANS	
Olaf Tryggveson (995–1000)	Olaf Saga
Olaf Haraldson (1015–1029)	Adam of Bremen

6. HUNGARIANS

Geza (974)	Simon de Kéza
Stephen (997–1038)	Life of Stephen

7. POLES

Mieszko (966)	Gallus Anonymus
Boleslav (992–1025)	Thietmar of Merseburg

8. BULGARIANS

Boris (864)	Life of Clement

9. RUSSIANS

Olga (959)	Nestorian Chronicle
Vladimir (988–1015)	Ilarion of Kiev

4

The Religious and Ideological
Profile of Russia

In the previous chapter I indicated the connection between the Christianization of Russia and the broader Christianization of Eastern and Northern Europe. Now we return to the theme of the formation of Russia's own religious image. In the Oration of Ilarion of Kiev this had reached not only a literary high point but also an 'ideological' balance between Christian universalism and religious patriotism.

The universalist aspect of Ilarion's view afterwards faded right into the background. Three centuries later, in the Moscow period of Russian history, Christian universalism was replaced by Orthodox exclusivism. Whereas in his Oration Ilarion wanted to give form to a sense of identity for his newly converted people within the world church, after him the religious self-awareness was ideologized and became the doctrine of the 'Third Rome' and the idea of 'Holy Russia'. In modern histories Ilarion is made the proto-Slavophile, and his oration is interpreted in terms of ideas of church and state which came into being only in the fifteenth and sixteenth centuries.[130]

Between the end of Kievan Russia and the rise of Moscow as the new centre of Russian power lies a period of political chaos and national adversity. As early as the twelfth century, the flying start of Christian culture in Russia in the eleventh century was followed by a setback in the form of civil wars between Russian rulers and by marauding expeditions of Turkish tribes from central Asia. The end of Kievan Rus' came about through the Mongol invasions, which began in 1223 and in 1240 struck the death blow to the old Russia with the destruction of Kiev. After that began the dark period in the Russian Middle Ages – apart from Novgorod, which lay to the north – which were only to come to an end in the middle of the fifteenth century.

During the long period of the heavy Tatar yoke, the designation used for the period of Mongolian occupation, there was no occasion for religious pride. People found comfort in the Orthodox Church, which despite the repeated devastation of church buildings during Tatar punitive expeditions was able to continue to function as an institution. The tie to the religion of the Russians in this period was there in the spirit of Christian humility and the sense that the disasters were a divine punishment for the people's own sinfulness. The expression 'for our sins' appears repeatedly in the accounts in thirteenth- and fourteenth-century chronicles of lost battles and plundering by the Tatars, and not as a pious cliché.

The feeling of Russia's own religious failings is powerfully expressed in the sermons of Serapion of Vladimir in the year 1270.[131] In five literary penitential sermons Serapion, bishop of Vladimir, castigates the un-Christian way of life of his people and calls himself 'your sinful father'. The Old Testament wrath of God is now being poured on the Russian people, which has still not turned to God: 'The divine seed in your hearts has not yet borne fruit.' Serapion makes it clear that the Russians, who 'already for forty years have lived in the slavery of the unbelievers', are in fact still themselves pagans in many respects. They believe in witchcraft and put people through ordeals by fire; they try to avert bad harvests with pagan rituals; and do not see that a famine which has already lasted for three years is a divine punishment for sins 'not only in Rus' but also among the Latins'. The Russians are in some respect even worse than the pagans, 'who do not kill one another's fellow-believers'.

And not only quarrels and rivalries among themselves but also generally human sins are widespread among the people that Serapion is addressing: avarice, fornication, conceit and unbelief prevail in the Russian land.

In their strict and sombre tone, Serapion's sermons are at the

opposite extreme from the optimistic tenor of Ilarion's eulogy to
the newly converted Russian people; they show the collapse of
the Christian land that Ilarion had depicted so evocatively.

> The churches of God are devastated, the sacred vessels, the
> venerable crosses and holy books are desecrated, the clergy
> have fallen victim to the sword, the bodies of the holy martyrs
> are fed as food to the birds, the blood of our fathers and
> brothers has drenched the land like an overflowing river, the
> power of our rulers and leaders has disappeared . . . many
> cities are uninhabited, our fields are overgrown with weeds,
> our greatness is diminished, our beauty has departed, our
> wealth has become the prey of our enemies, our work is the
> inheritance of the pagans and our land the property of
> strangers. We are put to shame by those who dwell around our
> land and we have become the mockery of our enemies, for we
> have called down upon ourselves the wrath of the Lord like
> rain from heaven.

The ideological contrast in Serapion's sermons is that between
pagans and Christians; here even some of the Russians form part
of paganism. In the accounts of the Mongolian invasion in the
chronicles the thematic opposition is that between the Christian
faith and the Orthodox people on the one hand and the enemy of
the Christians and the unbelievers on the other. This is the case,
for example, in the gripping account of the devastation of
Rjazan, in which 'the godless tsar Batu wants to seize the whole
Russian land and exterminate Christian faith and raze the
churches of God to the ground'.[132]

There were also Russian martyrs in this religious confrontation. Although most rulers yielded to some ritual and religious
demands on their obligatory visit to the khan, prince Michail of
Černigov and his boyar Feodor defended the faith to the death
(1246). The theme of Christianity and paganism comes clearly to
the fore in the account in the chronicle, which has the form of
a martyrology.[133] his visit to Khan Batu, Michail refused to
venerate the Tatar idols and a picture of Genghis Khan. He said
that 'Christians may not venerate creatures and idols, but only

the Holy Trinity, the Father, the Son and the Holy Spirit'. Michail was prepared to bow to Batu 'because God has entrusted the rule to you, but I will not bow before those to whom the others bow'. By 'the others' he means the Russian prince Boris of Rostov and his boyars, who begged Michail to yield, because otherwise he would face certain death. Thereupon Michail answered that he did not 'just want to be called a Christian and do the works of the pagans'. And with some central texts from the Gospels (Luke 17.33; Mark 10.36–38 and Matt. 10.32) he confirmed his readiness to 'suffer for Christ and to shed his blood for the Orthodox faith'.

This narrative is so special because there is as yet no mixture of Christianity with nationalistic or anti-Latin feelings. (As far as the latter are concerned, Michail had earlier enjoyed protection against the Tatars in Hungary, where his son married the daughter of the Hungarian king.) In this respect the narrative is unique among the thirteenth- and fourteenth-century lives of Russian rulers. It is also interesting historically that the Russian narrative about Michail of Černigov is confirmed by the Franciscan John of Piano Carpini, who at that moment was paying a visit to the Mongolian khan on behalf of Pope Innocent IV.[134]

Conflict with the West

In the above-mentioned writings the Russians are the defenders of Christianity against the threat from the East. But in the thirteenth century, as well as the opposition between Christians and pagans there is a new opposition, between Orthodox and Latins, and this quickly began to overshadow the other. Here we come to the break between Roman Catholics and Greek Orthodox, which only now began to have an influence on the religious self-image of the Russians. That was encouraged by two political and military events. The first was the plundering of Constantinople in 1204 by Genoese and Venetian crusaders and the appointment of a Latin emperor in the Byzantine empire. This event was experienced by the Orthodox world as a deep humiliation and as a visible expression of Latin arrogance. All the more striking is the fact that a Russian contemporary still does not see this as a Western plot against Orthodoxy. In his eye-witness account of the cruel plundering of the Constantinople by the crusaders he twice points out that the pope and the German emperor, who gave political support to the banished Byzantine pretender to the throne, had ordered the crusaders not to use violence against Constantinople: 'Do not wage war with the imperial city . . . do no harm to the Greek land.' According to the Russian author, the pope's view is that if Constantinople does not want the political candidate whom they support, then the crusaders must send him back to Italy and continue their journey to Jerusalem.[135] So there is still no general antipathy to the Catholic West.

That changes with the second military event, the crusade of the German Order in Livlandia and the conquest of the Russian city of Pskov. The Germans were defeated in 1242 by the Russians under the leadership of Aleksandr Nevskij, ruler of Novgorod. We can call this the first ideological confrontation between Russia and the Catholic West. Of course Aleksandr was not aware of the historic significance of the military clash, but as St Aleksandr Nevskij he has become the symbol for Russian Orthodox steadfastness against the efforts at Catholic infiltration in Russia.

In 1240 Aleksandr had already defeated the Swedes, who during their crusade for converting the Finnish tribes on the orders of Pope Gregory IX had attacked adjacent Russian territory over the river Neva.

In a Life written around the end of the thirteenth century, Aleksandr is portrayed as a typical Christian ruler in accordance with the hagiographical method of comparison with Old Testament and Roman predecessors: Aleksandr is called 'the power of Samson', 'the wisdom of Solomon' and 'the bravery of the emperor Vespasian, who subjugated the Jewish kingdom'.[136] With these gifts Aleksandr went against 'the king of a Roman land from the north', i.e. Sweden, and against 'those of the West', which is a reference to the Germans. In this fight the Russian ruler is compared with David, Moses and Joshua.

The Life makes mention of a delegation of two cardinals to Aleksandr in the name of 'the pope from great Rome', in which the pope calls on him to obey his teaching. Aleksandr replies that he already knows the whole history of salvation and the church, but 'we accept no instruction from you'. This passage refers to a letter from Innocent IV to Aleksandr Nevskij in 1248. In it the pope admonishes the Russian ruler 'to forsake the false way of corruption which leads to the damnation of eternal death ... and to recognize the Roman church as mother and to obey its pope'.[137] That is a rather tactless attempt on the part of Rome to achieve church unity with the Russians. It is a total disqualification of Orthodoxy for which Michail of Černigov had died a courageous death two years earlier. The pope promises Aleksandr that if he accepts this offer he will make him the equal of the other Catholic rulers. Possibly Innocent is suggesting bestowing the title of king on him, as did his successor Alexander IV on the West Russian ruler Daniil of Galicia. Alexander IV speaks just as sweepingly about Orthodoxy as 'the darkness of unbelief'.[138]

In the letter, Innocent called on Aleksandr to form a Christian front against the pagan Tatars, who were then also threatening central Europe, with the 'Brothers of the Teutonic house who are in Livlandia' (German Order of Knights). However, the Russian ruler rejected the approach and opted for a *modus vivendi* with the Tatars rather than a collaboration with the Western church against a common foe. Whatever Aleksandr's political calculations may have been, here is the first Russian expression of an assertive religious sense of identity, resulting in a concrete political decision against Western Christianity. In reaction to this, in 1258 Pope Alexander IV incited the Lithuanians to a crusade – which proved unsuccessful – against the Tatars and the Russians together. So here the pope was also making common cause with the pagans against other Christians, since at that time the Lithuanians were still pagans.

Aleksandr's rejection of the pope's approach is the first Russian political action against Western Catholicism. However, this defensive action on the part of the Russians was the mirror image of the Catholic repudiation of Orthodoxy, as is evident from the succinct choice of words by Pope Innocent. The unsubtle terminology in papal diplomacy is striking, but at that time in the Catholic Church it was already tradition to reject Orthodoxy completely. A letter from a Polish bishop to Bernard of Clairvaux from the year 1150 is an illustration of this.[139] In it Bernard, the preacher of the crusades, is asked to 'exterminate the godless rites and customs of the Ruthenians (= Russians) (*impios Ruthenorum ritus atque observantias extirpare*)'. And 'not only in Ruthenia, which is as it were another world (*quae quasi est alter orbis*), but also in Poland and Bohemia, the disorderly Slavs (*Slavos incompositos*) must be enlightened about the moral way of life', so that through Bernard the 'uncivilized barbarity is cultivated and inhuman people are tempered'.

These words of bishop Matthew of Cracow are quoted to make it clear that the attitude of the Catholic West was not much more open than the Orthodox East, and vice versa. And in any case the formation of the negative image of the East in the Latin West in the twelfth and thirteenth century was more definite than the other way round.

In this light, Aleksandr Nevskij still seems moderate in his answer to the pope. Nevertheless, as the first Russian ruler to have preserved the Russian land from Catholic influence, he has become an abiding symbol in the Russian Orthodox Church, which declared him a saint in 1546. In secular patriotism, too, he is honoured as a defender of Russian identity against the West. During the Second World War he was the church's symbol of the fight against the Germans, and despite the fact that he died as a monk, he was portrayed in armour. Even today, when according to many Russians the Russian national values are being threatened by modern Western influence, Aleksandr Nevskij's memory is kept alive. In 1992 there was a commemoration in religious nationalistic circles of the 750th anniversary of the battle against the German Order of Knights as an example of present-day wakefulness against the spiritual war being waged by the West. Aleksandr Nevskij figures as a kind of Russian

Mars, an Orthodox god of war, as the priest Georgij Čistjakov
has said in a critical review.[140]

In addition to Aleksandr Nevskij, there is another thirteenth-
century ruler who appeared as the defender of Russian
Orthodoxy and political independence. This is Dovmont of
Pskov, a Lithuanian warrior who in 1266 went over to
Christianity from paganism and was elected ruler of Pskov. He
married a granddaughter of Aleksandr Nevskij and like him
became a convinced defender of 'the holy church and the fatherland' against his pagan fellow-tribesmen of Lithuania and the
rising Catholic Germans in the Baltic. The latter are consistently
referred to in Dovmont's Life, which was written shortly after his
death in 1299, as 'people of the pagan Latin faith', 'pagan
Germans' or 'pagan Latins'.[141]

With his victory over the Catholic Swedes and Germans and
his rejection of collaboration with the pope, Aleksandr Nevskij
brought about a historical turning point in Russian history. He
not only consolidated the religious choice made by Vladimir of
Kiev but also made it the basis of the Russian sense of identity.
Now the political and cultural division of Europe, which was
caused by the Tatar domination, became a deliberate religious
division. Here the collaboration with the Tatar overlords was a
matter of political realism, but did not represent any religious
threat to Orthodoxy. As soon as the chance arose, the Russians
would also turn against the Asian oppressors. But that would not
be for around a century; then for the first time Moscow appears
on the political world stage.

Conflict with the Tatars

At the beginning of the fourteenth century the city founded on
the river Moskva, which had become a principality in 1276, was
able to gain the leading position among rival Russian principalities. In 1328 Ivan Kalita of Moscow gained the title grand prince
and was appointed tax collector over the other principalities
(hence his nickname Kalita, which means 'money bag'). In that
year the metropolitan also moved from Vladimir to Moscow;

this marks the beginning of the cohabitation of church leaders and political leaders in the Kremlin. It is also the beginning of a close collaboration between church and state in the construction of a unitary Russian state, or, as it says in the chronicles, 'the gathering of the Russian land'. The fourteenth and fifteenth centuries were to show a steady growth of the power of Moscow, through diplomacy, acquisition, marriage policy and the conquest of Tver, Pskov and Novgorod.

The first literary document in which the political and religious self-awareness of Moscow comes to the fore is the life of Dmitrij Donskoj, a leader who occupies a crucial place in mediaeval Russian history. In 1380 he defeated the Tatars and their Lithuanian allies in the battle of Kulikovo by the river Don (hence the name Donskoj). That was the first victory over the Tatar occupying forces, which were thought to be invincible, since their arrival one hundred and fifty years earlier. It was an enormous psychological boost for the Russian people and the first joint political and military action by the Russian principalities, which were divided among themselves. It was the salvation not only of the Russian state but also of the Christian church in Russia, a salvation from the Tatars who had meanwhile become Muslim, and had dropped their earlier tolerant attitude to the Orthodox Church.

Dmitrij Donskoj was revered as the defender of Orthodox Russia and more than that. His Life, written in the new panegyric style of Moscow hagiography, already contains some terms and themes which were to become stereotypes for the Russian political and religious self-awareness.[142]

Dmitrij is praised for his service to 'the whole of Orthodox Christianity'. In his eulogy the writer does not want to cite 'any examples from the writings of the ancient Greek philosophers . . . but to use holy scripture as I understand it as a mirror'. Then he produces a rich arsenal of Old Testament types of the Moscow prince, though most for the figures prove to be fragile foreshadowings: Adam, Seth, Enoch, Noah, Abraham and Isaac come off worse than Dmitrij. And so do the following people:

With whom shall I compare this grand prince, the tsar of the Russians? . . . Do I address you as Israel? But Israel strove with God, whereas you fought with foreign tribes, with the dishonourable sons of Hagar and the pagan Lithuanians, for the holy churches, through which you have made Christian faith as strong as the ladder to heaven . . . Shall I give you the name of Moses? But he was only ruler of the Hebrew people. And you in your principality had many peoples and your name has shone in many lands with grateful reverence.

For the Roman land praises Peter and Paul, the Assyrian John the Theologian, the Indian the apostle Thomas, that of Jerusalem James the brother of the Lord; the whole coastal region [viz. of the Black Sea] praises Andrew, the first to be called, the Greek land emperor Constantine, the Kievan land with the surrounding cities Vladimir. But you, grand prince Dmitrij, are praised by the whole Russian land.

It is interesting that in all his praise the author recognizes Dmitrij's modest knowledge of the Bible, but he is able to give it a positive twist: 'Although he did not master the divine scriptures to the last letter, he fulfilled it all in spiritual love of wisdom through his deeds.'

The closing line is a variation on the passage from Ilarion's *Oration on the Law and the Grace* that we already know. And right at the beginning of the Life the hagiographer had already associated Dmitrij with 'tsar Vladimir the new Constantine, who has baptized the Russian land'.

With these comparisons the line is laid down from the Old Testament leaders to the rulers of Moscow, which was to become a fixed theme in the Moscow ideology. How lively recollection of Dmitrij Donskoj still is in the present Russian Orthodox Church is evident from the fact that he was officially declared a saint in 1988, which was a canonical confirmation of the already existing veneration of him. Here the Russian church may have added a new nationalistic note to its concept of holiness, but the historical significance of Dmitrij Donskoj is beyond all doubt, for both the rise of the Russian state and the rest of Europe. For the young state of Moscow in 1380 it was a question of 'get on top or go under'. And for Europe the Russian conquest of the Tatars in 1380 was of the same far-reaching importance as Charles Martel's victory over the Saracens at the battle of Poitiers in 732 and Jan Sobieski's victory over the Turks in 1683. The difference is that neither Charles Martel nor Jan Sobieski was canonized, though the latter was given the title *defensor fidei* by the pope.

In addition to the bombastic Life of Dmitrij, which is very frugal with historical events, another two documents are devoted to the battle of Kulikovo, which are far more informative and expressive: *The Account of the Battle with Mamaj* and the famous epic *Zadonščina*. They are really more relevant to the Russian sense of religious identity than the pious Life.

That is already indicated in the complete title of the first narrative, which runs: 'The beginning of the account of how God gave the victory to the ruler and grand prince Dmitrij Ivanovič over the pagan Mamaj at the Don and how through the prayers of the most pure mother of God and Russian miracle-workers God put the godless sons of Hagar to shame.' The tone of this narrative is clearly religious, but this is combined in a balanced way with a mass of historical facts, realistic descriptions and dramatic tension. It is Russian in a religious but not in a national-istic way. The leitmotif is Christianity against the pagans or sons of Hagar or Ishmaelites, as the Muslim Tatars are called. Dozens of times in this lengthy narrative the expressions 'the Christian faith, all Orthodox Christians, the Christian people, the world of the Christians' occur over against 'the pagans, the godless, and Mamaj the persecutor of the Christians'. And although for the Russians it seems a hopeless task, the narrative speaks through-out of a biblical trust in God, there are repeated honest prayers, people are aware of their own sins and show a readiness to die for the cause of Christianity. Here too Old Testament com-parisons of Dmitrij with Moses and his victory over the Pharaoh, and with David and Gideon, appear, but without the pretensions of these metaphors in the Life. Here Dmitrij is a man with doubts and a sense of weakness. His requests for advice from Sergij of Radonež are mentioned repeatedly at length.

Reference is made to the baptism of Russia by Vladimir of Kiev and the duty he was then given to remain loyal to the faith. That not all Russians did that is evident from the betrayal by the rulers of Rjazan, who collaborated with the khan Mamaj. On the other hand two Lithuanian rulers also defended Christianity, despite the fact that their father, the grand prince of Lithuania, similarly chose to side with the Tatars.

The author of the narrative is aware of the great importance of the struggle: the future of Russia and Orthodox Christianity is at stake. However, the association of these two issues is not deepened in a nationalistic way. In other words, not the principality of Moscow but 'the Russian land' is made the goal. It is the equation which Christians, Catholic and Protestants have so often made in wars against one another in history: 'for faith and fatherland'.

The moment of battle itself is described in strongly religious terms and at the same time in realistic detail. Dmitrij takes the cross that is hanging on his chest and invokes it with words used by Constantine the Great. All the Russians cry out, 'God of the Christians, help us', and the Tatars invoke their gods. And that battle was fierce: people 'dealt cruelly with one another . . . and a great many thousand human souls created by God perished in the space of a single hour'. Initially the Tatars gain the upper hand, and the Russians are 'trampled down like grass'. But then the Russians send in their main force and 'with the power of the Holy Spirit' they succeed in felling the Tatars, 'as if they were cutting down a wood, and like grass under the scythe they perished under the horses' hooves of the Russian sons'. Then Mamaj, who senses defeat, begins to call on his gods, including the old Slavic gods Perun and Chor and 'his great helper Muhammad'. This is the only time that the Islamic identity of the Tatars is indicated more closely. The Slavic gods are mentioned to indicate the idolatrous character of Islam. But the Russians continue 'to leap on their enemies like wild beasts and to shear them like a flock of sheep'.

The victory was a hard one for the Russians: the human corpses lay 'like haystacks' in heaps and it took eight days to separate the Russian bodies from the Tatar bodies and give them Christian burial. According to the narrative, in total 253,000 Russians died out of 300,000. That is an exaggeration, but the number of 100,000 estimated by historians is enough to indicate the extent of the battle.

The other Old Russian document which deals with the battle of Kulikovo, the *Zadonščina* epic, also uses the religious paradigm. It begins with a biblical comparison between the two parties, who are traced back to sons of Noah. Japhet is the forefather of 'Orthodox Rus'' and Shem is the ancestor of the Eastern peoples, 'the pagan Tatars'. The term 'pagan' appears thirty times and the term 'Christian' ten. This religious perspective of *Zadonščina* is notable because the work derives much from the famous twelfth-century Song of Igor. That celebrates and bewails the battle against the Polovtsians of Asia which the Russians lost, but has no Christian framework of interpretation.

The Russian victory in Kulikovo did not finish off the Tatar-Mongols. Only two years later, in 1382, they returned under the leadership of Khan Toktamisj and set Moscow ablaze. And in 1395 the cruel Tamburlane was at the gates of the city. Moving chronicles were written about these traumatic events in the history of Moscow. The 'weeping of the church' in the chronicle of the devastation of Moscow by Toktamisj is emotional: the church bewails the death of her children and the disappearance of the splendid celebrations of the liturgy in church buildings which were once so beautiful.[143]

The threat to the city from Tamburlane has been associated with the most revered depiction of Mary in Russia, the icon of the Vladimir Mother of God. Prince Vasilij I and metropolitan Kiprian had the miraculous icon brought from the former capital, Vladimir, to Moscow, where it was greeted by great crowds of the population. The Muscovites attribute to her presence the sudden retreat of Tamburlane, which spared the population new slaughter.[144] Since 1495 the Mother of God has been regarded as the guardian of Moscow, and she is commemorated every year on 26 August. Later in Russian history the Vladimir icon was often invoked and carried through the city to avert political disaster, the last time in October 1993, when it was taken from the Tretjakov museum to avert the threat of a civil war.

The church's involvement in the struggle against the Tatars was very great and a matter of course. As I have remarked, in general the fourteenth-century metropolitans of Moscow play an important role in the consolidation of the Russian state and the growing national consciousness which was associated with it. Metropolitans Pëtr and Aleksij, both of whom were declared saints, were particularly important. It is related in the Life of Pëtr how he went through the territories of Kiev and Volhinia preaching to strengthen believers against the influence of the 'pagans of other beliefs' (*poganych inovercev*), i.e. the Catholics.[145] He also went through Tver, Moscow's rival, where he was badly treated, and to Vladimir-Suzdal. Finally 'he found a city which was distinguished for its gentleness, with a prince Ivan, the grandson of Aleksandr (Nevskij), one was a true believer'. Pëtr was buried in the Kremlin, and by miracles round his tomb 'God enlightened the land of Suzdal and the city which is called Moscow'. Shortly before his death Pëtr had transferred the metropolitan see of Vladimir-Suzdal to the new capital and urged Ivan Kalita to build the Uspenskij cathedral in the Kremlin, which has become the main church of Russian Orthodoxy.

His successor, metropolitan Feognost, was a less pastoral leader and put the political interests of Moscow above all else. On the orders of Ivan Kalita, who burned down the city of Tver in the name of the Tatars, Feognost excommunicated prince Aleksandr of Tver, thus also stigmatizing Moscow's rival ecclesiastically.[146]

The next metropolitan, Aleksij, was a powerful church leader, and for some years as regent of the young Dmitrij Donskoj he was also the political leader of Russia. He defended the position of Moscow above all against the power of Lithuania, which was increasing strongly at that moment; by then it had conquered the whole of western Russia, the Ukraine and the land of White Russia. Aleksij wanted the monk Sergij of Radonež to be his successor, but Sergij resolutely refused out of Christian humility.

However, Sergij continued to be an important moral support for the rulers of Moscow, especially for Dmitrij Donskoj in his struggle against the Tatars.

The failed Council of Florence

Around 1400 Moscow begins to take on an ecclesiastical profile over against the Byzantine empire. From now on, for the Russians the focal point of Orthodoxy began gradually to shift from Constantinople to Moscow. There had already been a good deal of friction with the patriarch of Constantinople over the nomination of metropolitans, as was again the case with the successor to Metropolitan Aleksij, but in general respect for the Byzantine emperor and the Greek mother church had remained.

1393 saw the first open challenge from Moscow to the Byzantine empire by grand prince Vasilij I. The occasion was authority over the Orthodox believers in the Russian territory ruled by Lithuania. The emperor and patriarch of Constantinople wanted to appoint their own metropolitan there, separate from Moscow. Vasilij I reacted with the church-political decision no longer to mention the name of the emperor during the celebration of the liturgy and to delete it from the diptychs (which contained the names of the dignitaries of the church and the empire who were to be commemorated in the liturgy). 'We have a church, but we do not have an emperor,' was Vasilij's position.

With this decision the ruler of Moscow came into direct collision with patriarch Antonios IV of Constantinople, since for the latter the emperor and the church were indissolubly bound together. He writes this in a letter to Vasilij which has become a historical document of Byzantine Orthodox ecclesiology.[147] The deletion of the 'divine' name of the emperor appeared to be an undermining of the church of Christ itself:

> The holy emperor has a great significance for the church. He is not an emperor like the other rulers and governors of a land . . . The emperors convened the ecumenical councils, and

through legislation they confirmed what the divine and holy canons say about the right dogmas and about the way of life of Christians . . . It is impossible for the Christians to have a church but no emperor. The imperial power and the church have a great unity and community, and it is quite impossible for them to be separated from each other.

This apologia for the emperor does not mean that the emperor is head of the church, for Antonios also says 'that the patriarch occupies the place of Christ and that he sits on the throne of the Lord himself'. But the letter is the most pregnant formulation of the famous symphony of church and state in the Byzantine world-view. And although the grand prince of Moscow, Vasilij, does not agree, ironically later the Russian tsars were to adopt this view of the church.

The next ecclesiastical clash with Constantinople took place on the occasion of the Council of Ferrara-Florence in 1439. This ecumenical council was meant to restore church unity between East and West, but for the Russian church it became not only a new endorsement of the break between Orthodoxy and Catholicism, but also the cause of a temporary break between Moscow and Constantinople.

At the council the patriarch and the emperor of Constantinople and most other Eastern bishops were behind reunion with Rome. So was the metropolitan of Moscow, Isidor, who was one of the most powerful advocates of union. From a Russian account of the journey to Florence, written by a Suzdal member of the Russian delegation, there seems to have been a benevolent attitude towards the Western Church.[148] This first Russian travel account of Europe is an objective and comprehensive account full of admiration of the material aspects of the German and Italian cities to which the Russian delegate went: the cultivated fields, the solidly built houses, efficient water supplies and well-stocked shops. A visit to a monastery in Lübeck also caused wonderment: at the realistic depiction of the Christmas event – 'the most pure virgin is so real' –, which is an interesting observation from a member of the Orthodox Church in which pictures are forbidden – for the many books in the monastery library and for the good food. Florence, too, evoked universal awe among the Russian travellers: not only the beautiful churches and strict monasteries but also the pilgrim houses so carefully looked after.

Little is said about the theological happenings at the Council. Here the author contents himself with a simple remark that after the restoration of unity the whole council sang and that metropolitan Isidor and twelve Greek metropolitans sat with the cardinals next to the pope, 'who sat on a golden throne as befits his rank'. He goes on: 'And on the same day Isidor and the Russian bishop Avramij received the pope's blessing before their return journey to Rus'.' It is not a very spiritual account, but at all events it expresses no hostility to the Catholic Church.

However, in addition to this account from 1440 another version of the Russian appearance in Florence has been handed down, written by Simeon of Suzdal; it is not clear whether he is the same person as the Suzdal author mentioned above. If that is the case, then he has now radically changed his view in a frontal rejection of the attempt at reunion and the Catholic Church as a whole. This version is included in the Moscow codex, a chronicle compiled at the end of the fifteenth century.[149] In contrast to the account mentioned above, this contains a good deal of theological information. Metropolitan Markos of Ephesus, who was in fact an opponent of union with Rome, is reported at length. He berates the pope so fiercely that the pope leaves the council along with all the cardinals and bishops and all the Italians and Germans. The teaching of the Catholic Church is said to be 'apostate, heretical, deceitful and lying'; in short, 'the Latins are no Christians'. The chronicle mentions that the pope bought the Greek patriarch and the Byzantine emperor and the metropolitan of Moscow with money, so that these have been covered with 'the darkness of unbelief' (the same expression as was used two centuries earlier in the opposite direction by pope Innocent IV in his letter to Aleksandr Nevskij).

Woe to this pernicious seduction, woe to this union of the

abomination with Greek Orthodoxy! How is the blackness of darkness taken for the living light? How will the right faith be united with the Latins? The emperor and the patriarch of Orthodoxy have yielded to the seductions of the Latin heresies, they are entangled in the net of gold, they succumb through the lies of Isidor.

After this the chronicler lapses into a tirade against Latin customs like the use of musical instruments in church, kneeling during the liturgy, and priests shaving their beards. And then there is an extensive quotation from the letter of the 'godless Isidor' about reunion, in which the eirenic tone of this letter is reproduced with striking objectivity. But the chronicler categorically rejects its content with a mention of the points of theological difference like the procession of the Holy Spirit, the use of unleavened bread in the eucharist and the doctrine of purgatory. Moreover the letter from pope Eugenius to Vasilij II is quoted and it is said that the ruler of Moscow was insensitive to it. Vasilij had Isidor arrested and deliberately let him escape in order to be rid of him; otherwise, according to the rules of the Orthodox Church, 'this corrupter of the church had to be burned or buried alive'. This prevented

Christianity from being turned into Latindom . . . by the unmasking of the deceitful enemy by the mighty Vasilij Vasil'evič, instructed by God, the tsar of all Russia radiant in piety, to whom God the Lord had given all this to grasp with understanding and to judge with wisdom.

On his return, Isidor did not in fact act very tactfully, provocatively entering Moscow with a Latin cross and surprising the unprepared believers in the Uspenskij cathedral in the Kremlin with mention of the name of the pope in the intercessions. But given the letter cited above, his intentions seem to have been honest.

The failure of Isidor's enterprise was not only the end of the last attempt at union between Rome and Moscow but also implicitly the Russian annexation of the Byzantine imperial claim to leadership of the church: it is the 'tsar' of Moscow, as Vasilij II is prematurely called in the chronicles, who determines the true faith, and not the head of the church. And here Vasilij II does what his father Vasilij I had formerly reproached the Byzantine emperor for doing.

With Vasilij II Russian caesaropapism has clearly come to the fore for the first time. It goes further than the nomination of bishops who favour particular political courses, as was the case in the German caesaropapism at the time of the investiture dispute. The rulers of Moscow concern themselves with the content of faith and give themselves an ecclesiological role. This is expressed in the words of a contemporary, who praises Vasilij because 'he has confirmed all his priests in the faith . . . has strangled the Latin heresy and not allowed it to flourish among Orthodox Christians'.[150]

In connection with the nomination of bishops, before the Council of Florence Vasilij II had already made critical comments about the nomination of the Greek Isidor as metropolitan of Moscow by the patriarch, passing over his own candidate, bishop Iona of Rjazan. Now that Isidor had been deposed and had fled, Vasilij II and the Russian bishops could immediately elect Iona as metropolitan of Moscow. That happened in 1448, and with it the Orthodox Church of Russia became autocephalous, independent. Now too the anachronistic reference in the title metropolitan 'of Kiev and all Rus'' was replaced by 'of Moscow and all Rus'', and that is how it has remained to the present day. When after the fall of Constantinople the patriarch and the whole of the Greek church again broke the union with Rome, Moscow also restored ecclesiastical contact with the patriarch, who recognized the *fait accompli* of the independence of the Russian church.

The Ukraine and White Russia, which had already belonged to the kingdom of Poland and Lithuania for around a century, were now also ecclesiastically cut off from Moscow and continued to belong to the patriarchate of Constantinople. In 1458 Kiev was given its own metropolitan. This made the break between this

Old Russian territory and Moscow Russia even greater. The Russian church was split, and the two parts of the Russian nation were alienated from each other. Now there came into being a distinctive Ukrainian identity which was not done away with by the incorporation of the territory in 1654 into the kingdom of Moscow and in the twentieth century was again to lead to a break with Moscow.

The independence of the Moscow-Russian church was a milestone in the religious sense of identity of the Russian state. This was rapidly followed by a political element as a consequence of the capture of Byzantium in 1453 by the Ottoman Turks.

The fall of Constantinople is described in an account by a Russian by the name of Nestor Iskander in that gripping atmospheric way which make the Russian chronicles such special literature.[151] It must have been almost an eye-witness account, but nothing more is known about the author, who presents himself as a Russian prisoner and slave of the Turks. The conclusion of the chronicle, with its philosophy of history, is important for our theme. In it Byzantine oracles and Old Testament prophecies are related to Constantinople, together with reminiscences from ancient Greek history.

> And this happened and was accomplished because of our sins: the unlawful Muhammad went to sit on the imperial throne, the most exalted of all kingdoms which have existed under the sun. And he began to rule over those who had ruled over the two parts of the world, he conquered those who the proud Artaxerxes had conquered . . . and conquered those who the wondrous Troy had conquered . . . But know well, accursed one, that when all has been fulfilled that was predicted by Methodius Patarskij and Leo the Wise and the signs about this city, then the following too will not pass by and will also be fulfilled. For it is written: 'The fair people together with those who founded this city shall gain the victory over all the Ishmaelites and shall take possession of the city of the seven hills together with those to whom of old it legally belonged, and the fair people will rule in the city of seven hills and

possess it, the sixth and fifth tribe, and they shall bear fruit in it and enjoy great abundance, and they shall take vengeance on the sanctuaries.

These are obscure statements, based on old Byzantine predictions of a rule of the Ishmaelites (the sons of Hagar, the Muslims) lasting for three hundred years, and an idiosyncratic interpretation of the visions of Daniel 7 and Ezekiel 38. The notion of a 'fair people' is based on a Greek and later Russian word-play on the name 'Roos' in Ezek.38.2. This speaks of a ruler of Roos [in fact the original Hebrew is *ros*, head], and this 'Roos people' can be translated into Greek as *rousios* people, that is 'fair people'. In Russian the Greek *rousios* is *rusyj*, and that in turn resembles *russkij*, 'Russian'. Finally, the original name 'Roos' is also the Byzantine name for Rus', the old name for 'Russia'. Thus by a double word play the Russian people can be identified as the fair people from the visions of Ezekiel.[152]

Naïve though this religious interpretation of history may be, it indicates the feeling of historical expectation that the Russians had in the second half of the fifteenth century. The fall of the Orthodox capital of the world, the new Rome, Constantinople, led among the Russians to the notion that they had been called to make good this shame on Christianity, or, as Nestor Iskander says, 'to annihilate and obliterate this evil and godless Ottoman faith and to renew and strengthen the whole Orthodox and unstained Christian faith'. This sense became the beginning of the notion that Moscow Russia has become the political and spiritual heir of the Byzantine empire, and that consequently the grand prince of Moscow is the new emperor/tsar.

Moscow and the fall of Constantinople

The conclusion that Moscow is the spiritual heir of Byzantium was drawn by Ivan III (1462–1505). Ivan III is the last great 'gatherer of the Russian land', who conquered Novgorod and thus added the extensive northern Russia to Moscow and violently eliminated Moscow's rival, Tver. In 1480 he also definitively rid Moscow of the Tatars, thus successfully completing what Dmitrij Donskoj had begun in 1380. He was urged on powerfully to settle things with the Tatars by archbishop Vassian of Rostov, who wrote a letter to the vacillating Ivan III. Vassian again uses Old Testament images for the Russian faith against the Tatars, but he goes one step further: as Moses and Joshua once freed Israel from the Pharaoh, Ivan must 'liberate the new Israel, the people named after Christ, from the accursed, ostentatious new Pharaoh, the pagan Achmed'.[153] Twice the Russian people is referred to as *novyj Izrail*, but it is also called on to do penance for its sins like the old Israel.

Victory over the Tatars was finally achieved without a struggle: the armies retreated, making Russia on balance master in its own land. But during the week-long confrontation at the river Ugra there was the same tension in Russia as there had been in 1380. The chronicle relating this event ends with a historic patriotic appeal to the 'Sons of Russia' to protect the fatherland from the fate that Bulgarians, Serbians, Greeks, Albanians, Croats and Bosnians have suffered from the Turks.[154] This is one of the first times that the term 'fatherland' (*otečestvo*) is used.

However, the most important ideological development is the parallelism between Moscow and Byzantium. The visible expression of this was the marriage of Ivan to princess Zoë Paleologos, the niece of the last Byzantine empire. She was living in Rome, and enjoyed the protection of the pope. The pope planned to marry her to the ruler of Moscow in order in this way to win him over to the church union with Rome which had been resolved on at the Council of Florence. Ivan in his turn could increase his international prestige enormously by a dynastic alliance with the Byzantine princess. The marriage went through, but the church union came to nothing because Zoë, in Russia called Sophia, became Orthodox again.

But the coming of Zoë did lead to an artistic convergence between Russia and Europe, an interesting footnote to the religious and ideological alienation between Russia and Europe. In keeping with the new political self-awareness, Ivan III developed the Kremlin into the majestic centre of the Russian state and church in the form which it now has. He did this with the help of Italian architects who came in Zoë's wake. That gave rise to the paradox that the Kremlin, *the* symbol of Russia's own political face, also came into being through Western architects: the Kremlin walls have the swallow capitals of the castles of northern Italy; the Palace of Facets outwardly resembles the Diamond Palace of Ferrara; the new Uspenskij Cathedral was built by Rudolfo Fioravante in authentic Russian style; and the Milanese architect Alevisio Nuovo made the Archangel Cathedral, the church in which the Moscow tsars are buried, a splendid combination of the Italian Renaissance and Russian architecture.

Ivan III now came to bear the Byzantine title 'autocrator' (Russian *samoderžec*) and informally also 'emperor (*car'*, tsar) and he adopted the Byzantine two-headed eagle as a coat of arms. Ivan was supported in his new status by the church. In 1492, in a circular letter, Metropolitan Zosima writes that 'God has now chosen grand prince Ivan Vasil'evič as the new Constantine for the new Constantinople, Moscow'.[155]

The great word has appeared. The Russian grand prince is the new Christian emperor and Moscow is the political heir of Constantinople. Moscow now begins to feel itself equal to the Western Roman imperial empire. The Western emperors and kings were as yet unwilling to recognize the title, but the fact is that these Moscow claims coincide with the rediscovery of Russia by Europe after centuries of isolation. Western diplomats now come to Russia, the most famous of whom is the Austrian Sigmund Herberstein. His travel account of Russia, *Rerum Moscoviticarum commentarii* (published in 1547), was an eye-opener for the West.

Before I develop the core theme of the Moscow ideology in more detail, I must first say something about Moscow's political rival, the city of Tver. Then it will prove that the notion in question is not an *idée fixe* of Ivan III but was just as much an ambition of the grand prince Boris of Tver. There is a writing in which Tver's claims to the spiritual legacy of Old Testament kings and Roman emperors clearly emerge: *Eulogy of the Pious*

Grand Prince Boris Aleksandrovič by the Humble Monk Foma.[156] It was written in 1453; it is not clear whether the author is the same as the monk Foma (Thomas) who took part in the Council of Florence as a delegate from Tver. This monk is actually named in the text, but is also known from other sources, and the council is directly related to the ruler of Tver in a flight of fancy.

The work is a bombastic eulogy of Boris of Tver, in which all the biblical and classical themes that we encountered in earlier lives of rulers have returned. Because the writing reveres Moscow's rival, it was not included in the official Moscow literature and for centuries was hardly known. However, it is illuminating as an anticipation of the Moscow ideology.

Tver proves to be the centre of the world: its ruler is 'revered from east to west . . . as far as the ruling city of Rome'. Boris is called a new Jacob, our new Joseph, another Moses, a new David, the equal of Solomon, a second Constantine, the successor to Vladimir, a new Jaroslav. He is compared with the emperors Tiberius, Augustus, Justinian and Theodosius, and given the titles emperor and autocrator. The old Israel, Constantinople, Kiev and Tver are all put on the same extended line. Foma draws this line from Israel via Byzantium and Kievan Rus' to Tver. The city of Tver is 'the new Israel', the people of Tver 'the new chosen people, led by the new Moses'. In no other Russian document is the eastward myth of Christianity so clearly expressed. But at the same time Boris appears to defend the unity with Rome.

Boris was invited by the Byzantine emperor John to defend both the true faith and the union with Rome at the Council of Florence. Boris sent his delegate Foma to do this. On this point the author Foma perplexingly goes over to the first person form of Foma the delegate: 'And I encountered here (= in Florence) pope Eugenius, and the holy emperor of Constantinople John and the ecumenical patriarch Joseph and the whole holy ecumenical council.' This council proves to be impressed by the purity of Boris of Tver's faith, and twenty Orthodox metropolitans begin to praise the grand prince of Tver. Quite apart from all the rhetoric, metropolitan Vissarion makes the interesting remark that 'there are many grand princes in Rus' but none has taken the trouble to send delegates to the holy council apart from grand prince Boris'. This sounds historical, since only Tver sent its own delegation.

Of course, court circles in Moscow did not like this glorification of Tver, since people made the same claims there. Another rival of Moscow, Novgorod, also had its own ideological declaration of identity, which later was also confiscated by Moscow. This is *The Story of the White Mitre*, written in the year 1490 by Dmitrij Gerasimov, translator and collaborator of archbishop Gennadij of Novgorod.[157] Gerasimov was sent to Rome by his bishop to get material with which to complete his translation of the Slavonic Bible. It is a curious narrative which begins with detective work in the papal library; its main theme is that after the fall of Constantinople, Novgorod has become the centre of Orthodoxy.

This is the content. When handing over the city of Rome to pope Silvester, the emperor Constantine had given him a white episcopal mitre, a symbol of the purity of faith. After Rome had departed from the true faith in the ninth century, the mitre was hidden and in the fourteenth century the pope wanted to destroy it. In a vision the pope was commanded to send the episcopal mitre to Constantinople. Patriarch Filotheos wanted to keep it there, but in a vision pope Silvester and the emperor Constantine predicted to the patriarch the fall of Constantinople to the Turks and commanded him to send the mitre to archbishop Vasilij of Novgorod. There it was put in the Sophia Cathedral as a sign that Novgorod had become the guardian of Christian orthodoxy.

The narrative is a Russian variant on the theme of the Donation of Constantine, the legendary gift of Rome to the pope by the emperor Constantine which was long believed in the West. The Russian legend expands the theme so that it becomes a *translatio ecclesiae*, a hand-over of the church, and of course changes the direction: back from Rome to Constantinople and on to Novgorod. The tone of the narrative is anti-Catholic. Pope

Silvester is highly esteemed, but the pope from after the break with Orthodoxy is called a forerunner of the Antichrist. When the pope heard that the episcopal mitre was going to Russia he became mad with fury, 'so much did he, the pagan, hate the Russian land, for the Christian faith which existed there that he could not bear to hear the name'.

Although Novgorod occupies the central position in this legend, the legend also contains general statements about Russia, namely that 'this land shall be called shining Rus' (*svetlaja rus'*), for it has pleased . . . God to fill it with the greatness of Orthodoxy'. And the following passage refers to all Russia:

> The old Rome has lost its glory and has lapsed from the Christian faith out of pride and self-will. In the new Rome, which is in Constantinople, the Christian faith will also perish through the violence of the sons of Hagar. But in the third Rome, that stands in the Russian land, the grace of the Holy Spirit shall shine out. And know well, Filotheos, that all Christian lands shall come together in the one Russian kingdom for the sake of the true faith.[158]

Here for the first time the expression 'the third Rome' (*tretij Rim*) is used, though without associating it with a particular city. However, rapidly the name of Moscow would be added, for it was neither Novgorod nor Tver, but Moscow which was to become the new centre of the Christian world.

5

Moscow, the Third Rome

Letters from Pskov

The doctrine of the Third Rome forms the ideological climax of
the political and religious awareness of Moscow and its theological apotheosis. The idea was worked out by the monk Filofei
(Filotheos) of Pskov in a letter to the Pskov representative of the
Moscow grand prince Vasilij III, a letter to Vasilij himself and a
letter to Ivan IV.[159] Pskov had just (1510) been subjugated by
Moscow, but despite its attachment to political independence, it
was strongly focussed on Moscow in religious terms because as a
frontier city it was constantly threatened by the Catholic Poles
and Lithuanians and the German Order.

The first letter was an answer to questions raised by Vasilij III's
Pskov delegate, Munechin, about the biblical chronology and
prophecies: *Letter against the Astronomers and the Latins*
(*Poslanie na zverdocëtcy i na latiny*). It gives an explanation why
the Byzantine empire perished and the Latin empire did not.
Filofei disputes Rome's argument that this is because Rome has
the true faith and God is still protecting her, ninety years after the
fall of Constantinople. No, already under Charlemagne and
pope Formosus Rome had deviated from the true faith through
the Apollinarian heresy, i.e. through the use of unleavened bread
in the celebration of the liturgy. For Filofei that is the greatest sin
of the Latin church, because he keeps reverting to it. He connects
this intrinsically unimportant matter with the fourth-century
teaching of Apollinarius about the corporeality of Christ.
So Rome may not be as devastated as Constantinople, 'but
her souls have already been imprisoned by the devil' since the

eighth century. The crucial passage occurs at the end of the letter:

> I would like to say a few words about the existing Orthodox empire of our most illustrious, exalted ruler. He is the only emperor on all the earth over the Christians, the governor of the holy, divine throne of the holy, ecumenical, apostolic church which in place of the churches of Rome and Constantinople is in the city of Moscow, protected by God, in the holy and glorious Uspenskij Church of the most pure Mother of God. It alone shines over all the earth more radiantly than the sun. For know well, those who love Christ and those who love God, that all Christian empires will perish and give way to the one kingdom of our ruler, in accord with the books of the prophet, which is the Russian empire (*rosejskoe carstvo*). For two Romes have fallen, but the third stands, and there will never be a fourth.

In the letter to Vasilij, Filofei calls him the 'governor of the holy, divine throne of the holy, ecumenical, catholic (*sobornaja*), apostolic church of the most holy Mother of God' (the name for the Mother of God denotes either the Uspenskij Church or the Russian Church as a whole), and he repeats precisely the formulations quoted above, with much emphasis on the fact that all former Christian kingdoms have come together in the Moscow kingdom and that this kingdom has no end. That is the fulfilment of Daniel 7.14.

The letter to Ivan IV, who had not yet come of age, at the beginning of 1540, is an exposition of the Revelation of John. Filofei illustrates the doctrine of the third Rome by means of the woman from Revelation 12. He makes this woman clothed with the sun and with the moon under her feet, which is taken as a symbol of the church, flee from the old Rome to the new Rome and finally to the third Rome 'in the new, great Russia'. Filofei explains the fact that the final destiny of the woman in Revelation 12.6 is a wilderness by saying that Russia was at that time still empty of faith because the apostles themselves had not preached in Russia. Filofei once again explicitly spells out for

Ivan his task in the church: 'Alone on earth the Orthodox, great Russian tsar steers the church of Christ as Noah in the ark was saved from the flood, and he establishes the Orthodox faith.' But Filofei does not succumb to moral pride. The conviction that the true faith is to be found only in Russia does not mean that there is no sinfulness. So now Rachel laments, 'not within the frontiers of Palestine but in the Russian land'.

The expression 'Moscow, the third Rome' began to lead a life of its own, and in histories was quoted in season and out of season, and above all used wrongly as a criterion for judging Russian foreign policy. However, no expansionist or messianic aims lay behind the doctrine of the third Rome. The Orthodox tsars never engaged in a war against the Latin world for their faith; they never made attempts to recapture Constantinople. The idea of the last Rome, of being the last Christian empire, was an eschatological notion: Russia had to preserve its rich store of faith in purity in the last phase before the end of the world, which had begun in 1492, or the year 7000 according to the Byzantine reckoning.[160]

Filofei of Pskov was the most striking representative of this Russian eschatologism, but not the only one. There were a number of speculations about the end time. If despite earlier expectations the world had not come to an end in 1492, at least its last period had dawned. The idea that Russia would crown world history as the last Christian empire fitted this sense.

This finalistic view of history had a remarkable parallel in a retrospective legitimation of the Moscow rulers. The family bond with the last Byzantine emperor was no longer sufficient; people looked for earlier points of contact with imperial traditions. This was done in a flowery literary work written by the first professional writer in Russia, Pachomij Logofet (from the Greek *logothetes*, 'one who puts into words'), who came from Serbia. In his *Account of the Rulers of Vladimir* he tells of a Byzantine transfer of imperial regalia by Constantine Monomachos to Vladimir Monomach, his Kievan son-in-law.[161] But Pachomij goes back even further; the Kievan dynasty of the Rjurikides is derived genealogically from a brother of the Roman emperor Augustus, of whom Rjurik is said to be a descendant. In this view even Babylonian rulers were seen as spiritual fore-fathers of the rulers of Moscow. Russia came to stand in a historical sequence of world empires, of Babylon, Persia, Macedonia, Rome and Byzantium. This was an Eastern *translatio imperii*, totally different from its Western counterpart.

It was unlike the Western version only in direction, for the formation of the political myth and the historiographical manipulations are the same in both cases. For a correct assess-ment of the ideological self-glorification of the Russian rulers it is good to reflect that there was also something of the same kind in European countries. Charlemagne and his court poets had a self-image like that of the later rulers of Moscow. As an illustration here is a Latin eulogy of Charlemagne:

> Most worthy Charles, my voice is too small for your works,
> king, love and jewel of the Franks, head of the world,
> the summit of Europe, caring father and hero, Augustus!
> You yourself can command cities: see how the Second Rome,
> new in its flowering and mighty extent, rises and grows;
> with the domes which crown its walls, it touches the stars![162]

What is said here of the new Western emperor, *caput orbis* and *Europae apex*, does not fall short of the claims of the new Christian emperor in Russia. And the description of Aachen as *Roma secunda* fits well with the Third Rome and the golden domes of the Kremlin. The only difference is that the Moscow grand prince is seven hundred years later than the Frankish king in his sense of imperial vocation.

There is also a striking contemporary European parallel to the formation of the Moscow sense of identity. By an Italian historian whom he employed, Henry VIII traced the English royal house back to the Trojan ruler Brutus.[163] John Foxe com-pares Queen Elizabeth in her church politics with Constantine the Great, who moreover proves to have had an English mother.[164] John Milton established an exclusive revelation by God to the English people, for in the new Reformed religion God had revealed himself 'first to us'.[165] And so England becomes the new Israel, the true Christian faith was only in England, and there battle is joined with the papal anti-Christ. These are all themes which we already know from the Russian chronicles.

Thus away from Moscow (and Kiev), there was indeed often talk in the Middle Ages of a *Constantinus redivivus* or *Augustus secundus*. But the reactivation of biblical images for later world rulers, which occurs so frequently in the Lives of Russian rulers, is not typical Russian Orthodox exegesis either. Some European authors, for example Dante, used even more colourful images than Russian hagiographers. Dante's seventh letter to the emperor is an almost blasphemous glorification of the German Henry VII, 'the late shoot of Jesse'. Dante addresses him with the words of John the Baptist about Christ: 'Are you he who is to come, or must we look for another?', and he 'raises his spirit to him' as to God and thought of him: 'Behold the lamb of God that takes away the sins of the world.'[166]

In sum, we can say that the religious and political ideology of Moscow is as much an exaggeration as that of other European kingdoms. There is no essential difference in the formation of political myth, the Christian sense of election, panegyric and titles. In both Western and Eastern Europe there rules an emperor, king or tsar, who is 'most pious (*piissimus* or *blagovernejšij*), 'beloved of God' (*deoamatus* or *bogoljubivyj*) and 'crowned by God' (*deocoronatus* or *bogovenčannyj*), and who emerges as 'defender of the faith' (*defensor fidei* or *chranitel' very*). Rome is everywhere, and the Old Testament heroes are the spiritual forefathers of every European ruler. Paradoxically, we can conclude that the ideology with which Russia gave itself a profile over against the West in the sixteenth century was itself confirmation that it stood in a common European Christian tradition, a confirmation of its European identity.

Ivan the Terrible and the church

Back to the situation of Moscow. The political legends about the descent of the tsars were included in compilations of sixteenth-century chronicles which are important for cultural history, like

The Russian Chronography of 1512 (from which Filofei of Pskov drew his inspiration), the *Nikon Codex* of 1558 and the brilliant *Illustrated Chronicle Codex* (*Licevoj letopisnyj svod*). This last collection of chronicles describes in ten volumes the history of the world from the creation to the year 1567 and illustrates it with 16,000 miniatures. This codex was in turn partially copied into a *Royal Book* (*Tsarstvennaja kniga*), just as richly illuminated, with corrections and additions by Ivan the Terrible, who in doing this established his own place in history. At the same time the Russian autocracy and tsardom was legitimated historically in *The Accession Book of the Genealogy of the Tsars* (*Stepennaja kniga tsarskogo rodoslovija*) and the coronation ritual for Ivan IV, both written by Metropolitan Makarij (1528–1563).

Metropolitan Makarij, who was a very active writer, not only wrote about the Russian rulers but also about the Russian saints of the previous five centuries in the monumental work *The Great Monthly Readings* (*Velkije Čet'i Minei*), twelve folios of 27,000 sheets of manuscript. This Russian counterpart of the Catholic *Acta Sanctorum* extends the Orthodox Russian empire into the hereafter, just as did the English church at the same time with John Foxe's *Book of Martyrs* (1563).

Metropolitan Makarij also substantially extended the number of Russian saints. In two years (1547–1549) he tripled the number of canonized saints, to sixty-one. This official canonization, which included many rulers, clearly had an ideological dimension: what was now tsarist Russia was also undergoing a revaluation in terms of the church. As a collaborator of metropolitan Makarij put it: 'It was necessary to show that the Russian church, although it entered history only at the eleventh hour, nevertheless through its zeal surpassed even the workers of the first hour.'[167] This way of thinking is diametrically opposed to the religious sense at the beginning of Christianity in Russia, Ilarion of Kiev's sense that the Russian people, the last workers to be called into the Lord's vineyard, were part of universal Christianity. Russian Christianity no longer stands on equal terms alongside the rest, but above them.

The sixteenth-century historical works provided a general religious garb for Moscow tsarism. The place of the tsar was laid down in the council decisions of 1551, the *Stoglav* (Hundred Chapters). They included the famous 'sixth novella' of the emperor Justinian on the symphonic relationship between *sacerdotium* and *imperium*, which was the basis for the collaboration between church and state in the Byzantine empire. However, the theological basis for the Russian autocracy was laid down by Iosif Volockij, abbot of Volokolamsk. Around 1500, Iosif Volockij led a monastic movement in the Russian church which argued for a strong link between church and state, a political theocracy. In particular the tsar had the duty as a servant of God to treat heretics harshly, as the 'apostolic' Constantine the Great had done. In a letter to Vasilij III, full of passionate words against the then active heresy of the 'Judaizers', Iosif calls the young tsar 'the ruler crowned by God' and 'self-ruling tsar and ruler'. The term 'ruler' (*vladyka*) is also a title by which bishops were addressed. Just as Constantine dragged Christianity from the abyss of hell by defeating the second Judas, Arius, so now the fate of Orthodoxy lies in the hands of Vasilij; unless he saves it from the Jewish heresy the whole of truly believing Christianity will perish as did former great empires, including the (monophysite) Armenian and Ethiopian and Roman empires.[168]

So that the monasteries can also play an active role in society, Iosif defends their ownership of lands. In his striving towards a theocracy Iosif is challenged by the former Athos monk Nil Sorskij and his 'monks without possessions', who led a more contemplative and poor monastic life and rejected the violent treatment of heretics. In 1503 a national council decided in favour of Iosif Volockij, creating the conditions for centuries of collaboration between church and state in Russia.

Ivan IV, the Terrible (1547–1584), made particular use of that. But he had yet another advocate, Ivan Peresvetov. If Iosif Volckij is the theologian of Russian autocracy, then Ivan Peresvetov is its blunt ideologist. He has been called the Russian Machiavelli. He had great esteem for the iron grip of the Turkish sultan. His writings are a plea for a theocratic dictatorship, exercised by the secular authority, which consists solely of the tsar/self-ruler. Peresvetov sees it as an important quality of the ruler that he embodies authority. The term *groza*, 'threatening', 'awe-inspiring', occurs many times in a letter to Ivan, and here Peresvetov anticipates the nickname *Groznyj*, 'Awe-inspiring', 'Terrible', which Ivan was later to be given by the people.[169] His view of the state is succinctly summed up in the sentence: 'May the true Christian faith in Russia be combined with Turkish justice!'[170]

After such a thorough theoretical and theological foundation for the tsardom, it was not difficult to present the concrete policy of Ivan the Terrible in the light of his function as defender of the Orthodox faith. Ivan's wars against the last Eastern and eternal Western enemy, the khanate of Kazan and the kingdom of Poland-Lithuania, are described in *The Conquest of the Empire of Kazan* and in *The Expedition of the Lithuanian King Stefan Batoryj against Pskov*. These are the last literary and historical works in which the scheme of Christian Russia against 'Muslim unbelievers' or 'the Catholic enemy of Christianity', now three centuries old, returns. The military battle against the West (Poland and later Sweden) was still to go on for another one hundred and fifty years, but that against the East was definitively decided in 1552; now the way to the Far East lay open for Russia. And thus there began not only an expansion of territory but also three centuries of Christian missionary work for the Russian Orthodox Church. It began immediately with the solemn baptism of the defeated khan of Kazan in the river Moskva, but significantly his wife refused to have herself baptized.

The unity between religion and politics and between church and state which took form in sixteenth-century Moscow does not mean that a symphony between secular and ecclesiastical power was achieved. However, that is how the pious Slavophile history imagines it. Ivan's father Vasilij was already criticized by the church for his divorce. This criticism did not come from the church leaders but from the theologian Maximus the Greek, an

Italian-Greek Athos monk, who was brought to Moscow in 1518 by the tsar himself as court librarian and translator. He was the first real scholar in the Russian church. However, the church did not welcome him with open arms. Maximus was accused of heresy by the conservative clergy because he corrected many translation mistakes in church texts on the basis of the Greek original. Moreover Maximus was a supporter of Nil Sorskij's ideas about relations between church and state. He wrote several treatises against the rising tsarist absolutism, including *Sermon which at Length and with Sorrow Expounds the Disorderliness and Violations of the Law by Emperors and Authorities of Recent Times*. Maximus was opposed to the omnipotence and arbitrariness of tsarism, not to the idea that Moscow tsar was the new Christian emperor. In his eulogistic letter to Vasilij III Maximus could still write that Vasilij 'can measure himself by the emperors Constantine the Great and Theodosius the Great, whose successor your majesty is', which is an interesting remark for a non-Rusisan.[171] Maximus had to pay for his scholarly and moral integrity with twenty-two years imprisonment. He wrote *Chapters of Instruction for Orthodox Rulers* for the young Ivan IV. However, that was to no avail.

The conflict between Ivan the Terrible and metropolitan Filipp was a dramatic one. In 1568, at the height of the bloody terror of Ivan's *opričnina*, the metropolitan reprimanded the tsar during a church service in the Kremlin. It was the first and last time that a Russian church leader openly criticized a tsar, and rarely has the hypocrisy of dictators attending the eucharist been indicated more clearly than with the words of Filipp to Ivan before the altar: 'We, O ruler (*gosudar'*), bring to the Lord (*Gospodu*) a pure and bloodless sacrifice for the redemption of mankind, and behind the altar Christian blood is shed and innocent men die.' And the proper position of a church leader over against worldly authority cannot be formulated more clearly than with the words: 'Ruler, I cannot obey your command more than that of God.'[172] Filipp also says that Ivan's accession has made Russia more unrighteous than any other people:

How long will you continue to shed the innocent blood of your faithful people and Christians? How long shall untruth reign in the Russian empire? Tatars and pagans, indeed the whole world, say that all people have law and truth, but they do not exist in Russia; throughout the world, transgressors who ask for clemency find it with the authorities, but in Russia there is not even clemency for the innocent and the righteous. Remember that although God has given you a high position in the world, you are still a mortal man, and God will require the innocent blood from your hands.[173]

Here the pious, righteous tsar, beloved of God, the new Christian emperor, is put in his place; here the myth of the third Rome is pricked. Some months later metropolitan Filipp was arrested and strangled in prison.

In the same spirit, Ivan the Terrible is criticized by his former friend the army commander Andrej Kurbskij. In 1564 prince Kurbskij fled from Russia to Lithuania, from where he carried on a polemical correspondence with Ivan and wrote a history of his rule. Kurbskij came from the intellectual circle around Maximus the Greek and like him was against the unlimited autocracy and identification of church and state.

Ivan gives an extensive (forty-page) defence of 'self-rule' in his reply to Kurbskij's first letter, which criticizes Ivan for his tyrannical government and transgression of Christian principles.[174] He is utterly convinced of his divine right, which he demonstrates with quotations from the Bible and church doctrine. Ivan was a tyrant with a strictly religious view of his task. He sees the tsardom as a divine commission and himself as head of the church and representative of God on earth.[175]

Ivan regards rebellion against him as rebellion against God himself, and Kurbskij's flight to Lithuania is a desertion to 'the enemy of Christianity'. Kurbskij answers Ivan's verbose letter, written in a bombastic and at the same time pedestrian style, briefly and pertinently, in accordance with the rules of Latin rhetoric which he had studied in Poland-Lithuania. He refers to the unscholarly nature of Ivan's biblical quotations, which make him seem ridiculous to the world outside Russia, where people 'have studied not only grammar and rhetoric but also dialectic and philosophy'.

Here for the first time a Russian himself points out the cultural difference between Moscow and the West: in the West people engage in philosophy and think critically. Kurbskij did great intellectual work on Russian territory which belonged with the Polish empire: he translated not only Greek church fathers but also Cicero into Russian and thus introduced the first pagan classical author to Russia. In a certain sense he was a bridge figure between the old mediaeval Russia and the modern humanistic culture with its emphasis on knowledge. But in his admiration of Western civilization Kurbskij remains faithful to the Russian nobility and to Orthodoxy. The first loyalty is evident from the remarkable narrow-mindedness with which he criticizes the foreign spouses of Ivan III and Vasilij III as evil spirits in the Russian tsarist genealogy.[176] Kurbskij defends the Orthodox Church against the Protestant church which was active in Poland at that time, against 'the Lutherans, Calvinists' and other 'blasphemers who dishonour God'.[177]

His faithfulness to Orthodoxy, together with his support of the Boyar nobility, is an important reason for his criticism of Ivan the Terrible. He accuses him of trampling Christian principles underfoot and of ruining the church in Russia. In this connection Kurbskij uses the expression 'holy Russian land' (*svjatorusskaja zemlja*) and 'holy Russian empire' (*svjatorusskoe carstvo)*, to indicate what the situation was like before Ivan's reign of terror.[178] Here Kurbskij introduces a tem which was later to have a magical ring among nineteenth-century Slavophiles as 'holy Russia' (*svjataja Rus'*); even more than the term 'third Rome' it became a key word in the formation of the national religious myth.

In contrast to 'third Rome', 'holy Russia' has no political implications. It is primarily an expression of a pious patriotism. But it can easily express a sense of religious superiority and later that also proved to be the case. Russia was not the only land in Europe to use the expression as such. 'Holy Russia' is comparable to the term *Italia sacra* used in Italy, the title of a church history commissioned by pope Alexander VII. [179] The expression 'holy Russian empire', which has more of a political ring, has its terminological counterpart in 'holy Roman empire', but in contrast to the latter never became an official name.

Andrej Kurbskij did not intend the terms to apply to the Russia of his time. He fervently challenged the absolutist autocracy of Ivan the Terrible and fervently defended Orthodoxy. If in romantic imagery his 'holy Russian empire' is not very different from Ivan's own 'Orthodox, truly Christian autocracy', his claim is quite different: it is directed to the past that is being destroyed by Ivan. Kurbskij mourns for the lost Christian Russia. Really Kurbskij sees the whole of world history as a lost religious paradise. Here East and West, Russia and Europe come to stand in a negative religious equilibrium. This is in itself a very sober look at past Christian glory, though it is motivated by nostalgia for the undivided Christian world. Kurbskij gave a splendid sketch of this picture of the world in a letter to the monk Vassian of the Caves Monastery of Pskov. [180] The letter forms a symbolic conclusion to the six-centuries quest by Russia for her place in the Christian world: Russia attained this place but then lost it again.

Kurbskij first looks to the East and asks what has become of India, Egypt, Ethiopia, Libya, Alexandria and the holy land of Palestine, areas which were known for their Christian faith. The Orthodox part of Europe is also part of the East:

Where is Europe, rich in the wisdom of the true faith? Where is the famous city of Constantine, which through its piety was the centre of the whole world? Where are the shining lands of the Serbs and Bulgarians, new in the faith, their great power and prosperous cities? . . . And if we now turn the eye of our soul to the Western lands, let us look and carefully consider: where is the capital Rome in which the successor of the apostle Peter, the old [i.e. before the schism] pope, lived? Where is Italy, that the apostles themselves converted; where is Spain, that the apostle Paul converted? Where is Milan in

which the great Ambrose administered pious government? . . .
Where is the great Germany? . . . It was wondrous to see how
they [the bishops at the councils] came together from the ends
of the earth as if borne on wings in order to establish the faith
and how their pious zeal was not deterred by the long journey,
the storms at sea and the cruelties of robbers. Where is all that
now? Are they not all driven asunder in a thousand heresies?
And after so much zeal and love of God they have become
irreconcilable enemies of those who have insight, even more
than the unbelievers.

But now look at us poor men! We barely know our forefathers, we live in a corner of the earth, we were not called to
glorious deeds, as heirs of the divine tenderness which God
showed time and again to the human race. And what summit
have we now climbed? We possess the books which the divine
Comforter has written, the Old and New Testaments, in our
own language. The bishops have power and respect and enjoy
peace in their churches. And if they want to give instruction on
the holy faith, then no one will hinder them here. Our whole
Russian land, from one end to the other, is like a pure field of
wheat: faith is there, the churches of God are dispersed over
the face of Russia like the stars in heaven, countless monasteries have been built. Tsars and rulers, as Orthodox as their
fathers, have been appointed judges and fighters by the Most
High.

But why do we oppose the goodness of God who wants
to make us fit for his heavenly kingdom? We close our ears to
his holy words and turn to his enemy. The authority which
comes from God devises unprecedented pains of death for the
virtuous. The clergy – we will not judge them, far be that from
us, but bewail their wretchedness – are ashamed to bear witness to God before the tsar; rather they endorse the sin. They
do not make themselves advocates of widows and orphans, the
poor, the oppressed and the prisoners, but grab villages and
churches and riches for themselves. Where is Elijah, who was
concerned for the blood of Naboth and confronted the king?
Where are the host of prophets who gave the unjust kings

proof of their guilt? Who speaks now without being embarrassed by the words of holy scripture and gives his soul as a
ransom for his brothers? I do not know one. Who will extin-
guish the fire that is blazing in our land? No one. Really, our
hope is still only with God.

This is a splendid combination of the vision of holy Russia
with an unmasking of the un-Christian reality. It is a good
summary of Russia's religious self-awareness, from the eulogy of
Ilarion of Kiev to the penitential preaching of Serapion of
Vladimir, from the sense of mission in the Lives of the rulers of
Moscow to the complaint of metropolitan Filipp in Kurbskij's
own time (the letter was probably written before 1568). The
survey of the Christian world at the beginning suggests the related passage in Ilarion's eulogy of Vladimir, though there is no
indication whatsoever that Kurbskij borrowed from it. But the
Russia of Ivan the Terrible is quite different from that of
Vladimir the Holy, and Kurbskij make that quite clear. This
letter of Andrej Kurbskij is just as worth being quoted per-
manently as the letter by Filofei of Pskov on the third Rome, but
it is hardly known.

Relations with the second Rome

The doctrine of the Third Rome and the tsarism with a religious
basis in the idea of the Russian state at the end of the sixteenth
century implied that Moscow had clear pretensions over against
the Greek mother church. On the other hand both Ivan IV
and metropolitan Makarij knew that only the patriarch of
Constantinople could bestow the title of emperor, as could the
patriarch of Rome in the West. In 1561, patriarch Ioasaf II
approved the title, which had been claimed in 1547. In so doing
he referred to the old family links of the Kievan rulers Vladimir
the Holy and Vladimir Monomach with the Byzantine emperors,
to the exceptional piety of Ivan IV and its importance for all
Christianity.[181] However, Ioasaf had also put the forged signa-
tures of other bishops to the document. Because of this he was
removed from office some years later.

The Greek church had still more difficulties with the strictly ecclesiastical claims of Moscow. That became evident in the case of the other title which Moscow wanted to have, but which had hitherto been refused it by the Greek Church, namely that of patriarch. Since the separation of church government from Constantinople in 1448, the head of the Russian church had only been a metropolitan, and on the recognition of the autocephaly *a posteriori* by the patriarch of Constantinople in 1461 the metropolitan of Moscow still did not receive the status of patriarch.

That happened only in 1589. Boris Godunov, brother-in-law and regent of the mentally handicapped son of Ivan the Terrible, Fëdor (1584–1598), was able to obtain the title by blackmail: the patriarch of Constantinople had become financially dependent on Russia to a considerable degree and in 1586 and 1588–89 patriarch Jeremias II himself went on begging trips to Moscow. The second time he got financial support in exchange for the title patriarch, and so metropolitan Iov of Moscow became the first Russian patriarch. This was not only an ecclesiastical but also an ideological victory for Moscow over Constantinople, since the doctrine of the Third Rome is explicitly mentioned in the document.[182] Filofei of Pskov's formulation of the three successive Romes was taken over literally. In passing it was recognized that Russia was the political heir of Byzantium by the twofold use of the expression 'our great Russian and Greek empire'.

The new position of the Russian church was canonically approved by all the Eastern patriarchs at a synod in Constantinople, and Moscow was added to Constantinople, Alexandria, Antioch and Jerusalem as the fifth patriarchate. That implies that although Moscow had taken over the political position of the Byzantine empire with the Moscow tsar as the new Christian emperor in the world, the new patriarch of Moscow had not assumed the first position in the Orthodox Church, nor even the third, for which Moscow had hoped. The patriarch of Constantinople remained the 'ecumenical' patriarch, the first among equals of the Eastern patriarchs. However, in practice all four patriarchs were financially dependent on Moscow for paying taxes to the Turkish rulers. The patriarch of Alexandria recognized the situation fully when in 1592 he made a financial appeal to the 'most Orthodox' Russian tsar, saying that 'the four patriarchates of the Orthodox speak of your rule as that of another, new Constantine the Great . . . and say that if there were no help from your rule, then Orthodoxy would be in extreme danger'.[183]

Thus in practice the tsar of Russia was also recognized outside Russia as the guardian of the whole Orthodox world and compared with Constantine the Great. But that was temporary. A century later, at a council in 1667, the Russian church had officially to surrender the doctrine of the third Rome in the presence of two Eastern patriarchs.

New repudiation of the West

During the first half of the seventeenth century the Russian church consciousness was strongly conditioned by the polemic against the first Rome, against the Roman Catholic Church. That had to do with the church union of Brest-Litovsk in 1596. In this union the Orthodox bishops in West Russia which belonged to Poland had recognized the ecclesiastical authority of the pope, as a result of which their Orthodox Church came to be under Rome while preserving the Slavonic language and liturgy. Thus Rome had after all achieved part of the aim of the Council of Florence. Of course the Russian Orthodox Church regarded this Union of Brest as an infiltration by Rome into its church territory, and to the present day it has remained a point of dispute between the Moscow patriarchate and the Vatican.

The opposition between Catholics and Orthodox was further intensified by the military intervention of Poland in the empire of Moscow during the dynastic crisis in the years 1605–1613 (the Time of the Troubles). In 1605 the Poles, with the support of the pope, put a pretender to the throne who was well disposed towards them, the false Dmitrij, on the throne of the tsars. The combination of Catholicism and Polish aggression led to a marked Russian xenophobia towards the West. It was seen as a plot against Orthodoxy, being carried out by king Sigismund III and pope Clement VIII via the false Dmitrij. Dmitrij had promised the pope that he would bring Russia under the pope's ecclesiastical authority. The war with Poland became a religious war for the Russians. In his detailed account of the Time of the Troubles Avraamij Palicyn expresses this anti-Catholic view. He refers to the Latins as 'the eternal enemies of the Christians' and 'the accursed pope of Rome' as 'an uncle of the Antichrist'.[184] The Polish invasion is seen in the light of the historical struggle between Rome and Russia:

> For from the years of Vladimir, who baptized the Russian land, to the present day the pernicious snake which has nested in the church of Italy has been raging around without rest . . . not only in Europe, a quarter of the world, but also in the East and the South and the North. And for many years its flattery has reached to Russia.[185]

Palicyn sums up Rome's most important attempts to lead people astray: the pope's exchange of correspondence with Aleksandr Nevskij (1248), a contact between the Swedish king Magnus Eriksson and the bishop of Novgorod (1347), the Council of Florence (1439), the papal delegate to Ivan the Terrible, Antonio Possevino (1581), and now the Polish intervention: four centuries of continual Catholic conspiracy, a view of history based on a hostile religious image.

After the murder of the false Dmitrij a year later, the Poles captured Moscow, but they could not occupy Sergeij's Trinity Monastery despite a long siege. When the Poles called on the defenders of the monastery to capitulate, they replied with a resolute rejection in religious terms: true believers against those who fought with God, light against darkness, truth against lies, and freedom against slavery.[186]

Meanwhile the Swedes, who were still seen as an advance post of the Latins, were conquering the north-west of Russia. This was one of the most dramatic phases in relations between Russia and Europe.

The total theological disqualification of the West emerges in a treatise in poetic form by Ivan Chvorostinin: *Exposition against the Blasphemous Heretics*.[187] In it the 'Western' and 'Eastern' churches are compared with Cain and Abel, and the differences between the two churches are worked out in this framework: the Western church is arrogant, greedy for domination, focussed on outward power and loves philosophy; the Eastern church is humble, pious, the victim of the Western church and faithful in teaching. The poem also sketches out a version of the eastward progress of Christianity in the person of the apostle Andrew, the 'Russian teacher'. He brought Christianity from Jerusalem via Byzantium to Kiev, and 'the church stands eternally for the whole of Christianity and the city of Kiev, the true flock chosen by God'.

Because this is a version of what was originally an anti-Catholic Ukrainian document, the transfer stops in Kiev. Of course in the Ukraine itself there was also fierce polemic from the Orthodox side, especially that of the learned bishop Meletij Smotrickij. He challenged the Catholic Church with the theological and philosophical knowledge that he had acquired as a student with the Jesuits. And that applies to a number of those who disputed the Union of Brest. For one of the results of the union was that for the first time Orthodox clergy in the Ukraine and White Russia could pursue studies at the Catholic seminaries and universities in Poland and Rome. This gave them a theological advantage over their Russian fellow-believers, a fact of which Peter the Great was later to make use in his church politics.

However, the Union of Brest failed as a bridge between East and West; it only increased the opposition. Neither of the two churches thought of getting closer, and of course the idea of sister churches did not yet exist. People thought only in terms of extending power and spheres of influence. The Catholic Church did not recognize the united church as perfect, and strove for a creeping Latinization. Conversely, the Orthodox Church always defended the idea of canonical territory, which coincided with the Russian state. After the Ukraine had again been incorporated into Moscow in 1654 in a semi-voluntary way within the framework of the ongoing war against Poland, the existence of the united church was threatened. At the beginning of the eighteenth century the state abolished it. But the Orthodox Church in the

Ukraine which fell under the patriarchate of Constantinople was put under the Moscow patriarchate. Thus Moscow would not tolerate any rival Orthodox jurisdiction in the land either; in this way the claim to be the Third Rome was once again expressed.

In the second half of the seventeenth century that led to new tension with the Greek mother church. However, the conflict now had a different nature. The Russian Orthodox Church was viewed with some suspicion not only by the Greek Church but also by the other Orthodox Churches, despite their financial dependence on it. The begging trips to Moscow were also voyages of discovery of the church for the Orthodox patriarchs: they saw how all kinds of church customs in the Russian land deviated from those of their own church. The amazement of Makarios, patriarch of Antioch, during a journey through Russia at the hours-long church services, the ritualism and the extremely strict fasts is well known.[188] And the Greeks always looked down on the theological ignorance in the Russian Church, its lack of Hellenistic culture, and its bad translations of the Greek liturgical texts.

Here the mistrust of the Greek Church by the Russian Church must have seemed particularly arrogant to the Eastern observers. The Russians mistrusted Greek Orthodoxy because it had its books printed in Catholic Venice, while the art of printing had barely penetrated Russia. At the council of 1551 the Russian Church had established the correctness of its liturgy and texts above those of the Greeks.

The Russian mistrust of their mother church in the seventeenth century went so far that Greek clergy who came to Russia were first 'trained' in a Russian monastery before they were admitted to communion. Greek merchants could not enter the Russian churches at all, because they might perhaps secretly be Uniates or perhaps even Muslims.[189]

Against this anti-Greek background the declaration of patriarch Nikon, 'I am a Russian but my faith is Greek', must have sounded like a curse to the simple Russian church people. But Nikon won the dispute over language in the Russian church, which lasted around a century. At the Council of Moscow in

1654 the mistakes in the age-old Russian translations were recognized and the texts corrected. Here the Russian church government implicitly abandoned its pretension to be the Third Rome over against the Greek mother church.

The Old Believers

The convergence of the Russian and Greek Churches was good for the integration of the Ukrainian Orthodox Church, which had never known the Moscow traditions, but it did lead to a deep schism in the Russian Church. Although the whole hierarchy agreed with the reforms of the council, a majority of the illiterate church people along with the village priests vigorously opposed them. These so-called Old Believers or Old Ritualists had an eloquent spokesman in archpriest Avvakum, who himself was far from illiterate. In 1667 he was excommunicated and put in prison, including twelve years in a pit, but his spirit remained unbroken. Eventually he was burned at the stake in 1682. His theological fanaticism was compensated for intellectually by his extraordinary vivid and sometimes laconic autobiography, a novelty in the Russian literature of the time.

The Old Believers thought that the official Russian church had lapsed into the Greek heresy. The faith of the Hellenes had now become as bad as that of the Latins: both were the work of the devil. Here it did not matter much that the differences of opinion with the Greeks did not concern dogmas but secondary matters, like the way in which the name Jesus was written, the direction of the procession round the church building, the number of alleluias in a prayer or whether the sign of the cross was made with two (or five) or three fingers. In the debate between Avvakum and the Eastern patriarchs at the council of 1667 we get the picture of Avvakum against the rest of Christianity, East and West. When the patriarchs say that the whole Christian world, 'our Palestine, the Serbs, the Albanians, the Wallachians (= Rumanians), the Romans and the Poles', make the sign of the cross with three fingers, Avvakum unshakeably maintains making the cross with two fingers:

You, ecumenical teachers! Rome has long since fallen and lies on the ground, and the Poles have gone under with her, for to the present day they have been enemies of the Christians. But with you, too, Orthodoxy became a varied mixture under the violence of the Turkish Muhammad. Nor is that surprising: you have become powerless. From now on you must come to us to learn: through God's grace we have the autocracy. Before the apostate Nikon the whole of Orthodoxy was pure and spotless in our Russia under the pious rulers and tsars, and the church knew no rebellion. But the wolf Nikon along with the devil introduced the tradition that one had to cross oneself with three fingers.[190]

The patriarchs use a remarkably broad summary of nations which embraces both Orthodox and Catholics. The acts of the council in fact speak of 'all Christian nations . . . from East to West'.[191] However, this makes no impression on Avvakum, and he will not yield before 'the great army of the Antichrist', as he calls the council fathers. Avvakum alone against the whole Christian world! This is not just a classic case of sectarian solipsism; it is also the ultimate consequence of the myth of the East: Russia is threatened in its Orthodoxy not only by Rome but also by Greece, both of whom are exerting their influence on Moscow from the Ukraine. In a letter to tsar Aleksej Avvakum points out to the tsar that the apostasy of Greece was already predicted in *The Story of the Novgorod White Mitre,* and that he, the tsar, is not fulfilling the religious obligation which according to the story rests on him as the guardian of the truth.[192]

Indeed the Old Believers turned away from the state, which they now saw as the fallen Third Rome. But the idea of Holy Russia was additionally cherished as a counterbalance to rejection by the state: the ordinary believers are now the elect people of the end time, who are being persecuted by a state which has become the Antichrist.

The Old Believers had a strong eschatological sense: now that the Third Rome had fallen, the end of time must have dawned. In the eschatologism and theological primitivism with which the

Old Believers condemned the established order as instruments of the Antichrist, they resemble the Puritan protest against the church and state in seventeenth-century England. There too believers turned against their own Anglican Church which – although itself a bulwark against Rome – was now put on a line with the Antichrist of Rome. However, they did not lose faith in the special election of the English people, any more than did their Russian counterparts. Schulte Nordholt says that the sense of national vocation is democratized in this religious opposition of the people to the state and the church hierarchy.[193] This socio-logical observation can also be applied to the Old Believers. And just as the Puritan idealism collided with the politics of Cromwell, so the efforts of the Old Believers came up against harsh oppression from the tsars. Here many thousands fell victim to the violence of the authorities and the collective self-immolation of groups of Old Believers.

In the meantime the church itself gave up the doctrine of the Third Rome, but for other reasons than the Old Believers. This happened at the Council of Moscow in 1667, which endorsed Nikon's church reform of 1654. At this council it was also declared that *The Story of the Novgorod White Mitre*, the ideo-logical source of the idea of the Third Rome, was a fabrication, which indeed it was. This explanation was not only an ecclesias-tical gesture towards the Greek Church but also a capitulation of the Russian Church leaders to the tsar. For the legend implicitly contained a theocratic claim to power on the part of the Russian Church which patriarch Nikon had tried to implement. Nikon wanted to put the authority of the church above that of the state and came into conflict with tsar Aleksej. The tsar supported Nikon's reform of the church completely, but would have nothing of his political ambitions. In contrast to the clash between Vasilij II and metropolitan Isidor two centuries earlier, the clash between Aleksej and Nikon was not a quarrel prompted by questions of faith but a political struggle for power. At the council which approved Nikon's reform of the church, Nikon himself was deposed as patriarch.

From now on it was finally all up with the symphony of

powers as it had always been imagined. But the result was not a separation of spiritual and worldly authority. The Council of Moscow in 1667 opened up the way for the structural caesaro-papism of Peter the Great. Here a new phase dawned in the Russian Constantinian principle of the state.

Before we go over to this new period in Russian history, first of all some closing remarks about the doctrine of the Third Rome. This no longer played a role in Petersburg Russia. Only in the twentieth century was it rediscovered, first as a brief ideological episode in 1948 and later in the 1990s as a nostalgic idea in post-Communist nationalism. In 1948 the formula was trotted out at a conference of the Eastern Orthodox Churches in Moscow. This conference was organized on the occasion of the commemoration of five hundred years of autocephaly in the Russian church and at the same time was meant as a Russian counterpart to the World Council of Churches, which was established in the same year. It was also a piece of propaganda on the part of Stalin against the Roman Catholic Church, with which he had come into serious conflict after the abolition in 1946 of the Uniate Church in the Ukraine. The notion of the Third Rome was mentioned three times in the speeches, twice by the delegations from Bulgaria and Poland, not by chance the only Orthodox delegations from Soviet satellite states. And once by a Russian theologian, who spoke of 'the famous and grandiose theory of the Third Rome'.[194]

As for post-Communist Russia, the Third Rome idea figures frequently in the ultra-nationalistic press like *Russkij Vestnik* (Russian Herald), *Sovjetskaja Rossija* and various party news-papers. The expression is used in the new ideological struggle against everything Western, in a way which can never have been intended by its inventor: so primitive is the mixture of mediaeval Muscovite, Petersburg-tsarist, Soviet state, religious patriotic and neo-Fascist ideologies. How permanent the ideological contribution will prove to be for the new sense of identity the future will tell.

6

The Religious Ambivalence of Petersburg Russia

Peter the Great forms a break in the history of Russian ideas; with him a new sense of Russian identity emerges. There is a paradigm shift from religious to secular ideas and there are symbols to legitimate the state and its autocratic authority. The new capital, St Petersburg, becomes the visible expression of this change. With the foundation of a new capital Peter also abandons the Third Rome idea geographically. But not the idea of Rome.

Back to the first Rome

Rome remains an ideological point of reference in the notion of the Russian state. However, it is no longer the second Rome but the first Rome to which reference is made, or ancient Rome takes the place of Orthodox Constantinople. Peter takes over Latin symbols: he replaces the title tsar by the Latin *imperator*, designates his state *imperia*, calls his advisory council *senat*, and makes the Latin *Rossija* the official name of his land in place of the Slavic *Rus'*.

Although the primary orientation is on imperial Rome, there are also all kinds of references to the Christian Rome. The name of the city, St Petersburg, was not just chosen because Peter was the patron saint of the tsar, but also to associate the apostle Peter with the new Russian capital. That was both a diminution of the religious significance of Moscow and a religious claim over against papal Rome. The adoption of the religious significance of

Rome is also evident from the cult of the second apostle of Rome, Paul, which is expressed in the name for the cathedral of the new capital, the St Peter and Paul Cathedral. This name was a break with the pious Russian tradition, which does not regard the two Roman apostles but Andrew as the patron of Russian Christianity. Thus St Petersburg is meant to be the new Rome, directly following on the old Rome, and passing over the second and third Romes.

Boris Uspenskij and Jurij Lotman have referred to this religious and semiotic transformation of the ideas of the Third Rome.[195] These authors have another argument. In addition to the name of the city and the cathedral, the coat of arms of St Petersburg also points to Rome, i.e. to the Vatican as the heir of Rome. The coat of arms of St Petersburg contains transformed motifs from the Vatican coat of arms: the crossed anchors in the Petersburg coat of arms correspond to the crossed keys in the Vatican coat of arms. And like the key bits on the two keys of the Vatican, the two anchors have their blades pointing upwards. Here we have a double symbolism. The anchor was not only the symbol of the new Russian fleet but also in baroque religious emblematics a symbol of the Christian faith and salvation through that faith.

However, the link with the Russian past was not completely cut. Peter strongly encouraged the cult of Aleksandr Nevskij and as early as 1704 planned a monastery in honour of the saint for the new capital; building began on it in 1712. In 1724 Peter had the bones of Aleksandr Nevskij brought from Vladimir to St Petersburg, and since then Aleksandr Nevksij has been regarded as the second patron saint of the city. In this way St Petersburg comes to be related to the thirteenth-century Russian ruler who conquered the Swedes and the Germans and thus defended Orthodoxy against Western Catholicism.

So it proves that the tsar who stands at the beginning of Russia's modern and secular history also wove religious elements into the new Russian state consciousness. We also see this in the writings of Peter the Great's most important ideologist, Feofan Prokopovič.

Feofan Prokopovič, a teacher of rhetoric and philosophy and later Rector at the Theological Academy in Kiev, poet and bishop, was an ardent defender of Peter's political and social renewal, and as preacher and advisor put himself completely at the service of the state. Never was there such political preaching in Russian churches, and never such erudite preaching. Prokopovič knew his classics; he had studied for three years at a papal college in Rome, and returned learned but also anti-Catholic. He had a theological sympathy for Protestantism.

Prokopovič was a representative of the Ukrainian-Slav renaissance, which introduced classical culture into Russia in the second half of the seventeenth century. His predecessors were Simeon Polockij and Sil'vestr Medvedev. In their odes the Moscow piety is already replaced by Latin rhetoric, and they found interested supporters in Peter's father tsar Aleksej and half-sister/regent Sofia. Here Peter and Prokopovič were not the first to open the doors to Latin culture in Russia, but they were the most energetic. Only in the time of Peter the Great does classical antiquity really begin to exert its influence on Russian literature and culture. This influence and the relationship between Petersburg and Rome is well expressed in the symbolism of the 'two bronze knights', a famous statue of Marcus Aurelius and an equally famous bronze statue of Peter the Great, in a study by M. Wes.[196]

Propokovič is the first representative of the early enlightenment in Russia, but he is against its liberal consequences. One scholar has described his paradoxical position as that of a '"latinizer" who hated the Roman Church, a humanist corrupted by the politics of monarchial absolutism, a man of religion who contributed mightily to the secularization of Russian culture and society'.[197]

Prokopovič's speeches are the literary expression of the broadening of cultural perspective in the new Russia. They are full of Latinisms, as a result of which Russian is enriched by dozens of words, and they put Peter the Great in a broad historical spectrum in which classical antiquity is as important as Old

Testament history. Reference is made both to Virgil and Homer and to the psalms. But despite all the comparisons with Greek mythological figures and Roman emperors, Peter the Great retains his Christian aura. There is merely a shift of accent in Prokopovič from 'Orthodox tsar' to 'Christian monarch' and 'Christian ruler'.

Before Prokopovič came to know Peter the Great, he had already alluded to his politics of renewal in the play *Vladimir* (1705). The play is about the introduction of Christianity into Russia. Christianity as a civilization is opposed to the backwardness of paganism. Here Vladimir the Holy can be seen as a prefigurement of Peter the Great and the stupid pagan priests as the conservative church opponents of Peter. But the play is also about Christianity, and there are some attractive religious fragments in the exposition of faith by the Greek philosopher missionary from Constantinople. This Greek philosopher-theologian does not just use biblical arguments but also points to non-Christian voices to establish the truth of the faith: Plato is quoted and Epicurus is rejected, and reference is made to the prediction of 'the old sibyls and Hellenic virgins'.[198]

Orthodoxy is not central in the later panegyric sermons of Prokopovič but rather the Russian state, the acts of Peter, autocracy as a form of government, the metamorphosis of Russian society, and the appearance of Russia on the European stage as 'an apocalyptic vision'.

Peter the Great's court preacher

Peter got to know Prokopovič during his visits to Kiev in 1706 and 1709. On the second occasion Prokopovič addressed Peter in the Sofia Cathedral after his victory in Poltava over the Swedish king Charles XII. Prokopovič showed his rhetorical talent there: he compares the victory over the Swedes with the victory of the Greeks over Troy and with the Roman siege of Carthage and David's victory over the Philistines; Peter himself is compared with Heracles who dismembered a seven-headed serpent and Samson who dismembered a lion, and even with

Mars.[199] This repertory is quite different from that in the pious
Lives of the Moscow rulers.

Prokopovič had made a great impression on Peter with this
speech, and in 1716 Peter brought him to the new capital as an
advisor. There Prokopovič gave his first speech on the occasion
of the birth of Peter's son and the heir to the throne, and this
immediately became an ideological act of birth of the new
Russia.[200]

In this speech Russia is compared with other lands inside and
outside Europe. A European and world perspective is unfolded in
which Russia is no longer treated as unique. In this speech the
geographical horizon of the new, Petersburg Russia is well
brought to the fore.

Prokopovič says that Russia may count itself fortunate to have
a hereditary monarchy. It is in good historical company with the
Assyrian empire, the Medes and Persians, Israel, the Egypt of the
Pharaohs and the Ptolemies, the Macedonian and Illyrian
empire, ancient Africa, and 'our forefathers the Scythians and
Sarmatians'.

And let us also look to the present. Beginning with Europe,
there are Spain, Gaul, England, Germany, Denmark, Sweden,
etc. They all have a monarchy, they all have a hereditary
sceptre. Go to Africa and the same order exists: Fez, Tunis,
Algeria, Tripoli, Barka and great Ethiopia, the Abyssinian
people and the other states on the crescent. Go to Asia:
Turkey, Persia, India, China and Japan are just the same. We
hear the same about America, which is called the new world.

All states with another form of government, namely a republi-
can democracy, an aristocracy or a monarchy with an elected
head of state, 'are not to be envied'. These include the Polish
republic, which 'has broken its golden fetters', Venice with its
intrigues, Genoa, the Belgian Confederation, and the free
Hanseatic cities. And the same is true of the Roman republic in
antiquity, with its consuls and later dictators, whose cruel power
is far worse than the monarchy, and with its many rebellions.

'And it is evident from all this how much sounder autocracy is for human society.'

Perhaps this is the first time in a Russian text that there is such a wide geographical summary: the whole world comes into view. This geographical survey illustrates the end of the narrow-minded Moscow perspective on the world and also the exclusive religious foundation of tsarism: Russia does not stand alone with its monarchy; it is an objectively better form of government, as Prokopovič also makes clear in his speech. Here Peter primarily emerges as a European monarch in place of the Orthodox tsar.

Here it is not the Christian heritage of the Byzantine empire but historical and political-philosophical arguments which are used to justify the Russian state order. This is still the best of all monarchies, for nowhere is there such a powerful and enterprising monarch as Peter the Great. The renewal of education, the modernization of government, the promotion of offices, the creation of a fleet, the foundation of a new capital and military successes are seen both as unique personal deeds of Peter and as proofs of the effectiveness of the autocratic monarchy.

This is quite a pragmatic argument for autocracy. But Feofan Prokopovič was also a theologian. And in his well-known speech *On the Authority and Honour of the Tsar* (1718) he in fact provides theological support for the authority.[201] It is a Palm Sunday sermon, and the entry of Christ into Jerusalem is the occasion for defending the monarchy as a divine institution. Did not Christ show his accord with the monarchy by this triumphal entry? The sermon becomes a biting attack on theologians who reject the absolutism of the ruler with a reference to the New Testament freedom from the Law which Christ is said to have brought, or to the way in which Christ puts the divine authority above worldly authority. This category extends from the pope, who puts the spiritual power above the emperor, to the Anabaptists, who reject any state authority. It is also an attack on of a Christian spirituality which rejects earthly glory and human praise and teaches gospel humility and sobriety. Prokopovič thinks this kind of criticism a biblical interpretation by Pharisees, pseudo-theologians and hypocrites. Here he is alluding to ecclesiastical opponents of Peter who had gathered around his son Aleksej (who was to be tortured to death that same year on Peter's orders).

Prokopovič gives a whole series of biblical quotations to defend authority as coming from God, even when it is exercised by bad and unbelieving kings, like Cyrus, Nebuchadnezzar, Nero and all the other Roman emperors before Constantine the Great. How much more are Christians then obliged to show obedience to 'the ruler who truly believes and truly judges . . . who is like a father'. But here too there is a rational argument to reinforce the theological argument: God has placed authority in the natural laws, so that 'even atheists argue that God is to be preached among the people because otherwise the people would rebel against the authorities'.

The whole argument culminates in a challenge to the 'papist spirit' according to which the church is exempt from subjection to the authority of the state. And to 'the curse, the doom of our time', (Enlightenment) ideas about human freedom and the restriction of the God-given authority of the tsar. Here we see the paradox of Prokopovič's and Peter's social renewal: the modernization and Westernization of Russian society goes hand in hand with an ideological consolidation of tsarist absolutism.

That is quite clearly the case in Peter the Great's policy towards the Orthodox Church, of which Prokopovič was the architect. We must include this church policy in Prokopovič's overall verdict on Peter's religious mandate, or rather in Prokopovič's religious verdict on Peter generally. That is a comparison, often used, between Peter the Great and the apostle Peter, which fits well in the semiotic bond between Petersburg and the first Rome which was mentioned earlier.

In a sermon from 1718 Prokopovič relates Peter, 'the first of the Russian tsars', to his patron saint Peter, 'the first of the apostles'.[202] Like the latter, tsar Peter has an 'apostolic vocation . . . And what the Lord has commanded your patron and apostle concerning his church, you are to carry out in the church of this flourishing Russian empire.' That is a far-reaching theological comparison. The comparison takes on a more literary and allegorical character when Prokopovič compares Peter's journeys abroad with Peter's fishing in the Sea of Galilee. Just as the latter, on Jesus' orders, must not remain on the sea shore but cast his nets into the deep and thus obtain a rich catch, so Peter is not to remain on land but to go to sea, where he 'will have a rich catch for the salvation of Russia'. And at the end of the sermon there is the prayer that Christ will be graciously present 'in this city of Peter' as he was 'in Peter's ship'.

Prokopovič mentions the actual religious policy of the tsar in two speeches which he gave after the tsar's death. In a first brief speech Peter the Great is called the David and Constantine of the Russian church and his church government is praised: the establishment of synodical church government, the fight against the schism of the Old Believers, against superstition and for the improvement of the training of clergy.[203] The second commemorative speech is longer, given on the festival of the apostle Peter, six months after Peter's death. There archbishop Prokopovič speaks about Peter's foreign policy in a religious context, and about the failed sea battle against the Turks in the Sea of Azov:

> And so he proved to be the defender not only of his fatherland but of all Christianity. He gave himself completely to this cause. He had the fixed purpose of smashing and killing the Muslim dragon or at least driving it out of the Eastern paradise. And those efforts would not have been hopeless had you, dear Europe, overcome your fixed habit, namely of disunity and mutual envy, and if in this communal catastrophe you had not envied one another but come to his aid.[204]

A friendly rebuke of Europe, though Prokopovič goes on to say that it was the school in which Peter learned.

In this speech Prokopovič once again calls the dead tsar 'apostle' as the climax of his status: 'In our Peter, in whom we first saw a great knight (*bogatyr*), and then a wise ruler, we now already see an apostle. As such, as a Christian tsar, God has shown him.'[205]

Before we go on to discuss Peter's concrete church policy, first
a few more remarks about the religious imagery relating to Peter
the Great later in the eighteenth century. This went even further
than that of Feofan Prokopovič. All the great Russian writers
of the century attribute divine properties to him. Michail
Lomonosov writes in 1750, 'He is a god, he was your god,
Russia!', and compares the birth of Peter with the birth of Christ.
So does Sumarokov (1768), who calls Kolomenskoye, Peter's
birthplace, 'the Russian Bethlehem'. Gavriil Deržavin (1776)
says: 'Like God, great through his providence, he oversaw all
from his being . . . Did not God descend from heaven into him?'
Aleksandr Puškin says that 'God's awesomeness' radiated from
Peter.[206]

But there is also a completely opposite religious evaluation of
Peter, as apostate and Antichrist. Of course Peter was Antichrist
for the Old Believers, who saw in him confirmation of their
pessimistic expectation of the downfall of Orthodox Russia.
However, after initially persecuting the Old Believers, in 1716
Peter gave them the right of existence, as second-rate citizens
who had to pay double taxation. Other believers also saw Peter
the Great as the Antichrist and were put to death for this. One of
them was Grigorij Talickij, who circulated a pamphlet against
Peter as early as 1690, in which he called Moscow a new Babylon
and Peter the Antichrist.[207]

Chef de l'église

Peter the Great was no Antichrist, but he was not a second
apostle Peter either, though that is how he was described not
only by Feofan Prokopovič but also already in a 1702 school
book ('as the rock Peter on whom Christ has built the
church').[208] The tsar's church policy had baneful consequences
for the Russian Orthodox Church in the next two centuries.
With his ecclesiastical reform of its government Peter had put the
church completely in his own hands and made it a structural and
bureaucratic extension of the state. In 1721 he gave the church a
new statute, the notorious Spiritual Regulation (*Duchovnyj*

Reglament), which the church historian Igor Smolitsch has called the capitulation document of the Russian church.[209] As early as 1700 Peter forbade the election of a new patriarch and in 1721 he abolished the office. In place of this he created a collective leadership of twelve members, the Most Holy Synod. The members were nominated by the tsar. Moreover Peter also appointed a top official as the 'tsar's eye and ear': he attended all the gatherings of the synod, determined the agenda and had to approve any decision. This new function was denoted by the German name *oberprokuror*.

Feofan Prokopovič drafted this government structure, which was alien to the nature of Orthodoxy, and he wrote the Spiritual Regulation. He himself became the vice-president of the synod; metropolitan Stefan Javorskij, who had been the caretaker since the death of the last patriarch in 1700, became the powerless president. Like Prokopovič, Javorskij came from the Orthodox Academy in Kiev and was trained by the Jesuits in Poland, but theologically and spiritually he was at the opposite pole from Prokopovič. Unlike the latter he had some sympathy for Catholic theology, and he criticized Peter over ethical questions like his divorce and the killing of his son Aleksej. He was also against the abolition of the patriarchate, but was nominated president of the synod against his will; in this way Peter further humiliated his timid critic.

Although he was in fact head of the church, the tsar or 'the monarch of all Russia' was not called 'head of the church' in the new church statute and the formula of oaths for the bishop, but 'supreme judge (*krajnij su'dja*) of the spiritual college (= synod)' and 'protector and guardian of Orthodoxy' (*zaščitnik i chranitel' pravoslavija*).

Earlier, Prokopovič had said in a treatise that since Constantine the Great, the emperor has an episcopal function in the sense that he oversees the bishops, and he calls the emperor himself 'bishop of the bishops' (*episkop episkopov*').[210] According to Prokopovič a patriarch was superfluous and as reprehensible as a pope. In the Church Regulation Prokopovic put forward a theological and practical argument for abolishing the function of the patriarchate. The theological reason is that a collective leadership is more in accord with the conciliar spirit of Orthodoxy. He calls this government *sobornoe pravitel'stvo*, speculating on the double meaning of the Russian term *sobor*, which stands for both council and synod. The pragmatic reason is disillusioning: believers would identify too easily with a recognizable church leader, and in cases of conflict between tsar and church would be inclined to take the side of the patriarch. That danger was not present with a collective in which there was no place for a clear leading figure.

Collective synodical government was a Lutheran innovation introduced by Peter into the Russian Church. Only if the synod had been able to operate independently was it still the lesser evil. However, as a result of the *oberprokuror,* a kind of minister of religious affairs, the Russian church was wholly stripped of its spiritual garb. Not only was the *oberprokuror* a layman, often a general, but in addition most *oberprokurors* were not interested in Orthodoxy. They were either deists or freemasons or atheists or Protestant pietists, except for the pious Pobedonoscev, and all of them, including the pious and reactionary Pobedonoscev (1880–1905), obstructed any possibility of theological and social renewal in the church, down to 1917.

With the abolition of the patriarchate the Russian church came to stand outside the tradition of Eastern Orthodoxy, for there was always also a patriarch in all the episcopal synods in the Orthodox Church. The prayer in the liturgy for the 'ecumenical patriarch of Constantinople' was also abolished. However, by a tendentious presentation of things Peter obtained the agreement of the Eastern patriarchs, who also had no other choice in view of their financial dependence on Russia. Ironically this was the same situation as that in 1589 when they had agreed with the establishment of the Moscow patriarchate.

Thus we can also see Peter the Great's religious and ideological ambivalence in his concrete church policy: on the one hand a break with the Orthodox tradition and a further distancing from Constantinople, while on the other the Byzantine caesaropapism is implemented in its last consequences. The tsar who drove away the stuffy clerical atmosphere of Moscow by the Western sea breeze in St Petersburg, who modernized the training of the Russian clergy and introduced Western philosophy, had himself installed as a high priest and thus reinforced the traditional Constantinopolitan church-state system.

This church-state structure remained throughout the rest of tsarist Russia. That was also the case under Catherine the Great, who despite her German Protestant origins outwardly identified herself completely with Russian Orthodoxy and the church-state tradition. In her correspondence with Voltaire she called herself *chef de l'église grecque,* and acted accordingly by having the only critic of her church policy, metropolitan Arsenij of Rostov, put to death. That was one of the contradictions in Catherine's policy, which despite her interest in Enlightenment ideas and the modern state order was not ready to put any of these ideas into practice.

A more general remark needs to be made about Catherine the Great in this connection. Although Catherine was the first to intend to subject Russia to a basic law modelled on the West, the *Nakaz,* in which she explicitly stated that 'Russia is a European state' (art.6), she in fact removed Russia further from European political culture by extending serfdom and by condemning writers (Radiščev). As for the political and intellectual convergence of Russia and Europe, the reign of Catherine the Great was a missed opportunity for Russia, however profitable it may have been in other areas. The German tsaritsa, with her European erudition and love of Russia, was better fitted to bridge the political and ideological gulf between Russia and Europe, actually to make Russia 'a European state', than anyone else. It was all the more a missed opportunity because after Catherine no Russian leader expressed this European ambition again until Michail Gorbachev, whose 'European house' idea was a comparable break with the national tradition to Catherine's formulation.

Back to the problem of church and state. Catherine's successor, tsar Paul, officially adopted the title 'head of the church' (*glava cerkvi*) in his accession law of 1797. But that was meant more in a metaphorical sense, in order to indicate that the

Russian emperor must adhere to the Orthodox faith, and thus cannot be Catholic or Protestant.[211]And Paul himself had Catholic leanings, while his successor Alexander I was Protestant.

Alexander I was the only tsar to distance himself from the ecclesiastical veneration of the tsar, which seemed to him to be blasphemous. He personally ordered the synod to forbid all bishops to express such reverence 'which befits God alone' towards him.[212] Nevertheless his successor Nicolas I was again called 'image of God' by metropolitan Filaret, under whom a law was also laid down, albeit in an appendix, that the tsar is 'the head of the church'.[213]

With his repudiation of Byzantine religious titles and signs of honour, tsar Alexander I caused a breach in the myth of the East and in Peter the Great's church policy, though everything went on as before. Alexander is a special tsar from the religious and ideological perspective for yet another reason. He was the first tsar to give up the Orthodox exclusiveness in favour of a broader view of Christianity. He entered into a Christian alliance with his Western fellow monarchs, namely the Austrian emperor and the king of Prussia, the so-called Holy Alliance. This was meant as a common Christian front against revolutionary France. As political saviour of Europe in the battle against Napoleon, Alexander also wanted to be its spiritual saviour, by defending Christian values against the atheistic ideology of the revolution. From the perspective of the age-old Russian religious self-image this really did break through the myth of the East. Orthodox Russia no longer stood as the only true Christian nation over against Catholic and Protestant Europe, but stood with Catholic Austria and Protestant Prussia over against a common threat to Christianity. However, Russia in the person of Alexander I took the initiative.

The religious principles which Alexander adopted as the basic of his alliance were ethical and pietistic and not ecclesiastical by nature: Christian love of neighbour, justice, the conviction that all men are brothers and that the three participating states should regard one another 'as members of one and the same Christian people . . . as three provinces of one and the same people'.[214] The Holy Alliance was not a great political success; nevertheless it was an important break in the Russian religious and political ideology.

Shortly after Alexander I there was also to be a change in the Russian religious self-image backed up by a philosophical argument. That happened through Alexander's former envoy in Paris and Russia's 'first philosopher', Pëtr Čaadaev. His unmasking of the myth of the East for the first time explicitly raises the question of the relationship between Russia and Europe.

7

Unmasking the Myth in the Nineteenth Century

Čaadaev's City of the Dead

In 1836, an article appeared in a Russian journal by the philosopher Pëtr Čaadaev which caused a shock in the Russian cultural and political world. Never before in Russian history had the problem of Russia and Europe been formulated more sharply than in this article and, intellectually, Russia would never be the same again. Čaadaev's *Philosophical Letter* became the opening shot for a debate on Russian identity between the Slavophiles and the Westernizers which lasted for decades and in this respect largely compensated for the publication ban which was immediately imposed on the author by tsar Nicolas I.

Thematically, Caadev's article is just as important for the Russian history of ideas as Ilarion's *Oration on the Law and the Grace* eight centuries earlier. It discusses the same question, Russia's religious and historical destiny in relation to the Christian world, but now with a dramatically different conclusion from that of Ilarion. And it is almost as unknown among historians of Western ideas as Ilarion's treatise, despite the fact that Čaadaev's work was originally written in French and stands in the European currents of German romanticism and French traditionalism. As a Russian who wrote in French and thought in terms of German romanticism, an Anglophile with Roman Catholic leanings, Pëtr Čaadaev occupies an original place in the history of European ideas.

Pëtr Čaadaev is praised and criticized in his own land as a

cosmopolitan Russian, but supporters and opponents alike recognize him as the first Russian philosopher. Čaadaev was also special politically: progressive but anti-revolutionary. On the one hand he would have nothing of the French Revolution; on the other he had an antipathy to the barbaric political system in his own land and spoke out powerfully against serfdom. He was the first person in Russia to do this out of Christian conviction and the second to do so in writing after Aleksandr Radiščev, who had to pay for his standpoint in 1790 with exile.

In 1821, Pëtr Jakovlevič Čaadaev (1794–1856) resigned from government service to travel in Europe and devote himself to philosophy. He did not leave much of a literary *oeuvre*: eight essays in letter form, *Lettres philosophiques addressées à une dame* (1829–1830), the beginnings of a number of articles, and an extensive intellectual correspondence with prominent figures from the Russian and European intelligentsia.[215] Čaadaev could not get his *Philosophical Letters* published, but in 1836 the first slipped past the censor. The author immediately became known on a national scale, but tsar Nicolas was furious. The censor was dismissed as rector of Moscow University, the editor of the journal *Teleskop* was banished to Siberia, the journal itself was closed down and Čaadaev declared to be mentally ill; a lifetime ban on publication was imposed on him. A year later Čaadaev reacted to this with a work *Apologia of a Madman*. But Russia had been rudely woken from its philosophical sleep, and the myth of the East was fundamentally weakened.

In the discussion of Čaadaev's thought which now follows I shall quote at length from the first *Philosophical Letter,* in which the author gives his verdict on Russia.

The problem is that we never grew up with other peoples, that we do not belong to a single great family of the human race, either to the West or to the East, and that we do not have the tradition of either the one or the other. We stand as it were outside time, and the world-wide upbringing of the human race has not reached us. The wonderful bond of human ideas in the succession of generations and the history of the human spirit, which has brought this spirit throughout the rest of the world to its present status, has had no influence on us at all. Truly, what has for long already formed the essence of life and society is still only theory and speculation for us.

Čaadaev thinks that the Russian people did not undergo the stages of growth which brought the other nations to adulthood and that it did not develop any historical consciousness and fruitful ideas. The Russian past knows nothing but barbarism, superstition and the Tatar oppression which shaped the Russian mentality. The Russians live from one day to the next, without memories and without a view of the future, without regulations and clear convictions. The people endures everything in animal-like passivity or sometimes tries something out in a chaotic way, as it were a natural eruption, which goes away again as quickly as it arose. Russia has no historical links with anyone; it is put in the world 'like a lawless child'. The whole of Russian culture is merely an importation of neat and clear ideas which are applied wrongly; it is imitation without organic integration into every-day Russian reality: 'We grow but do not mature, we move forward but on a crooked line which does not reach its goal.' That is the deplorable position of Russia in the general develop-ment of mankind, whereas Russia, Čaadaev cryptically adds, has after all been created to offer something to mankind.

After this sketch of Russia's isolation in the world, Čaadaev describes the connection with the other peoples, especially with Europe. He does so from a view of the peoples as collective persons.

The peoples of Europe have a common physiognomy, a family feeling (*physionomie commune, un air de famille*). Despite the general division of these peoples into a Latin and a Teutonic branch, into southern and northern types, there is a common bond which unites them all in one and the same group, as is clear to anyone who has steeped himself in their general history. You know that it is not so long ago that the whole of Europe called itself Christendom (*que toute l'Europe s'appelait la Chrétienté*) and that this word has a meaning in public law. In addition to this common character, each of these peoples has its own special character, which is a matter of history and tradition, that form the legacy of the ideas of these peoples. But each individual has a part in the common heritage, and without difficulty and in a natural way collects during his lifetime the knowledge which is disseminated in society and adapts to it. Make for yourself the comparison with what happens among us and judge for yourself: what elementary ideas can we get in everyday converse, in order to use them in one way or another as a guideline in life? Note that the issue here is not one of study or reading, of literature or science, but simply the contact between intellects (*intelligences*). It is about the ideas which surround the child in the cradle and accompany him at his play, which the mother imparts with her caresses; which finally penetrate to the marrow of his bones, in the form of all kinds of feelings together with the air that he breathes, and which form his moral nature before he enters the world and society. Do you want to know what kind of ideas these are? They are the ideas of duty, justice, law and order. They derive directly from the events which have made the society there; they form the building blocks of the social world of those lands. That is the atmosphere of the West; it is more than mere history or psychology; it is the physiology of the European man (*la physiologie de l'homme de l'Europe*).

These civil virtues are lacking in Russia, as a result of which the form of its society is so different from that in the West. Čaadaev sees another essential difference in the lack of a philosophical tradition in his land. Not only do 'we all lack a certain method of the spirit and a certain logic, and the syllogism of the West is unknown to us'. In the distant past, too, Russia did not have any wise men who gave the people direction, whereas the primitive peoples of Europe, like the Scandinavians and Germans, had their skalds and bards. In short, Russia is one great spiritual void, and that is all the more remarkable, given that Russia could have been a link between two great cultures.

Situated between the two great parts of the world, between the
East and the West, leaning on China with one elbow and on
Germany with the other, we should have allowed the two
great principles of human intelligence, imagination and reason
to come together in us. We should have united the histories of
the whole earth in our civilization. But providence has not
assigned us this role. Far from it, it seems to have been uncon-
cerned about our fate. By excluding us from its beneficent
influence on human reason, it has left us entirely to ourselves;
it in no way wants to involve itself in our affairs, nor does it
want to teach us anything. The experience of the ages does not
stand before us. Periods and generations have gone past
without leaving us anything. Looking at ourselves, we can
say that in our case the universal law of mankind has been
abolished. Standing alone in the world, we have given nothing
to the world and taken nothing from it. We have not added a
single idea to the total of human ideas; we have not contributed to the progress of the human spirit in a single respect,
and the progress that we have made, we have spoiled. From
the first moment of our social existence nothing has come
forth from us that was of use for the general well-being of
mankind; not one useful thought has taken root in the sterile
soil of our fatherland; not one great truth has arisen from
our midst; we have not taken the trouble to invent anything
for ourselves, and of all that others have invented we have
only taken over the deceptive appearance and excessive
luxury . . .

To be noticed at all we have had to extend from the Bering
Sea to the Oder. Once a great man thought to bring us civilization;[216] to give us a pledge of the Enlightenment he threw over
us the mantle of civilization. We assumed the mantle but never
arrived at Enlightenment. Another time a great monarch, who
encountered us in his glorious mission, led us as conquerors
from one end of Europe to the other.[217] When he returned
home from his victorious way through the most enlightened
lands of the world, we took with us only crazy ideas and fateful errors which led to an enormous disaster that put us back

half a century.[218] Usually there is something in our blood which works against any real progress . . .

I cannot stop wondering about this void, this perplexing isolation of our social existence. That is certainly partly to blame for our incomprehensible fate, but here without doubt we must also partly speak of human guilt, as in the case of everything which takes place in the moral world. Let us again ask history: it alone gives an explanation of the peoples.

And then Čaadaev comes to the fundamental explanation of the unhappy fate of Russia, namely Byzantinism, Russia's choice of Byzantine Christianity in the tenth century and the isolation from world Christianity which followed: missing the boat of Western, Latin civilization. In saying this Čaadaev took the ground away from under the Russian sense of identity and at the same time created a ideal picture of Christian Europe, which came into being out of the confrontation of the barbarians with Christianity. He unfolds a grandiose view of Catholic Christianity, in which his philosophical idealism and intellectual sense of religion converge.

What did we do when out of the struggle between the energetic barbarism of the Northern peoples and the lofty thought of religion the structure of modern civilization arose? Driven by a fatal destiny, we went into wretched Byzantium, a subject of deep contempt among these peoples, in search of the moral code that had to define our upbringing. Shortly beforehand an ambitious spirit[219] had detached this family of peoples from the universal brotherhood; so what we got was an idea distorted by human passion. But the life-giving idea of unity was then permeating all of Europe. Everything arose from it and everything came together in it. The whole intellectual movement of the time was merely focussed on the realization of the unity of human thought, and every impulse derived from this powerful need to arrive at a universal idea that is the genius of the modern time. Alienated from this wonderful principle, we became the prey of conquest.[220] And when we had been liberated from the foreign yoke, had we not been separated from the human family we could have profited from the ideas which had arisen among our Western brothers at this time. But instead of that we lapsed into an even greater slavery, hallowed as that was by the very fact of our liberation.[221]

How many bright rays were already shining in the darkness that covered Europe at that time! The majority of the knowledge of which the human mind is now proud was already there in embryo in people's minds; society had already taken a fixed form, and falling back on pagan antiquity Christianity had rediscovered the beauty which it had hitherto lacked. But nothing of what was taking place in Europe penetrated to us, imprisoned in our schism. We had nothing to do with the great events of the world. The eminent qualities with which religion had endowed the modern peoples and which, from the perspective of sound reason, had raised them as far above the old as the latter stand above the Hottentots and the Lapps; the new forces with which it had enriched the human intellect, the customs which through subjection to an unarmed authority were as gentle as they had formerly been cruel – we had nothing of this in our land. When Christianity made its majestic progress on the way that its divine founder had marked out, and took the generations with it, we did not stir ourselves, despite the fact that we called ourselves Christians. When the whole world was building itself up, nothing was being built up among us: as of old we hid in our huts of wood and straw. In a word, we did not fulfil the new destinies of the human race. Even though we are Christians, the fruit of Christianity has not ripened among us.

The Christian religion does not just reveal itself as a moral system, contained in the perishable forms of the human spirit, but as an eternal divine power that is universally at work in the world of the intellect, the visible effect of which must be a constant lesson for us. That is the real significance of the dogma that is addressed in the symbol of faith in a universal church . . .

But, you will say, are we not Christians and cannot we be

civilized in a non-European way? Yes, we are doubtless Christians, but are not the Abyssinians Christians, too? And one can of course be civilized in a different way from Europe; are not people civilized in Japan, and even more so than in Russia, if one may believe one of our fellow-countrymen?[222] But do you think that the order of things of which I have just been speaking is realized in the Christianity of the Abyssinians and in the civilization of the Japanese, and that this forms the final destiny of the human species? Do you really think that these foolish deviations from the divine and human truths will bring heaven on earth?

Two very different things must be distinguished in Christianity: one is its effect on the individual and the other its effect on the universal intelligence. They are mixed in a natural way in the supreme reason and necessarily result in the same end. But our limited gaze cannot encompass the span of time in which the eternal plans of the divine wisdom will be realized. We must make a distinction between the divine action that manifests itself in a particular time, in a human life, and the divine action that fulfils itself in infinity. On the day of the final consummation of the work of redemption, all hearts and minds will simply form one feeling and one thought, and all the walls which divide the peoples and the communities of faith will fall. But before that moment it is important for everyone to know his place in the order of the universal vocation of Christians, that is, to know what means there are within him to work for the attainment of the goal that is set before the whole of human society.

Čaadaev sees the characteristic feature of Europe as its active participation in this historical movement towards the unity of humankind, which at the same time is the saving movement of Christianity. He sees a first realization of it in the Catholic Middle Ages, of which he gives an evocative picture in the following passage:

All the nations of Europe held each other by the hand on their journey through the ages. They are also doing this now to take a particular direction; they constantly encounter one another on the same way. To see the family aspect in the development of these peoples one need not even study history: read Tasso and you will see how all these people lie at the foot of the wall of Jerusalem. Remember that for fifteen centuries they had one language with which they addressed God, one moral authority, one single conviction in life; imagine how for fifteen centuries, every year, on the same day at the same hour, in the same words and all at the same time, they raised their voices to the supreme Being to celebrate his praise in the greatest of his benefits: a wondrous harmony, a thousand times more sublime than all the harmonies of the physical world. Given that this atmosphere in which the people of Europe live, and which is the only one in which the human species can attain its final destiny, is the result of the influence which religion has exerted on them, it is clear that if the weakness of our faith and the inadequacy of our doctrine has hitherto kept us outside this universal movement in which the social idea of Christianity is being developed and formulated, and has thrown us back into the category of people who can profit from Christianity to the full extent only indirectly and far too late, it is clear that we must try with all possible means to breathe new life into our faith and to give ourselves a truly Christian impulse. For it is Christianity alone which has brought all this to pass there. That is what I mean when I say that among us the upbringing of the human race must begin again.

'There' is Europe, a simple place name with an almost magical resonance for Russia.

Philosophical Catholicism

With his ideas, Čaadaev became the catalyst for the ideological debate between Slavophiles and those inclined towards the West which was never again to cease. However, he himself stood above the divide, as later did Vladimir Solov'ëv, whose thought is in the same religious universalistic direction as that of Čaadaev. Both represent a third current in the nineteenth-century Russian ideological debate, that of religion and Europe. In contrast to the nationalistic Slavophile current and the revolutionary and atheistic supporters of the West, it was religious and non-violent with a leaning towards Europe. It is a minority current, but one which opens up a completely new perspective for Russia. It is the only one that laments the division of the church between Russia and Europe and propagates the idea of Christian universalism.

Pëtr Čaadaev does that more for philosophical than for ecclesiological reasons. That becomes clear in the following essay-letters in which he develops further his philosophical beginnings about the unity of mankind from his first letter. Then it proves how closely Čaadaev's thought is related to the philosophy of Friedrich Schelling, with whom Čaadaev had personal contact in 1825. He thinks in the spirit of Schelling's idealism, but replaces Schelling's rationalism with Christianity as the guiding force of history. When Čaadaev later, in 1832, heard of Schelling's new philosophy of revelation, he wrote in a letter to Schelling how pleased he was that Schelling had arrived at 'the great idea of a fusion of philosophy and religion'. He says that the fundamental effort in his intellectual work has always been 'to contribute to the building of the temple in which all human beings will one day have to unite in order, in perfect knowledge, to worship the evident God'.[223] Čaadaev confesses to Schelling that with this idea he felt alone 'in the intellectual wilderness of my land' but later experienced that 'the whole thinking world is progressing in this direction'. But that is happening outside Russia and therefore the most recent work of Schelling is still unknown, 'for however powerful your work is, esteemed sir, it does not reach our latitudes . . . We belong to another solar system.'

Because Čaadaev does philosophy from a Christian salvation-historical perspective, he rejects the rationalistic constructions of history in abstract idealist philosophy with their unfounded, mechanistic idea of progress, and also the pagan starting points of antiquity and the Renaissance. So here Čaadaev is explicitly presenting himself as a Christian thinker. He does not reject just atheistic philosophical thought but also religious idealistic thought which begins from a mechanistic self-revelation of the divine reason. For Čaadaev the personal revelation of God in Christ is central. On the other hand, with his striving for a reconciliation between rationalism and Christian revelation, he goes beyond the limits of theology. He himself is aware of his special position and confesses that his religion 'does not coincide with the religion of theologians . . . It is the confession of the Fénelons, Pascals, Leibnizes and Bacons.' He knows that he is not an 'authentic Catholic', but he feels at home in 'the Catholic philosophy' which 'regards the kingdom of God not only as an idea but also as a fact'.[224] And in a letter in which he explains his attitude to the Bible he calls himself 'not a theologian, not a scribe, but an ordinary Christian philosopher'.[225] Čaadaev never went over to the Catholic church, but he was what Russians call a *filokatolik*, a 'Catholicophile', a sympathizer with Catholicism.[226]

Čaadaev's basic idea is that human civilization, world history, is moved forward by a striving for unity, a unity in which all the intellectual and moral forces of humanity converge. This striving for progress is not deterministically enclosed in history, but has been put in it by the Creator, who also guides this process through salvation history. The incarnation of God was the definitive turning point in history. With the birth of Christ, the striving of the universal intelligence took on an irreversible impulse which leads to the consolidation of the kingdom of God on earth. Čaadaev already expressed that belief in the Latin motto above the first philosophical letter: *adveniat regnum tuum*.

The universal temple in which all men will one day unite is the Roman Catholic Church, to which Čaadaev constantly refers without denoting it by that adjective. Čaadaev's concept of the church is more philosophical than theological. For him the church is primarily a moral and civilizing force which has the divine task of uniting mankind over and above the dividing lines of nations and races. The cosmopolitan Catholic Church with its centralizing role fulfils God's command best. Čaadaev criticizes the Protestant churches because they have failed to recognize the fundamental Christian task of bringing about the unity of mankind: 'The Reformation set the world back into the disunion of paganism, and restored the great national individualities.' This denial of the Christian task is not counterbalanced by the fact that in other areas the Reformation brought specific progress for mankind.[227] According to Čaadaev, the splitting of mankind by Protestantism is continued in the tendency towards fragmentation within the Protestant churches themselves: they constantly fall apart into smaller churches and in so doing constantly move further away from the goal of unity. It is the consequence of the rejection of the two symbols of Christian unity, the eucharist, 'the wonderful invention of Christian reason, which as it were materializes the souls in order to be able to unite them better', and the papacy. Of this Čaadaev says:

> Even if, as people say, the papacy is a human institution – as if things of this extent can be made by human hands – what difference does that make? What is certain is that at that time it emerged in its essence from the true spirit of Christianity and that at present as the visible sign of unity it is still the sign of reunion ... Who is not amazed when he sees that despite all its evils, all its disasters, all its own mistakes and guilt, despite all the attacks on the faith and even the unprecedented victory of unbelief, it still stands, more powerful than ever? Stripped of its human glitter it has only become stronger.[228]

Čaadaev values the papacy more as a symbol of human unity and continuity than as a doctrinal authority, as all Rome is. With Čaadaev, too, the eternal Russian fascination with Rome lives on, but now in another way: not to commandeer it ideologically, but on the contrary to recognize it in its own worth. Čaadaev pours out his heart philosophically in a letter to his friend Aleksandr Turgenev, who adopted a more sceptical attitude on a visit to the eternal city:

Rome is no ordinary city, no heaping up of stones and people, but an immeasurable idea, a grandiose fact . . . Rome is the bond between the old world and the new, and it is utterly necessary that there should be such a point on earth to which all men can look now and then with the aim of coming into contact in a concrete and tangible way with all the memories of the human race . . . How can you not bow before this attractive symbol of so many centuries? . . . But then the pope, the pope! What about that? Is he too not just an idea, a pure abstraction? Look at this old man, sitting in a gestatorial chair or under a baldachino, with his triple crown, today just as a thousand years ago, as if nothing in the world had changed; really, what is the man here? Is it not an almighty symbol of time – not the time which ticks on but the time which is immovable, through which everything goes but which itself remains indestructible and in which and through which everything is accomplished . . . An imperishable spiritual monument.[229]

For Čaadaev, Christianity, Catholicism and Europe are indissolubly connected. Catholic Christianity made Europe what it is; it brought it from pagan social barbarity and gave it a spiritual unity as a first step towards the universal unity of mankind intended by the Creator. 'L'Europe est encore la Chrétienté', says Čaadaev like a Russian Novalis ('Christianity or Europe').[230] Perhaps it seems that Čaadaev identifies Christian universalism with Europe, but a Eurocentric picture of the world was universal in nineteenth-century philosophy of history and historiography. And after all, Čaadaev has more right to speak than Novalis, because Novalis is speaking from a *Western* European perspective which he takes for granted, with the unknown Russia outside his mental horizon. By contrast, Čaadaev is looking far beyond his natural horizon and encompassing all Europe.

More strongly, where Novalis thinks not only Eurocentrically but also in terms of German nationalism, by giving his country a preferential role in Christian Europe, Čaadaev's attitude is in principle anti-nationalistic. His Christian preference is for England, which in his view has best realized the Christian idea of progress.[231] Here Čaadaev is speaking as an admirer of the English political institutions (he had been to England and in Moscow was a frequent visitor to the English club), because in terms of church history England does not of course fit into his Catholic picture of Europe under the leadership of the pope. But that fact is compensated for by the legal recognition of Catholics in 1829 which Čaadaev could just mention in his first philosophical letter. Elsewhere, however, Čaadaev does not conceal his abhorrence of the 'tyrant Henry VIII with his hypocrite Cranmer', whom he thinks responsible with other reformers for the disappearance of religious unity in Europe.[232]

Despite the differences from the German romantics, Čaadaev also has a clearly Eurocentric view of the world. In the sixth letter he expresses this: European civilization is destined to outlive the Chinese, Japanese, Indian, Arab and Mexican cultures. These last have lost their creative verve and have become stationary. However, Čaadaev rejects what we would now call Western cultural imperialism, as is evident from a remark in his first letter about the materialistic civilization of the United States which is about to destroy the culture of the Indians.

His attitude towards Muslim culture is really ambiguous. Despite the fact that Čaadaev calls Ottoman Islam cruel and barbarous and thinks European culture superior to Islamic culture, he has a strikingly positive assessment of Muhammad, and he assigns Islam an important role in the spiritual history of mankind; Islam has made pagan polytheism disappear in its territories and as a monotheistic religion has come to prepare the way for Christianity. Islam also has its inspiration in Christianity, and God uses Islam as an indirect way of drawing out the notion of the unity of mankind.[233] The hostility between the two religions which developed later through wars cannot destroy the spiritual affinity.

For all his idealization of the Catholic Middle Ages, Čaadaev also sees the bad sides of mediaeval Europe, the wars of religion and the burnings at the stake. However, he believes that the

European nations have ultimately come out of these bloody conflicts better than Russia, where no such conflicts of opinion took place, and where from a spiritual perspective nothing but a deadly silence has prevailed. Even in the Europe of his time Čaadaev sees 'not just reason, virtue and religion, far from it', but 'despite all the imperfection, evil and lawlessness in present-day European society it is nevertheless true that to a certain degree the kingdom of God has been realized because it contains the principle of a continuous progress'.[234] And that is entirely lacking in Russia.

A new opportunity for Russia

Čaadaev seldom speaks explicitly about the Orthodox Church in his own land: it is clear that it shares in his criticism of the Byzantine and Russian spiritual void. Only in the second philosophical letter does he criticize it directly: the 'social idea', what forms the essence of Christian society, is completely lacking in the Russian Church. Christianity even proves to have had an adverse social effect in Russia, for serfdom was introduced into Russia after its acceptance of Christianity, namely in the sixteenth century whereas slavery in Europe, which came from Roman times, had disappeared under the influence of Christianity. 'Just let the Orthodox Church explain why it has not raised its maternal voice against this abhorrent abuse of one half of the nation by the other.'[235]

Here Čaadaev is putting his thumb on the sore point in relations between Russia and Europe, as he had done in the first letter, and this is the core of his social and religious criticism of his own country: Russia is not a constitutional state. As he puts it elsewhere: 'How could even the most elementary concepts of justice, laws and other forms of legality take roots under a government which from one day to the next could turn the whole population from free men into slaves?'[236] And Čaadaev formulates the difference between Russia and the contemporary United States sharply on this point. The problem of serfdom is worse in Russia than in the United States, where the wretched situation of the slaves and the corruption of the slaveowners is far more visible. Russian serfdom is integrated into society and accepted, and the phenomenon is not felt to be a scandal. In the United States slavery is based on ethnic differences, but in Russia there is not only no racial difference between free men and slaves, but there is not even an visible difference between the behaviour of peasants who are serfs and free peasants! The whole of Russian society is marked by the stamp of unfreedom. The notion of freedom does not exist.[237]

Despite his extremely negative verdict on Russia, Pëtr Čaadaev does not write off his own land. And despite his Europeanism he loves his land. He makes that clear in his defence *Apologie d'un fou* (1837), which he prefaced with a motto which is a remark by the English writer Samuel Taylor Coleridge: 'O my brothers! I have told most bitter truth, but without bitterness.' In this writing Čaadaev introduces more nuances into what he says about Russia, but he does not essentially take anything back. He urgently presents his vision of the connection between love of fatherland, Christian universalism and individual responsibility. It is a work against nationalism, against collective passions, against the populist view that public opinion represents truth. Love of truth stands above love of fatherland, and the way to God does not go through the fatherland but through truth. The author makes a moving plea for a critical love of fatherland without retrograde utopias and fantasies of the future, and says of himself that he loves much of his land, but 'not with closed eyes, bowed head and pursed lips'.[238]

Čaadaev does see a place for Russia in history, despite the fact that it has stood outside European civilization for so long. This can, paradoxically enough, give Russia a good starting point because it does not have the same self-seeking interests and established prejudices as those of Europe. 'We face every new idea as *esprits vierges*.'[239]

In fact Russia has already deliberately taken a new course and is now playing an indispensable role in European history thanks to Peter the Great, for whom Čaadaev is full of praise. Čaadaev expresses his deep conviction 'that we are called to solve the majority of social problems and to bring to fulfilment the ideas which arose in the old society'. At the end he also mentions the Orthodox Church, almost in passing, 'this church that is so humble and sometimes so heroic – which is some consolation for the emptiness of our chronicles'.[240]

So here Čaadaev makes an interesting leap of thought: Europe is a lesson for Russia, but once taught, Russia can make a unique contribution to Europe. Čaadaev already alludes to this in his first letter when he says that Russia has 'a great lesson for the world'. This observation and those in the *Apologia* seem to go in the Slavophile direction. And later in fact Čaadaev toned down his hard line in the first philosophical letter on Byzantium. In a discussion with A. Chomjakov in 1843, Čaadaev recognizes the positive role of Byzantium in the Christianization of Russia: 'From flourishing Byzantium holy Orthodoxy shines out for us', and he points to the unique non-violent way in which Christianity was introduced into Kievan Russia under Vladimir. But at the same time he emphasizes that Byzantium was at that time still linked with Rome and that eleventh-century Russia had bonds with most European cities: there was 'a feeling of common Christian citizenship'.[241]

It seems paradoxical, but despite incidental inclinations towards moderate Slavophile standpoints in the later writings, up to his death Čaadaev continued to produce his blunt criticisms of the nationalistic delusions of the Slavophiles. It is certainly paradoxical – though the fact can be evaluated positively – that Čaadaev did not emigrate to the West, and that despite his admiration for the Catholic Church he did not go over to that church. He continued to live in the Necropolis, the City of the Dead, as he called the place from which he sent his first philosophical letter. As an intellectual phenomenon Čaadaev was not only a paradox but also a personal refutation of the intellectual void that, he claimed, existed in Russia. And even the cultural void no longer existed in his time, in which 'the gracious genius of Russia', as Čaadaev called his friend Aleksandr Puškin, had for the first time brought the country to the top of European literature.

Be this as it may, Pëtr Čaadaev is certainly original, and he played a decisive role in Russian intellectual history. The Westernizers completely subscribed to his progressive social views but rejected his religious view of society, and the Slavophiles valued both his social views and their religious starting points, but of course rejected the Catholic implications.

The tragedy of Čaadaev was that by his Catholic inclinations he isolated himself from those who celebrated him for his criticisms of serfdom and despotism. Even Puškin distanced himself from his friend on this point and reversed Čaadaev's view of Christianity: it was Russia which rescued Christianity for Europe by holding back the Mongolian hordes at the cost of being centuries behind Europe.[242]

Aleksandr Turgenev could not reconcile himself to Čaadaev's Catholic notions either. He equally had leanings toward Europe but thought that the way to European religious unity lay through Protestantism, which he regarded as the authentic expression of Christianity. He mockingly called the pope 'the Dalai Lama on the Tiber'.[243]

Finally, N. Nadeždin, who had published the first philosophical letter in his journal *Teleskop*, also began to think differently from Čaadaev. Even more strongly than Čaadaev himself did in his *Apologia*, he saw a great advantage in the Russian time-lag behind Europe: in contrast to Europe, torn apart by political passions, 'as children we still have an unripened virginity of the soul in which a wise hand need sow only the seeds of truth and prosperity'.[244] Or in another metaphor: the West is burned out, while Russia needs only to wait for a favourable wind to kindle her fire. Nadeždin believes that the young Russia will ultimately overtake the old Europe.[245] With this thought, which already has resonances of the Slavophile (and later Soviet Communist) motif of 'catch up and overtake', Nadeždin evolved towards the opposite pole from Čaadaev, who had formerly been like-minded.

The core of Čaadaev's view, the Catholic idea of unity, did not catch on at all in Russia. Certainly there were some like-minded figures who in fact went over to Catholicism. They included

Čaadaev's friend Ivan Gagarin, who later became a Jesuit: he published three philosophical letters and the *Apologia* in France after Čaadaev's death.[246] Another well-known Russian Catholic was Vladimir Pečerin, a colourful representative of the Russian intelligentsia. He dropped a career as professor of classical languages at the University of Moscow and went to the West, his only baggage a very good knowledge of languages and a burning hatred of his fatherland. That was in 1836, some months before the publication of Čaadaev's first philosophical letter. In Belgium, Pečerin became a priest and member of the congregation of the Redemptorists. After twenty years as a successful preacher he left the monastery, disappointed at its stifling atmosphere. After that he worked another twenty-five years as a priest in England and Ireland and died in 1885 without ever returning to Russia.

Pečerin corresponded with the leading Russian Westernizers A. Herzen and N. Ogarëv, but he has become known through his dazzling and ironic memoirs in the form of letters. The book could not be published in nineteenth-century Russia and only appeared in 1932 under the title *Zamogil'nye zapiski* (*Letters from Beyond the Tomb*).[247]

In the 1830s Pečerin had opted for Catholicism under the influence of the social Christianity of the French priest Lamennais. Even when he had become disillusioned by it, he remained faithful to Catholicism all his life. But he in no way spared the Catholic Church his mocking criticism of everything which no longer pleased him. In particular the hierarchical character of the church, including the papacy, had to suffer. Here Pečerin contrasts sharply with Čaadaev. This is what he says about Pope Pius IX in 1848:

What a strange change! The conservative, aristocratic court church, the close friend of all despots, which with its mantle has covered centuries of the abuse of power, has been re-created in a furiously revolutionary democratic church: her priests have become demagogues, leaders of the ignorant, restless plebs; from high on his holy throne the archpriest himself incites the peoples to rebel against the law and the authorities.[248]

He even differs from Čaadaev in his evaluation of Catholic Rome as a symbol:

> In Rome everything bears the stamp of total exhaustion, decay, sleepiness, as if everything is seized with paralysis: yet people act as though they are aroused and want to pose as being fresh and youthful . . . That reminds me of the Polish countess whom I saw in Chmelnik in 1823; she was in her seventies, but she made herself up with a mild rouge and went around with her breast half bared, dressed as a girl of sixteen. That is the Catholic Church in its present taste.[249]

Čaadaev and Pečerin: two views of the Catholic Church by two original Russians: one values it highly but remains faithful to the Orthodox Church nevertheless; the other admires it initially even more, to such a degree that he is converted to it and even becomes a priest. He later criticizes it for all the things for which he had formerly admired it, but remains an active member of the church. This illustrates the complex relationship between Russia and the Catholic Church. However, nothing is known of any contact between Pečerin and Čaadaev, though between 1849 and 1853 the latter did engage in polemic over Catholicism with the Slavophiles F. Tjutčev and A. Chomjakov. And Čaadaev's writings remained unpublished in Russia until the beginning of the twentieth century.[250]

The revaluation of Čaadaev at the end of the 1980s

Like many religious thinkers from Russian history, Pëtr Čaadaev also experienced scholarly rehabilitation and even a revival in post-Communist Russia. During the Soviet period, while he was not banned, his significance was measured exclusively in social and political terms.[251] In the second half of the 1980s his religious ideas were also freely discussed. Various editions of the *Philosophical Letters* appeared in a short period and many articles were devoted to Čaadaev.[252]As with the rediscovery of Ilarion of Kiev, here there were discussions about the religious content of the writer's works and about whether or not there were new forms of 'ideological adaptation' of the rediscovered Russian thinker. Especially the editors of the two new editions carried on an interesting discussion; there is something to be said for the standpoints of both of them in it.[253] B. Tarasov emphasizes the central Christian starting point in the thought of Čaadaev, against what he called ' the unconscious Soviet habit' of marginalizing it. However, Z. Kamenskij refers to the ambivalent character of this Christianity and relativizes Čaadaev's Catholicism.

Alongside this positive revaluation (with the usual differences in interpretation) there is also a new ideological reaction to Čaadaev from the ultra-nationalistic side which reflects his ideas. In 1995 a book appeared which was intended as a 'textbook for forming the Russian national consciousness'; in it everything that is 'un-Russian' is rejected in a venomous way.[254] In addition to freemasonry, Zionism, cosmopolitanism, communism, Catholicism and nihilism this includes the 'fantasies' of Čaadaev (*Čaadaevščina*). All this ultimately amounts to the same thing: the denial of 'holy Russia'.

The publication in 1993 of a manuscript by the Orthodox theologian Sergej Bulgakov from 1922, *U sten Chersonisa* (At the Walls of Cherson), was a quite unexpected form of rehabilitation of Čaadaev's thought.[255] The title refers to the old Greek city of Cherson on the Crimea where Prince Vladimir of Kiev was said to have been baptized in 988. Four Russians, a fugitive from Bolshevik Russia, a lay theologian, a monk and a parish priest engage in a vigorous debate over whether or not the consequences of Russia's choice of Greek Christianity and isolation from the Roman Catholic word church was a fateful one.

This theme of Čaadaev's (*Čaadaevškoe*) had become topical for Bulgakov when he saw how the isolated church in Russia was annihilated by the Bolsheviks. In the book, in the person of the fugitive, Bulgakov expresses Catholic sympathies and abhorrence of the nationalism of the Orthodox Church. The parish priest also argues powerfully for reunion of his church with Rome. But the lay theologian, who is to be identified as Sergej Nilus, a Slavophile and antisemite from the beginning of this century, and the monk, express a militant anti-Catholic standpoint.

Although in 1940 Bulgakov rejected his 'inner Catholicism' as a spell he had been under, he did not burn the manuscript. As a result he has left us a book which is special in both genre and content, in which he fills Čaadaev's view with authentic theological and ecclesiologial arguments and develops it further into an ecumenical view of the church. It has become a compelling church-historical argument in which both supporters and opponents of the Catholic Church have an equal say. There are theological statements which have preserved their value for present-day Russian Orthodoxy, relations between the Orthodox Churches and the Catholic-Orthodox ecumene.

As a conclusion to this chapter I shall quote a historical remark by Bulgakov which also lost none of its topicality, namely that when Russia accepted Christianity there was still no confessional division between East and West and that therefore with Orthodoxy, Russia

> accepted the universal Christian faith and we became a branch of the one Ecumenical Church. As a result we were not only born to eternal life but also destined to a historical existence as part of the one Christian Europe in which Christian culture must be kindled. Here Russia is born as a Christian European land which had its particular way and particular fate, though these were indissolubly bound up with the fate of the whole of Christian Europe . . . The pagan and barbarian of yesterday becomes a *homo christianus*, and in the perspective of what was then a still mysterious and dark future at the same time that means a *homo Europeus*.[256]

But by fate and without its own doing, in the schism of 1054 Russia was 'separated by a Chinese wall from Christian Western

Europe'. In 1917 the wall was raised even higher, but now that it is some years since this communist ideological wall of division disappeared, the old religious dividing line in Europe must not be reactivated. Therefore Pëtr Čaadaev's thought of Christian unity still remains topical in present-day discussion of the unity of Europe, despite its outdated philosophy of history.

8

The Slavophile Reformulation
of the Myth

With his attitude, Pëtr Čaadaev set off an intensive debate within the Russian intelligentsia about the national character of Russia and the definition of its place in Europe. However, this debate between the so-called Slavophiles and those inclined towards the West demonstrated how much Russia was already thinking in the general frameworks of thought of the European philosophy of history. Not only did those with leanings towards the West orientate themselves on French Enlightenment philosophers and socialists like Saint-Simon and Fourier, on Hegel, Feuerbach, the English positivists and various philosophers of law, but the Slavophiles too developed their national self-awareness with the help of Herder, Schiller, Schelling, Hegel and French traditionalists. Russia became a new shoot on the European philosophical stem, which in turn enlarged the wealth of European ideas.

It is impossible to discuss the many writings of the Slavophiles separately here. But in contrast to the period before 1800, there are many studies and surveys of nineteenth-century Russian thought.[257] Here I shall content myself with the main theme and the most important representatives of the thought of the Slavophiles.

Like the Westernizers, the Slavophiles did not form a homogeneous group. They can be divided into 1. the early or classic Slavophiles, 2. the state nationalists, 3. the pan-Slavists and 4. the eccentric Byzantinophile Konstantin Leont'ev.

Classic Slavophiles

The early Slavophiles were romantic Russophiles who saw the restoration of the old Russia, with the typical Russian village community of peasants and the central position of the Orthodox Church in society, as an alternative to the bureaucratic and repressive Russia of tsar Nicolas I. They wanted the abolition of serfdom, and limitations on the power of the tsar, but not its abolition. They rejected the revolutionary and liberal ideas from the West. Their criticism of Europe related to its prevalent individualism, political antagonism (the formation of parties), legal formalism, philosophical rationalism, atheism and materialism. Over against this they put authentic Russian values like a sense of community (*obščinost'*), a 'natural' sense of justice, philosophical 'wholeness' (*celostnost'*) and Orthodox religion. They developed these elements into distinctive characteristics of a distinctive 'national disposition' (*narodnost'* and *samobytnost'*, terms which are translations of the German *Volkstümlichkeit* and *Eigenart*).

The most important Slavophiles, Ivan Kireevskij and Aleksej Chomjakov, were gifted thinkers who used their knowledge of Western philosophy to define Russia's identity. Chomjakov for the first time spelt out the Russian concept of the church as distinct from the Roman Catholic and Protestant concepts. He accused the former of being based on the despotic unitary principle of the papacy, and the second of being a reaction to this which was heading towards anarchy. Over against these he set the harmonious union of unity and freedom in the Orthodox Church, which he designated with the term 'community' (*sobornost'*). Although his own church did not just accept it from the lay theologian Chomjakov, the term has now become *the* way of stating the Orthodox view of the church.

The Slavophiles were not blind to the bad sides of Russian society and the state, and they also saw positive elements in European society, which they knew from their own travels and from study in Germany and Paris. All this indicates that they do not stand outside Europe, nor did they want to isolate Russia from Europe. Indeed it is not the criticism of Western political and religious institutions, though this contains notions worth considering, but the dream of a 'holy Russia', which makes Slavophilism a new mutation of the myth of the East. However, of all the four currents mentioned it did this in the most nuanced way, and articles like Kireevskij's 'On the Character of European Culture and its Relation to the Culture of Russia' (1852) and Chomjakov's reaction to it, 'On Humboldt', along with his 'On the Western Communities of Faith', are interesting critiques of culture.

One special Slavophile was the erudite art expert Vladimir Odoevskij. In his philosophical collection of short stories *Russian Nights* (1844), as a Russian Faust he goes in search of universal knowledge, which consists in a reunion of European culture with the 'Slav spirit'. And in his uncompleted novel of the future, *The Year 4438*, he expresses his belief that the rising Russia, which has learned much from the older West, is in its turn called to rescue that same West, which is now succumbing to materialism and internal divisions, in an East-West synthesis of faith, science and art and a universal European brotherhood.

State nationalism

Alongside the romantic Slavophiles there were the supporters of state nationalism. That was the official ideology of tsarism under Nicolas I which was propagated in teaching. The basis of this state education was the ideological triptych of autocracy, Orthodoxy and nationhood. The teaching was given more as a pragmatic policy than from idealistic motives, and was directed against ideas that undermined the state from the West, which was fomenting revolution. It did not imply a break with Europe; from 1815 on Russia formed an integral part of the European state system. Russia stood for the conservative part of Europe, for which Nicolas I also felt responsible. And his 'state ideologist' Sergeij Uvarov, the minister of education, enjoyed European culture and often preferred speaking German and French to his mother tongue.

A more inspired ideologist for state patriotism was the historian Michail Pogodin, whom I already quoted at the beginning of this book. In 1845 he wrote an article, making opportunist use of conceptions of A. Thierry and F. Guizot; this contrasted the love of peace in the formation of the Russian state with the expansionist principle in the formation of the Western European feudal states. According to Pogodin, the Russian state had at one time come into being as a consequence of a voluntary invitation to the Norsemen to govern the land of Russia. That led to a development of the Russian state system which was free of antagonism.[258] Pogodin believed that Russia, together with the other Slav peoples, was called to create a new Christian society in Europe, recognizing that while the attainments of the other European peoples were great, they had developed one-sidedly. Here Russia would bar the way to the influence of materialistic America which, while richer, was spiritually poorer. Pogodin was the first to express the notion of a union of Slav peoples under the leadership of Russia, here anticipating pan-Slavism.

The writer Nicolaij Gogol was also close to official nationalism, although he himself said that he stood above the parties. In 1847 he published a book, *Selected Passages from Correspondence with Friends*, in which he showed an ardent belief in Russia's religious and political superiority over the West. He defended absolute autocracy, serfdom and the church's role as servant of the state. Here the satirist who was celebrated everywhere flabbergasted the whole Russian intelligentsia and contradicted the breadth of his earlier cultural thinking.

The Moscow professor of literature Stepan Ševyrëv also reverted to a being a convinced anti-Westerner and patriot. From 1841 onwards, in a series of articles, he slated the corrupt influence of the 'rotting West' on Russian culture, having previously been an ardent admirer of German romanticism and steeped himself for years in European literature – which he continued to do.

Pan-slavism

The third nationalistic current was that of pan-Slavism. This was a politically expansionist outgrowth of romantic Slavophilism and a Russian commandeering of Polish and Czech pan-Slavism. It arose as an ideological compensation for the Russian defeat in the Crimean War (1853–1854), which put an end to the position of power which Russia had held in Europe since 1815. Adherents included some prominent literary figures like Fëdor Dostoevskij and the poet Fëdor Tjutčev. Here we see the same paradox as with Gogol: great artists and cultural cosmopolitans prove to be ideologically naïve and narrow-minded in their political views.

Dostoevskij set down his political belief in his *Diary of a Writer*. For him, pan-Slavism, the liberation of the Orthodox brother peoples in the Balkans and their reunion with Russia, however passionately argued for, was not a goal in itself. It was a step towards 'panhumanism', universal brotherhood in Europe, realized by the 'all-humanity' of the wide Russian soul. Dostoevskij's view of the relationship between Russia and Europe is a complicated one. On the one hand he speaks critically about the 'churchyard of Europe', on the other he states powerfully that 'Europe is our second fatherland'; on the one hand he disparages all that is French, German, Polish, Jewish, Catholic and Protestant, on the other he argues for a synthesis of European culture with Russian culture on a higher level. Dostoevskij saw Peter the Great and Puškin as the embodiments of this synthesis.

The most systematic ideologist of pan-Slavism was the biologist and cultural philosopher Nikolaj Danilevskij. He developed a cyclical theory of culture in which Slav culture was the last in a series of eleven (Egyptian, Chinese, Babylonian, Indian, Iranian, Hebrew, Greek, Roman, Arab, German-Romance). The present-day type of culture, Catholic-Protestant German-Romance, is, he argued, coming to an end and will be replaced by Slav culture. Despite the fact that Orthodoxy is an important characteristic of Slav culture, Danilevskij's pan-Slavism is not primarily based on religion but on a scientific morphology of culture, set out in his book *Russia and Europe* (1869). Danilevskij sees the Slavic cultural type explicitly not as a European variant, and unlike Dostoevskij he rejects the possibility of a synthesis of European and Slav culture. He is also the only one to formulate an imperialistic pan-Slavistic programme for Russia: the formation of a 'Pan-Slavic union', embracing the whole of Eastern Europe, including Hungary, Rumania, Greece, and Constantinople, the historical capital of Orthodoxy, recaptured from the Turks.

Danilevskij is certainly the most extreme Slavophile and anti-Westerner to have reformulated the myth of the East. But in his establishment of the cultural and racial superiority of Russia he does not fall outside the Western intellectual sphere: England and the United States also had their versions of racial Darwinism. In the year that Danilevskij's book appeared, Charles Wentworth Dilke published his *Greater Britain*, which celebrates the grandeur of the Anglo-Saxon race; somewhat later Josiah Strong's *Our Country* appeared in America, and Karl Pearson and Cecil Rhodes expressed similar ideas.[259]And in his vision of the decline of the West Danilevskij anticipated Oswald Spengler.

The Byzantinophile variant

This last is also the case with the fourth variant of the Slavophile theory of history and culture. This is formed by the original thinker Konstantin Leont'ev. A doctor by training and a diplomat by profession, Leont'ev was also a writer and provocative intellectual who in his essays on the philosophy of culture attacked both the Slavophile religious and romantic view of society and pan-Slavist sense of mission and modern Western European civilization. Leont'ev set out his unconventional views in a two-volume collection *The East, Russia and Slavdom* (1885–1886); the 1873 essay 'Byzantinism and Slavdom' is the most important piece in it.

Leont'ev contrasts mediaeval Byzantine culture and not a separate Slav culture with modern European culture. He criticizes Danilevskij's racial cultural typology and the associated notion of progress, and his own theory of the strong and weak sides of a civilization applies to any civilization. Leont'ev sees the development of civilization as a tripartite biological-naturalistic process with growth, blossoming and decay. Or it is a development from the phase of 'primary simplicity' towards the blossoming phase of 'unity in complexity' and then to the phase of decay into a 'secondary simplification'. The phase of the blossoming of a civilization consists in as great a cultural and social variety as possible, though this is held together by a tight religious and political unity. The West had reached this stage in the Catholic Middle Ages and Renaissance, which Leont'ev values very highly, but the civilization of the Byzantine empire was even more colourful. Since the eighteenth century the stage of decay, the 'secondary simplification', has begun in Europe. That is a consequence of the liberal notion of equality and the democratic levelling down, which in the nineteenth century was still enforced by Socialist egalitarianism. All this leads to an overcoming of bourgeois mediocrity, which is the end of the creative period of a culture.

Leont'ev is an ultra-conservative romantic and an aesthete with an elitist view of culture. He will have nothing to do with modern society with its bourgeois plebeianism, utilitarianism and social conformity. Russia must not go this way, but backwards to its historical roots, which lie in Byzantine culture with its social hierarchy, imperial and church splendour, and despotism and artistic wealth. Leont'ev's deepest incentive is an aesthetic hedonism, on the basis of which he judges politics and religion. In so doing Leont'ev deliberately turns out to be a reactionary ideologist who is not only against democracy but also against educating peasants and against railways. He arrives at 'an "aesthetic" apotheosis of inequality reminiscent of Nietzsche'.[260]

Apart from the reprehensible social consequences of Leont'ev's concept of culture, this concept contains elements which intrinsically are philosophically interesting, in so far as it shows up the mechanistic notion of progress in both socialist and liberal bourgeois ideologies. In fact Leont'ev has a pessimistic view of mankind and also gave notable prognoses of the totalitarian development of socialism. And his anxiety about a trivial mass culture has also not proved completely unfounded.

Konstantin Leont'ev also foresaw European unification, the fusing of the European states into 'a federal republic . . . And many who do not really want this believe in such an outcome as an unavoidable evil.' Leont'ev explains this development in terms of 'the crazy religion of thinking in terms of prosperity (*evdomenizm,* eudaemonism)' with its slogan of '*le bien-être materiel et moral de l'humanité*'. This striving for unity provoked in Leont'ev a fear of cultural impoverishment. He feared that the old capital cities of Europe would be swept off the map because formerly they had been centres of hostility between the European nations, and that the monarchies would disappear in favour of 'a banal workers' republic'. Leont'ev asks himself:

> What price must be paid for such a fusion? Will not a new pan-European state have to dispense in principle with recognizing all local differences? . . . In any case France, Germany, Italy, Spain, etc. will cease to exist as states; they will become districts of the new state as former Piedmont, Tuscany, Rome and Naples have become districts for Italy, and as now Hessen, Hannover and Prussia have themselves become districts of pan-Germany; they will become for pan-Europe what Burgundy and Brittany have long become for France![261]

According to Leont'ev, the cultural complexity of Europe cannot be maintained in a Europe which has been democratically levelled down, but only in the various monarchistic states of Europe. Leont'ev also indicates what Russia must do in this situation with relation to Europe; it must think 'less of prosperity and more of strength'. In any case, Russia must stand strong over against Europe; if the new 'federal West' becomes strong, then Russia must defend its independence over against Western pressure from a strong internal position; and should the West lapse into anarchy, then Russia must help the West and rescue what is worth rescuing, 'namely what has made the West great: the church, whatever church it is, *the state*, the remains of poetry and perhaps . . . *learning itself!* . . .(Not a tendentious learning, but a *strict, sad* learning!).'[262]

Leont'ev also judges the church from his aesthetic stand-point. It then proves that for him the confessional dividing line between Catholicism and Orthodoxy is subordinate to his cultural philosophical criterion of 'unity in complexity'. Leont'ev's preference is of course for strict Byzantine Orthodoxy: the 'black Christianity' of the monks of Mount Athos and the Russian Optina monastery.[263] He despises the moralizing and sentimentally religious Christianity of Dostoevskij and Lev Tolstoj, and is sarcastic about their 'pink' Christianity, which preaches a universal brotherhood and 'humanizes' Christianity. For Leont'ev God is the strict Pantocrator, and an 'ascetic and dogmatic Orthodox believer' is pessimistic about human nature.

For Leont'ev, unity and authority were essential aspects of the church. On this point Leont'ev differed radically from Chomjakov's 'church democracy', which he thought to be a 'nationalistic Protestant heresy'. In the light of his aesthetic principle of unity Leont'ev had great esteem for the papal magisterium, and he sardonically expresses his agreement with the doctrine of papal infallibility:

> If I were in Rome, I should not hesitate to kiss not only the hand but also the slipper of Leo XIII . . . Roman Catholicism suits my unabashed taste for despotism, my tendency to spiritual authority, and attracts my heart and mind for many other reasons.[264]

An interesting ecumenical remark for an Orthodox, but it is not meant in that way. And for Leont'ev the present-day papacy would no longer be adequate either. In our time he might perhaps have felt more akin to Khomeini.[265] But it remains an interesting remark for a strict Orthodox, which is what in the end the cultural hedonist Leont'ev also was. Shortly before his death in 1891 he entered the monastery of the Trinity at Sergiev Posad, where he combined his aesthetic faith with an ascetic existence.

Konstantin Leont'ev was not the last voice in the polyphonic

nineteenth-century Russian debate on Russia and Europe. That
role fell to someone at the opposite pole, Vladimir Solov'ëv. He
produced a devastating criticism of the Slavic particularism of
Danilevskij and Leont'ev, and also otherwise rejected any religious nationalism in principle. In his own work Solov'ëv
removed the ideological dimension from the notion of Russian
identity and entered into a thoroughgoing dialogue with Western
philosophy. In so doing he brought Russia philosophically to a
European and world level, where it had already been glittering
throughout the century with its great poets and writers from
Puškin to Tolstoj. With his work (and literally with his death in
1900) Vladimir Solov'ëv concluded the nineteenth-century
debate between Slavophiles and those with inclinations towards
the West and resolved the Russian identity with a conscious
intellectual integration of Russia into Europe. But his philosophical professionalism puts Solov'ëv outside the theme of this
book.

Conclusion

The religious sense of identity of Russia described in this book was increasingly challenged at the beginning of the twentieth century and rivalled by a secular current which saw quite a different role for Russia in the world. And when this current, Russian Communism, had seized power, it did everything it could to destroy the religious elements in the Russian national consciousness. But in the meanwhile, without being aware of the fact, it itself continued the myth of the East in a secularized and perverted form. However, despite the unmistakeable agreement in the national psyche between Russia's Slavophile-religious and Communist-ideological sense of exclusiveness, we must not forget the essential differences. That is, of course, not only the diametrical opposition between the Christian and the anti-religious content but also the difference in form: where the religious myth never knew a form of expansionism outwards – even the pan-Slavist variant remained religious fantasy – the Communist form was outspokenly aggressive.

After the fall of Russian Communism in 1991 the old religious national consciousness returned as a basis for renewed Russian identity. It is striking how quickly Russian society again linked up with the religious and ideological thought of the time before the Soviet period. It really already began in 1988, at the millennial commemoration of the conversion of Russia. However, that was still an 'ideology-free' rediscovery of Christianity, as authentic as the first discovery of Christianity in Kievan Russia of the tenth and eleventh centuries. But just as the original Russian Christianity from the thirteenth century narrowed down and became a national ideology, so too Orthodox Christianity has become increasingly ideologized in post-Soviet Russia. It has become a repetition of Russian history, but at an accelerated tempo.

The year 1997 became a culmination of these tendencies. In September of that year two events took place which restored Russian Orthodoxy to its central position in the national sense, visual and legal. These were the completion of the Cathedral of Christ the Redeemer in Moscow (see the illustration on the cover of this book) and the introduction of a new law about religious freedom. Both matters were the subject of years of discussion in which many arguments were presented for and – as a minority voice – against a national form of Christianity, as we have met this in previous chapters.

On the long parliamentary conflict centring on the law about religion, all that needs to be said here is that the law passed on 26 September 1997 gave legal priority to Russian Orthodoxy so that it had a stronger position over against 'foreign' churches and new religious movements. Whatever practical arguments one can adduce to support the Russian Orthodox Church in its restoration as an institution after decades of oppression under the Soviet government, and to protect theologically illiterate people against all kinds of pseudo-religious sects, the division of Christian churches into 'national' and 'foreign' goes against the nature of Christianity.

The myth in stone

The Cathedral of Christ the Redeemer is a spectacular expression of the national religious revival of Russia. It is a rebuilt nineteenth-century church in the centre of Moscow which had been blown up by Stalin in 1931. When the plan for rebuilding was raised at the beginning of the 1990s it was regarded by many observers as technically and financially impossible. But at an un-Russian pace involving continuous building work day and night, the exterior of the church was completed in three years, so that on 3 September 1997 it could be solemnly brought into use by patriarch Aleksij and president Yeltsin. That happened on the occasion of the celebration of the 850th anniversary of the existence of Moscow. This also provided a patriotic context for the ecclesiastical event. Even the expression 'Third Rome' was used by the patriarch in the church journal *Moskovskij Cerkovnij Vestnik*, to underline the religious and historical status of Moscow. The original church of Christ the Redeemer had been built to commemorate the Russian victory over Napoleon, so it was also a military monument. That fact again indicates that the cathedral has not only a religious but also an ideological significance.

Because of the central place of the rebuilt Cathedral of Christ the Redeemer in the consciousness of the present-day Russian church and state, it is worth looking briefly at this new national symbol. From a Christian perspective one must criticize the nationalistic interpretation and ideological exploitation of Christianity associated with the rebuilding. Orthodox Christianity is so focussed on Russian culture and identity that the character of Christianity, which transcends nation and ethnicity, threatens to be lost. But all the other arguments against the rebuilding of the cathedral, financial, aesthetic, pragmatic and political, are easy to refute. So I want to defend the rebuilding of the cathedral, despite my rejection in principle of the underlying ideology. In so doing, while maintaining my criticism of the myth of the East, as in previous chapters, I want to relativize it historically by referring to related, albeit less explicit, phenomena in the West.

The high building costs, in this case $200,000,000, can easily be objected to in the case of any cathedral. The money can always be devoted to social needs, and from this perspective any mediaeval cathedral is socially irresponsible. But even from a contemporary perspective, Moscow is not the only city to spend money on a religious prestige object while there are great humanitarian needs in the city. The biggest church in the world, St John the Divine, has been under construction all this century in New York, which is not a city without social problems. And the enormous Cathedral of Sts Peter and Paul in Washington should not be completed, if the abolition of poverty is a moral condition for building churches.

As for the aesthetic argument, the Cathedral of Christ the Redeemer, built in the nineteenth-century neo-Russian style, is not in fact the most attractive from the perspective of the history of art. But that applies to several famous churches in the neo-style, especially the neo-Byzantine Sacré Coeur in Paris. That church radiates the same religious triumphalism by its pomposity. In terms of beauty, Sacré Coeur and Christ the Redeemer fall far short of their older sisters, Notre Dame and the Uspenskij Cathedral in the Kremlin, but both have left their stamp on the silhouette of the city.

The practical argument is that from a pastoral perspective the church is superfluous: it will seldom be full, and moreover there are enough churches in the centre of Moscow, as opposed to the expanses of modern suburbs in which there is not a single church building. This utilitarian argument is of more universal application than the first two: are not most churches empty in all city centres, and is not even Rome full of empty churches?

The political argument, that the secular authorities, government and city administration (Mayor Yuri Luzhkov is the driving force behind the rebuilding) should not be involved in the rebuilding of the cathedral is short-sighted. The authorities destroyed the church with the explicit aim of humiliating Russian Orthodoxy, and it is testimony to a sense of shame or at least good fashion that the authority is taking steps to reverse this shameful act. It is no more than just that it should also contribute to the costs.

No, the only tenable criticism of the rebuilding does not relate to the building itself but to the false religious mystique surrounding it. Here the Moscow patriarch could have performed an authentic religious action with the rebuilding, by presenting the cathedral not as a symbol of rising Russia but as a house of prayer for all Christians, which is what the American government and the Episcopal Church mean Washington Cathedral to be. But such a generous gesture is far above the Christian capacity for imagination in the Russian Orthodox Church, and would also require of the state a greater moral sense than is shown by its present indirect confession of guilt. This is also dictated by political and nationalistic considerations.

A less loaded symbol of the restored national identity which is more valuable for the history of art is the religious reconstruction of Red Square. Here the Kazan Church (1992) and the Gate of the Resurrection with the chapel of the Iverskaja icon of the Mother of God (1995) have been rebuilt. These were also demolished by Stalin to make room for military parades and Party demonstrations. The restoration and use of these buildings by patriarch, president, prime minister and mayor together could be interpreted as a symbolic forswearing of the state by Communism.

As for Red Square and the Kremlin, this centre of government of the Russian capital remains a special architectural expression of the typical Russian relationship between church and state. No other capital in the world has such a religious setting for its centre of political power. The six churches within the walls of the Kremlin, the Hall of Facets with its frescoes of Russian holy rulers, used for receiving heads of state, Red Square with the striking Pokrov Cathedral, the picturesque Kazan Church and the heavily visited Iverskaja Chapel, with the dominant presence of the gold-domed Cathedral of Christ the Redeemer in the vicinity, is an expression which has grown up in history of a special religious-national sense of identity, which will retain its cultural value even without the ideological implications of the myth of the East.

Bibliography

A. *Sources*

Abbreviations

AQDG   Ausgewählte Quellen zur Deutschen Geschichte des Mittelal-
        ters, Darmstadt 1958–1988.
MGH   Monumenta Germaniae Historica, Epistolarum, Berlin 1928.
MPH   Monumenta Poloniae Historica, ed. A. Bielowski, Warsaw
        1960 (reprint of 1864 edition).
PG   Patrologiae Cursus Completus, Series Graeca, ed. J. P. Migne,
        Paris 1857–1866.
PLDR   Pamjatniki Literatury Drevnej Rusi, ed. L. Dmitriev and D.
        Lichačëv, Moscow 1978–1994.
SRH   Scriptores Rerum Hungaricarum, ed. E. Szentpetery, Budapest
        1937.

*Actes de la conférence des chefs et des réprésentants des églises orthodoxes
    autocéphales réunis à Moscou 8–18 Juillet 1948*, Vol. 1, Moscow 1950.
Adalbert of Trier, *Continuatio Reginonis*, AQDG VIII.
Adam of Bremen, *Gesta Hammaburgensis Ecclesiae Pontificum*, AQDG,
    Vol. XI.
Annales Hildesheimenses, MGH, Scriptorum I.
Anonymi Gesta Hungarorum, SRH, Vol. I.

Bujnoch, J. (trans.), *Zwischen Rom und Byzanz. Leben und Wirken der
    Slawenapostel Kyrillos und Methodios nach den pannonischen Legenden
    und der Klemensvita*, Graz 1958.
Bulgakov, S., *U sten Chersonisa*, St Petersburg 1993.
Bruno of Querfurt, *Epistola ad Henricum regem*, MPH, Vol. I.

Čaadaev, P. J., *Polnoe sobranie sočinenij i izbrannye pis'ma*, ed. Z. A.
    Kamenskij, Moscow 1991, Vols 1–2.
—, *Stat'i i pis'ma*, ed. B. N. Tarasov, Moscow 1987.

Čerepnin, L. (ed.), *Skazanie Avraamija Palicyna*, Moscow 1955.
Chibnall, M. (ed.), *Ecclesiastical History of Orderic Vitalis*, Oxford 1980.
Choždenie na Florentijskij sobor. PLDR, Vol. 4.
Christiansen, E. (trans.), *Saxo Grammaticus, Books X-XVI*, Oxford 1980.
Chronica Polonorum Vincentii Cracoviensis Episcopi, MPH, Vol. II.
Chronicon Monacense, SRH, Vol. II.
Chronicon Posoniense, SRH, Vol. II.
Chronicon Roskildense, Scriptores Minores Historiae Danicae Medii Aevi, ed. M. Gertz, Copenhagen 1917.
Chvorostinin, Ivan, *Izloženie na eretiki-zlochul'niki*. PLDR, Vol. 12.
Colgrave, B. and Mynors, R. (eds), *Bede's Ecclesiastical History of the English People*, Oxford 1969.
Constantine Porphyrogenitus, *De Cerimoniis Aulae Byzantinae*, PG 112.
— *De Administrando Imperio*, PG 113.
Cronica Galli Anonymi, MPH, Vol. I.

Danilevskij, N., *Rossija i Evropa*, Moscow 1991.
Dante Alighieri, *On World Government* (De Monarchia), trans. H. W. Schneider, New York 1957.
Darrouzès, J., *Notitiae Episcopatuum Ecclesiae Constantinopolitanae*, Paris 1981.

Ellis Davidson, H. (ed.), *Saxo Grammaticus. The History of the Danes*, Cambridge 1979.
Eremin, I. P. (ed.), *Feofan Prokopovič, sočinenija*, Moscow 1961.

Fedotov, G., *Svjatoj Filipp mitropolit moskovskij*, Moscow 1991.
Franklin, S. (trans.), *Sermons and Rhetoric of Kievan Rus'*, Harvard Library of Early Ukrainian Literature, Vol. V, Harvard 1991.

Gogol, N., *Vybrannye mesta iz perepiski s druz'jami*, Pol. sobr. soč., Vol. 8, Leningrad 1952.
Gregory of Tours, *Historiarum Libri Decem*, AQDG, Vol. II.
Gudzij, N. (ed.), *Žitie protopopa Avvakuma im samim napisannoe*, Moscow 1960.

Hauptmann, P., and Stricker, G. (eds.), *Die Orthodoxe Kirche in Russland. Dokumente ihrer Geschichte (860–1980)*, Göttingen 1988.
Heinrichs, A., (ed.), *Olafs Saga Hins Helga. Die 'Legendarische Saga' über Olaf den Heiligen*, Heidelberg 1982.
Helmold of Bozau, *Chronica Slavorum*, AQDG, Vol. XIX.
Holder, A. (ed.), *Saxonis Grammatici Gesta Danorum*, Strassburg 1886.
Hollingsworth, P. (ed.), *The Hagiography of Kievan Rus'*, Harvard Library

of Early Ukrainian Literature, Vol. II, Harvard 1992.

Ilarion of Kiev, *Slovo o zakone i blagodati*, PLDR, Vol. 12.
— *Slovo o zakone i blagodati*, Bogoslovskie Trudy 28.

John of Plano Carpini, *Geschichte der Mongolen und Reisebericht 1245–1247*, translated into German by F. Risch, Leipzig 1938.
Johannis VIII Papae Epistolae, MGH, Epistolarum VII (Karolini Aevi V).

Kara-Murza, A., and Poljakov, L., *Reformator. Russkie o Petre I*, Ivanovo 1994.
Karamzin, N., *Istorija gosudarstva rossijskogo*, Vol. 1, Moscow 1989.
Kartašëv, A. V., *Vossozdanie Svjatoj Rusi*, Paris 1956.
Kawerau, P. (ed.), *Arabische Quellen zur Christianisierung Russlands*, Osteuropastudien der Hochschulen des Landes Hessen, II, 7, Wiesbaden 1967.
Kurbskij, A., *Istorija o velikom knjazje Moskovskom*, PLDR, Vol. 8.

Labunka, *Mytropolyt Ilarion i joho pysannia. Metropolita Ilarion ejusque opera*, Rome 1990.
Lavrov, P. (ed.), *Materialy po istorii vozniknovenija drevnejšej slavjanskoj pis'mennosti*, Leningrad 1930 (Slavic Printings and Reprintings, ed. C. H. Schooneveld, The Hague 1966).
Legenda S. Stephani Regis Major et Minor atque Legenda ab Hartvico Episcopo Conscripta, SRH, Vol. II.
Leont'ev, K., *Izbrannoe*, Moscow 1993.
Libellus de Institutione Morum, SRH, Vol. II.
Lur'e, J., Rykov, J., and Lichačëv, D. (eds), *Perepiska Ivana Groznogo s Andreem Kurbskim*, Leningrad 1979.

Malinin, V., *Starec Eleazarova monastyrja Filofej i ego poslanija*, Kiev 1901.
Mango, C. (ed.), *The Homilies of Photios of Constantinople*, Cambridge, Mass., 1958.
Matthaei Cracoviensis Episcopi Epistola ad s. Bernardum Abbatem Clarevallensem. De suscipienda Ruthenorum conversione, MPH, Vol. II.
Müller, L. (ed.), *Des Metropoliten Ilarion Lobrede auf Vladimir den Heiligen und Glaubensbekenntnis*, Wiesbaden 1962.
—, *Die Werke des Metropoliten Ilarion*, Forum Slavicum 37, Munich 1971.

Nitsche, P. (ed.), *Der Aufstieg Moskaus: Auszüge aus einer russischen Chronik*, Vol. 2, Graz 1967.

Otto van Freising, *Chronica sive Historia de Duabus Civitatibus*, AQDG XVI.

Pečerin, V., *Van over het graf*, Amsterdam 1990.
Photii Encyclika Epistola and *Epistola ad Michaelem Bulgariae Principem*, PG 102.
Poslanie na Ugru Vassiana Rylo, PLDR, Vol. 5.
Povest' o stojanii na Ugre, PLDR, Vol. 5.
Povest' o našestvii Tochtamyša, PLDR, Vol. 4.
Povest' o Novgorodskom belom klobuke, PLDR, Vol. 7.
Povest' o razorenii Rjazani Batyem, PLDR, Vol. 3.
Povest' o Temir Aksake, PLDR, Vol. 4.
Povest' o vzjatii Car'grada krestonoscami v 1204 godu, PLDR, Vol. 3.
Povest' o vzjatii Car'grada Turkami v 1453 godu, PLDR, Vol. 5.
Povest' vremennych let, PLDR, Vol. 1.

Sathas, C. (ed.), *The History of Psellus*, London 1899.
Serapion of Vladimir, *Slova*, PLDR, Vol. 3.
Simonis de Kéza Gesta Hungarorum, SRH, Vol. I.
Skazanie o Dovmonte, PLDR, Vol. 4.
Skazanie o knjazjach Vladimirskich, PLDR, Vol. 6.
Skazanie o mamaevom poboišče, PLDR, Vol. 4.
Skazanie o ubienii v orde knjazja Michaila Černigovskogo i ego bojarina Feodora, PLDR, Vol. 3.
Slovo o žitii velikogo knjazja Dmitrija Ivanoviča, PLDR, Vol. 4.
Smirennogo inoka Fomy slovo pochval'noe o blagovernom velikom knjaze Borise Aleksandroviče, PLDR, Vol. 5.
Solov'ëv, V., *Saint Vladimir et l'état chrétien*, Deutsche Gesamtausgabe der Werke von Wladimir Solowjew, ed. L. Müller, Vol. III, Freiburg im Breisgau 1954.
Stephani V Papae Epistolae, MGH, Epistolarum VII (Karolini Aevi V).
Sumnikova, T. A., *Idejno-filosofskoe nasledie Ilariona Kievskogo*, Vol. 1, Moscow 1986.

Thietmar of Merseburg, *Chronicon*, AQDG, Vol. IX.
Turgenev, A. I., *Političeskaja proza*, Moscow 1989.

Vita S. Clementis Bulgariae Archiepiscopi, PG, Vol. 126.

Widukind, *Res Gestae Saxonicae*, AQDG, Vol. VIII.

Zadonščina, PLDR, Vol. 4.
Zimin, A., and Lichačëv, D. (eds), *Sočinenija I. Peresvetova*, Moscow and

Leningrad 1956.
Zimin, A., and Lur'e, J. (eds), *Poslanija Iosifa Volockogo*, Moscow and
  Leningrad 1959.
Žitija sv. Petra mitropolita. Makarij, *Istorija russkoj cerkvi*, Vol. IV, St
  Petersburg 1886.
Žitie Aleksandra Nevskogo, PLDR, Vol. 3.

B. Literature

Alpatov, M. A., *Russkaja istoričeskaja mysl' i zapadnaja Evropa (XVIII-
  pervaja polovina XIX v)*, Moscow 1985.
Andreyev, N., 'Kurbsky's Letters to Vas'yan Muromtsev', *The Slavonic and
  East European Review* 23, 1955, 414–16.
Angenendt, A., *Kaiserherrschaft und die Königstaufe. Kaiser, Könige und
  Päpste als geistliche Patrone in der abendländischen Missionsgeschichte*,
  Berlin 1984.

Benz, E., *Endzeiterwartungen zwischen Ost und West. Studien zur
  christlichen Eschatologie*, Freiburg 1973.
Boer, P. den, *Europa. De geschiedenis van een idee*, Amsterdam 1997.
Buslaev, F., *Russkaja chrestomatija*, Moscow ⁹1904, Slavic Printings and
  Reprintings, ed. C. Schooneveld, The Hague and Paris 1969.

Cherniavsky, M., *Tsar and People. Studies in Russian Myths*, New Haven
  1961.
Čistjakov, G., 'Vojna glazami christianina', *Russkaja Mysl'*, 29 August
  1996.
Cracraft, J., 'Feofan Prokopovich', in J. Garrard (ed.), *The Eighteenth
  Century in Russia*, Oxford 1971.

Derjagin, V., *Al'manach bibliofila*, Moscow 1989.
— Ilarion, *Slovo o zakone i blagodati*, Moscow 1994.
Dvorkin, A., *Ivan the Terrible as a Religious Type*, Quellen und Studien zur
  orthodoxen Theologie 31, Erlangen 1992.

Ioann, Metropolitan, *Samoderžavie Ducha. Očerki russkogo samosoznanija*, St Petersburg 1994.

Fedotov, G., *The Russian Religious Mind*, New York 1946.
Förster, R. H., *Die Idee Europa 1300–1946*, Quellen zur Geschichte der
  politischen Einigung, Munich 1963.

Gualdo, G., and Sbriziolo L. (eds.), *Italia Sacra. Studi e documenti di storia ecclesiastica*, Rome 1960–1970.
Gudzij, *Chrestomatija po drevnej russkoj literature*, Moscow ⁸1993.
Gulyga, A., 'Poiski Absoljuta', *Novyj mir* 1987, no. 10, 245–53.

Ignatow, A., *Das russische geschichtsphilosophische Denken. Grundmotive und Resonanz*, Berichte des Bundesinstituts für ostwissenschaftliche und internationale Studien 5–1996, Cologne 1996.
Isaev, I., and Zolotuchina, N., *Istorija političeskich i pravovych učenij Rossii XI-XX vv*, Moscow 1995.

Judah Hallevi, *Kitab Al Khazari*, trans. H. Hirschfeld, London 1905.

Kamenskij, Z. A., 'O sovremennych pročtenijach P. Ja. Čaadaeva', *Voprosy filosofii*, 1992, no. 12.
Kämpfer, F., 'Beobachtungen zu den Sendschreiben Filofejs', *Jahrbücher für Geschichte Osteuropas* 18, 1970, 1, 1–46.

Langeler, A., *Maksim Grek, Byzantijn en humanist in Rusland*, Amsterdam 1986.

Maslin, M. (ed.), *Russkaja ideja*, Moscow 1992.
Moldovan, A. M., *Slovo o zakone i blagodati Ilariona*, Kiev 1984.

Naarden, B., '"En een vierde zal er niet zijn." Moscow als het Derde Rome', *Spiegel Historiael* 32, 1997, 70–81.
Nolthenius, H., *Muziek tusen hemel en aarde. De wereld van het Gregoriaans*, Amsterdam 1981.

Obolensky, D., *The Byzantine Commonwealth*, London 1971.

Pascal, P., *La vie de l'archiprêtre Avvakum écrite par lui-même*, Paris 1938.
Platonov, O., *Russkaja civilizacija*, Moscow 1995.
Podskalsky, G., *Christentum und theologische Literatur in der Kiever Rus'*, Munich 1982.
Poljakov, L., *Filosofskie idei v kul'ture drevnej Rusi*, Moscow 1988.

Rietbergen, P., *Dromen van Europa*, Amersfoort 1994.
Robinson, M., and Sazonova, L., Commentary in *Voprosy literatury*, 1989, no.9, 236–53.
Rose, K., *Grund und Quellort des Russischen Geisteslebens. Von Skythien bis zur Kiewer Rus'*, Berlin 1956.
Rozov, N., 'V načale bylo slovo', *Trudy otdela drevnej russkoj literatury* 48, 1993, 88–95.

Schaeder, H., *Moskau, das Dritte Rom. Studien zur Geschichte der politis-chen Theorien in der slawischen Welt*, Darmstadt 1957.

Schulte Nordholt, J. W., *The Myth of the West*, Grand Rapids, Michigan 1995.

Sipovskij, V., *Istoričeskaja chrestomatija po istorii russkoj slovesnosti*, Petrograd 1915.

Smolitsch, I., *Geschichte der russischen Kirche 1700–1917*, Vol. 1, Leiden 1964.

Stender-Petersen, A., *Geschichte der russischen Literatur*, Munich 1957.

Studies in Soviet Thought, Vol. 32, 1986, no 4.

Stupperich, R., 'Kiev, das zweite Jeruzalem', *Zeitschrift für Slavische Philologie* 12, 1935, 332–54.

Tarasov, B. N. (ed.), *Cena vekov. P. Ja. Čaadaev*, Moscow 1991.

—, 'Prostranstvo mysli Petra Čaadaeva', *Literaturnaja gazeta*, 11 March 1992.

Uspenskij, B. A., *Izbrannye trudy. Semiotika istorii, semiotika kul'tury*, Moscow 1996.

Vodoff, V., 'Pourquoi le prince Volodimir Svjatoslavič n'a-t-il pas été canonisé?', in O. Pritsak (ed.), *Proceedings of the International Congress Commemorating the Millennium of Christianity in Rus'-Ukraine*, Cambridge, Mass. 1990, 446–66.

Walicki, A., *The Slavophile Controversy. History of Conservative Utopia in Nineteenth-Century Russian Thought*, Oxford 1975.

Wes, M. A., *Tussen twee bronzen ruiters. Klassieken in Rusland 1700–1855*, Baarn 1991.

Wessels, A., *Europe: Was it Ever Really Christian?*, London 1994.

Zamaleev, A. F. (ed.), *Rossija glazami russkogo. Čaadaev, Leont'ev, Solov'ëv*, St Petersburg 1991.

Zernov, N., *The Russians and their Church*, London 1945.

Notes

1. E. Benz, *Endzeiterwartung zwischen Ost und West: Studien zur christlichen Eschatologie*, Freiburg 1973, 91.
2. Otto von Freising, *Chronica sive historia de duabus civitatibus*, VII, 35, Ausgewählte Quellen zur deutschen Geschichte des Mittelalters (henceforth AQDG), Vol. XVI.
3. For example, A. Wessels, *Europe. Was It Ever Really Christian?*, London 1994.
4. J. W. Schulte Nordholt, *The Myth of the West. America as the Last Empire*, Grand Rapids, Michigan 1995.
5. A. Angenendt, *Kaiserherrschaft und die Königstaufe. Kaiser, Könige und Päpste als geistliche Patrone in der abendländischen Missionsgeschichte*, Berlin 1984.
6. R. H. Förster, *Die Idee Europa 1300–1946. Quellen zur Geschichte der politischen Einigung*, Munich 1963, 11.
7. P. Rietbergen, *Dromen van Europa*, Amersfoort 1994; P. den Boer, *Europa. De geschiedenis van een idee*, Amsterdam 1997. Rietbergen mentions Russia only in a passing and cautious reference to the interest in Europe on the part of Peter the Great and Catherine the Great, and with an interesting quotation from William Penn in 1693 about the inclusion of the Russians and Turks in a future European parliament (79 and 81). Den Boer relates Russia to Europe only after the Holy Alliance of 1815, but then does so quite explicitly (102–4).
8. In speaking of the early mediaeval Russian state we are faced with a terminological problem which is very tricky after the division between Ukraine and Russia in 1991. Until recently the name of the Kievan empire, *Rus'*, could, for convenience's sake, be translated by 'Kievan Russia'. Now, however, one must consistently speak of *Rus'* to make a distinction from the later Russia centred on Moscow, *Rossija*. The continuity between the two kingdoms was presented in too linear a way by Russian historians, but wrongly denied by Ukrainian historians. Perhaps one can also indicate the difference by speaking in the first case of the *Russian land*, thus using a similar distinction to that between the *Frankish land*, which was not yet France, and the later *France*.

9. '*Omnes hee naciones preter Pruzos christianitatis titulo decorantur. Diu enim est ex quo Rucia credidit . . . Quibus autem doctoribus ad fidem venerint, minime compertum habeo, nisi quod in omnibus observantiis suis Grecos magis quam Latinos imitari videntur. Nam Rucenum mare brevi in Greciam transmittit.*' Helmold of Bozau, *Chronica Slavorum* I, AQDG, Vol. XIX.

10. Chapters 1, 2 and 4 were published in a rather different form in the journal *Het Christelijk Oosten* 47, 1995; 48, 1996; and 49, 1997. Chapter 3 was published in *Exchange* 26, 1997.

11. *Povest' vremennych let* [Narrative of Bygone Years], Pamjatniki Literatury Drevnej Rusi (henceforth PLDR) [Monuments of the Literature of Ancient Rus'], Vol. I. There is an English translation by S. H. Cross and O. Sherbowitz-Wetzor, *The Russian Primary Chronicle*, Cambridge, Mass., 1953, to which I am indebted here.

12. *Povest'* under the year 955.

13. *Povest'* under the year 945.

14. *Žitie Konstantina'* [Life of Constantine], chs VIII–IX, in P. Lavrov, *Materialy po istorii vozniknovenija drevnejšej slavjanskoj pis'mennosti* [Texts from the History of the Oldest Slavonic Literature], Leningrad 1930. There is a German translation in J. Bujnoch, *Zwischen Rom und Byzanz. Leben und Wirken der Slawenapostel Kyrillos und Methodios nach den pannonischen Legenden und der Klemensvita*, Graz 1958.

15. Judah Hallevi, *Kitab Al Khazari*, translated from the Arabic by H. Hirschfeld, London 1905, 40–5.

16. P. Kawerau, *Arabische Quellen zur Christianisierung Russlands*, Wiesbaden 1967, 15–18 (Arabic text and German translation). The other Arabic source, Ibn al-Atir, 28–30; the Armenian source, Stephen of Tarom, 43–4.

17. Adalbert of Trier, *Continuatio Reginonis*, under the year 959. See also 960 ('*episcopus genti Rugorum*'), 961, 962 ('*Rugis episcopus*') and 966, AQDG, Vol. VIII. The arrival of *legati Rusciae* at the court of Otto is also mentioned in the *Annales Hildesheimenses* under the year 960, where Adalbert of Trier is mentioned as the bishop who was sent. Monumenta Germaniae Historica (henceforth MGH) Scriptorum, I, p. 60.

18. *List S. Brunona do Henryka II cesarza* [Letter from St Bruno to emperor Hendrik II], Monumenta Poloniae Historica (henceforth MPH), Vol. I, 224.

19. Thietmar of Merseburg, *Chronicon*, VII, 72–74, AQDG, Vol. IX. From Thietmar we also learn that the German missionary bishop for Russia mentioned by Adalbert of Trier must have been Adalbert himself, *Chronicon*, II, 22.

20. *Povest'* under the year 980.
21. Kawerau, *Arabische Quellen* (n.16), 25.
22. Gregory of Tours, *Historiarum Libri Decem*, II, 30, AQDG, Vol. II.
23. *Bede's Ecclesiastical History of the English People*, ed. by B. Colgrave and R. Mynors, Oxford 1969, II, 9 and 11.
24. N. Karamzin, *Istorija gosudarstva rossijskago* [History of the Russian State], Moscow 1989 (originally 1816), Vol. I, ch. 9.
25. *Povest'* under the year 1037.
26. *Moravsko-Pannonskie žitija Konstantina i Mefodii* [Moravian-Pannonian Lives of Constantine and Methodius], in P. Lavrov (ed.), *Materialy po istorii* (n.14).
27. 'Litteras denique Sclaviniscas a Constantino quondam philosopho repertas, quibus Deo laudes debite resonent, iure laudamus et in eadem lingua Christi Domini nostri preconia opera et opera enarrentur, iubemus; neque enim tribus tantum, sed omnibus linguis Dominum laudare auctoritate sacra monemur . . . Nec sane fidei vel doctrine aliquid obstat sive missas in eadem lingua Sclavinica canere sive sacrum evangelium vel lectiones divinas novi et veteris testamenti bene translatas et interpretas legere aut alia horarum officia omnia psallere, quoniam qui fecit tres linguas principales, Hebream scilicet Grecam et Latinam, ipse creavit et alias omnes ad laudem et gloriam suam.' Bulla *Industriae tuae* of June 880, MGH, Epistolarum, VII (Karolini Aevi V), 223–4. With this letter Pope John VIII revoked his letter to Methodius of June 879, in which, urged on by Frankish opponents of Methodius, he had forbidden him to celebrate mass 'in barbara, hoc est Sclavina lingua', ibid., 161. After the letter of 880 John VIII in another letter, in March 881, again defended Methodius against his slanderers, ibid., 243–4.
28. *Povest'* under the erroneous date 898.
29. The last sentence is not in the letters of Pope John VIII.
30. 'Divina autem officia et sacra mysteria ac missarum sollemnia, quae idem Methodius Sclavorum lingua celebrare praesumpsit . . . nullo modo deinceps a quolibet praesumatur', MGH, Epistolarum, VII, 357.
31. *The Homilies of Photios, Patriarch of Constantinople*, trans. and ed. C. Mango, Cambridge, Mass. 1958, 88, 96 and 98.
32. Centuries later, this event would be celebrated in the Russian Orthodox Church as the feast of Mary the Protection: *Pokrov*.
33. *Patrologia Graeca* (henceforth *PG*), Vol. 102, cols. 736–7.
34. Kawerau, *Arabische Quellen* (n.16), 3.
35. 'aemula sceptri Constantinopolitani, clarissimum daecus Graeciae', Adam of Bremen, *Gesta Hammaburgensis Ecclesiae Pontificum*, II, 22, AQDG, Vol. XI.
36. *Constantini Porphyrogeniti Imperatoris De Administrando Imperio*,

IX, PG, Vol. 113, cols 170ff.

37. *De Cerimoniis Aulae Byzantinae*, II, PG, Vol. 112, cols 1108–12.
38. D. Obolensky, *The Byzantine Commonwealth*, London 1971, 189.
39. *Povest'* under the year 955.
40. J. Darrouzès, *Notitiae Episcopatuum Constantinopolitanae: texte critique, introduction, notes*, Paris 1981, 122 and 343.
41. *The History of Psellus*, Greek text edited with critical notes by Constantine Sathas, London 1899, 129–31.
42. Obolensky, *Byzantine Commonwealth* (n.38), 225. *Povest'* under the year 1043.
43. According to the *Povest'* under the year 1051. On his nomination as bishop, Ilarion also wrote a confession of faith, a correct variation on the Niceno-Constantinopolitan Creed with emphases on the doctrine of the two natures of Christ.
44. Old Russian text in Ludolf Müller, *Des Metropoliten Ilarion Lobrede auf Vladimir den Heiligen und Glaubensbekenntnis* (a new edition based on the original edition of 1844, with an introduction and commentary), Wiesbaden 1962. A text-critical translation by Müller was published in 1971: L. Müller, *Die Werke des Metropoliten Ilarion*, Forum Slavicum 37, Munich 1971. In making this translation, Müller used the revised edition by N. N. Rozov, which appeared one year after his own edition of the text, in *Slavia* 32, Prague 1963, 141–75. It was not until the end of the 1980s that the modern Russian translations of the oration were published: in 1986 by T. A. Sumnikova, *Idejno-Filosofskoe Nasledie Ilariona Kievskogo* [The Philosophical Heritage of Ilarion of Kiev], Part 1, Institut Filosofii AN SSSR, Moscow; in 1987 by A. Belickaya, *Bogoslovskie Trudy* [Theological Works] 28, 315–43); in 1989 by V. Deryagin in *Al'manach Bibliofila* [The Bibliophile's Almanac], Moscow 1989, 155–207. In 1990 an Ukrainian translation was published in Rome: M. Labunka, *Mytropolyt Ilarion i joho Pysanja. Metropolita Ilarion ejusque Opera*. In 1991 an English translation was published: S. Franklin (trans. and introd.), *Sermons and Rhetoric of Kievan Rus'*, Harvard Library of Early Ukrainian Literature V, Harvard 1991. I am much indebted to Franklin's translation.
45. These Jews had come from the Khazar kingdom which was subjugated by Kiev in 966. Not until the twelfth century would an anti-Jewish outbreak take place in Kiev.
46. G. Fedotov, *The Russian Religious Mind*, New York 1946, 92.
47. Following the Septuagint, Ilarion uses two terms for 'nation': *jazyk* for a pagan nation (Greek *ethnos*) and *ljudie* (Greek *laos*) for a converted nation, nation of God. See Müller, *Die Werke* (n.44), 62–7.
48. Müller, *Die Werke* (n.44), 15.

49. Ilarion designates Vladimir by the title *kagan* (khan), a Turkish-Tatar appellation, customary, for example, among the neighbouring people of the Khazars. The Russian rulers are mostly given the title of *knjaz'* (prince). The best Western equivalent for *kagan* is 'king'.

50. Russian for Basil, the name of the then Byzantine emperor, adopted by Vladimir out of respect for the emperor who had functioned as an indirect godfather.

51. A missive (*poslanie*) to Prince Izyaslav Yaroslavich. Its authenticity is disputed, but the sharp anti-Latin tone is typical of the later period. See G. Podskalsky, *Christentum und Theologische Literatur in der Kiever Rus' (988–1237)*, Munich 1982, 91 and 180–4.

52. Next to a single use of 'orthodox' (*pravoslavnyj*), the term 'of the true faith' (*pravovernyj*) occurs twice (44.27 and 47.27), a term which is more general than the term *pravoslavnyj*.

53. For this see Müller, *Die Werke* (n.44), 80–6.

54. The Mother of God Church was destroyed by the Mongols in 1238, but the Annunciation Church on the Golden Gate and the great Sophia Cathedral are still standing.

55. *Povest'* under the year 1015 ('a new Constantine'); *Čtenie o žitii i pogulbenii blažennuju strastoterpca Borisa i Gleba* [Lecture on the Life and Death of the Blessed Passion-Sufferers Boris and Gleb] in the introduction ('a second Constantine has appeared in Rus''). Translation in P. Hollingsworth (ed.), *The Hagiography of Kievan Rus'*, Harvard 1992.; *Pamjat' i pochvala knjazju ruskomu Volodimiru* [Memoir and Eulogy of the Russian Prince Volodomir]; translation also in Hollingsworth.

56. Life of Constantine (Cyril), ch. XIV, in P. Lavrov (ed.), *Materialy po istorii*; Photios, *Epistola ad Michaelem Bulgariae Principem*. PG, Vol. 102, 659; Gregory of Tours, *Historiarum* II, 31.

57. Georgij is the baptismal name of Jaroslav the Wise.

58. Irina is the baptismal name of the Swedish princess Ingigerd, wife of Jaroslav. Because she died in 1050 the Oration must have been given before that year.

59. In the Life of Clement of Bulgaria the comparison is also applied to the late conversion of the Bulgarian nation, *Vita S. Clementis Bulgarorum archiepiscopi*, PG, Vol. 126, 1201. There is more about this in the next chapter.

60. In the prayer the term *milost'*, 'mercy', appears several times. In his always meticulous translation Müller translates *milost'* in this section incorrectly by *Gnade* (grace), which is all the more inconsistent in view of the theme of the address: law and grace (*blagodat'*). This may also lead to theological misunderstandings, because in the prayer *milost'* ('mercy') is set over against 'works', whereas the latter, as is now

suggested, stand over against *blagodat'* ('grace') in a more Pauline sense. S. Franklin's not always precise English translation has the correct rendering, mercy.

61. For explanations see V.Vodoff, 'Pourquoi le prince Volodimir Svjatoslavič n'a-t-il pas été canonisé?', in O. Pritsak and I Ševčenko (eds), *Proceedings of the International Congress Commemorating the Millennium of Christianity in Rus'-Ukraine*, Cambridge, Mass. 1990, 446–66.

62. The complete title runs: 'Memorial and Eulogy of the Russian ruler Volodimir, how Volodimir is baptized and has his children baptized and the whole Russian land from one end to the other, and how Olga the grandmother of Volodimir is baptized earlier than Volodimir. Written by the monk Jakov.' The precise date of the composition of this text is not known: estimates for various sections range from the end of the eleventh to the thirteenth century. There is an English translation with a text-historical introduction in P. Hollingsworth, *Hagiography of Kievan Rus'* (n.55).

63. The passages about the conquest of Cherson, and also other passages from the life of Vladimir, are taken over by the author of the Memorial direct from the Nestorian Chronicle.

64. For this see R. Stupperich, 'Kiev, das zweite Jerusalem', *Zeitschrift für Slavische Philologie* 12, 1935, 332–54.

65. A. M. Moldovan, *Slovo o zakone i blagodati Ilariona* [Oration on the Law and the Grace by Ilarion], Kiev 1984.

66. PLDR, Vol. I, p. 17.

67. N. Gudzy, *Chrestomatija po drevnej russkoj literature* [Anthology of Old Russian Literature], Moscow [8]1973, 31–3. This fragment is obviously taken from an anthology from before 1917, since it is exactly the same as the one in V. V. Sipovskij, *Istoričeskaja chrestomatija po istorii Russkoj Slovesnosti* [Historical Anthology of the History of Russian Wordcraft], Petrograd 1915, 53–5. At that time the *Slovo* was called *Slovo o vetchom i novom zavete* [Oration on the Old and the New Testament]. The fragment in this anthology of 1915 in turn goes back to a still older one from 1904: F. Buslaev (ed.), *Russkaja chrestomatija* [Russian Anthology], Moscow [9]1904, 114–18 (republished in Slavic Printings and Reprintings, ed. C. H. van Schooneveld, The Hague and Paris 1969).

68. The translations already mentioned by T. Sumnikova, A. Belickaja and V. Derjagin. The translation by Sumnikova was also published in L. V. Poljakov, *Filosofskie idei v kul'ture drevnej Rusi* [Philosophical Ideas in the Culture of Old Rus'], Moscow 1988.

69. In 1987 Arsenij Gulyga expressed his bitterness about the tragic fate of Ilarion's Oration in Soviet times and he acknowledged 'to my shame

... that I, a Russian professor in my sixties, read this real jewel of old rhetoric for the first time in German on a visit to L. Müller in Tübingen', *Novyj Mir* 1987.10, 249.

70. *Voprosy Literatury* [Problems of Literature], 1988.12, 130–75 and 1989. 9, 236–53.

71. I. Isaev and N. Zolotuchina, *Istoria političeskich i pravovych učenij Rossii XI-XX vv* [History of Political and Juridical Theories in Russia between the Eleventh and the Twentieth Century], Moscow 1995, 9–18.

72. M. A. Maslin (ed.), *Russkaja ideja* [The Russian Idea], Moscow 1992, 18–37. V. J. Derjagin (ed.), *Ilarion, Slovo o zakone i blagodati*, Moscow 1994.

73. Maslin, *Russkaja ideja* (n.72), 19.

74. PLDR, Vol. XII, book 3. A year previously, in 1993, N. Rozov, who had published the Old Russian text abroad in 1963, deplored in a fine article that Ilarion's *Slovo* was not included in the series. N. N. Rozov, 'V načale bylo slovo' ['In the beginning was the word'], *Trudy otdela drevnej russkoj literatury* [Works of the Department of Old Russian Literature], St Petersburg 1993, Vol. 48, 88–95.

75. The most recent edition is N. Karamzin, *Istorija gosudarstva rossijskago* [History of the Russian State], Moscow 1989, Vol. 1, 15.

76. A. Turgenev, *Političeskaja proza* [Political Prose], Moscow 1989, 36.

77. N. Gogol, *Vybrannye mesta iz perepiski s druz'jami* [Selected Pieces from Correspondence with Friends], Leningrad 1952, 417–18.

78. Most recent edition, N. Danilevskij, *Rossija i Evropa* [Russia and Europe], Moscow 1991.

79. A. Kartašëv, *Vossozdanie Svjatoj Rusi* [The Restoration of Holy Russia], Paris 1956, 31.

80. 'Saint Vladimir et l'état Chrétien', in *Deutsche Gesamtausgabe der Werke von Wladimir Solowjew*, Freiburg im Breisgau 1954, III, 94–131.

81. Gregory of Tours, *Historiarum Libri Decem* II, 29–31, AQDG, Vol. II.

82. In the seventh-century chronicle of Fredegar, which also takes over the narrative by Gregory of Tours, as a proof of Clovis' religious fervour is added the fact that after hearing the account of the passion of Christ at the baptismal ceremony Clovis exclaims: 'If I had been there with my Franks, I would have avenged the injustice', *Chronicarum Quae Dicuntur Fredegarii Libri Quattuor III*, 21, AQDG, Vol. IVa.

83. *Bede's Ecclesiastical History of the English People (Historia Ecclesiastica Gentis Anglorum)*, ed. B. Colgrave and R. Mynors, Oxford 1969, I, 25–6.

84. Ibid., II, 9–14.

85. That the opposite can also happen appears from an account by Bede (II,

15) about king Raedwald of Kent, who rejected the Christian faith under the influence of his pagan wife.

86. Widukind, *Res Gestae Saxonicae,* I, 15, AQDG, Vol. VIII.

87. Adam of Bremen, *Gesta Hammaburgensis Ecclesiae Pontificum* I, 12, AQDG, Vol. XI.

88. For convenience's sake I shall call Vladimir king as well. In the Western Latin chronicles the Russian word for 'ruler' is usually translated by *rex* (sometimes by *dux),* and in the Old Norse by *konong.*

89. *Chronicon Roskildense,* ch.I, Scriptores Minores Historiae Danicae Medii Aevi, ed. M. Gertz, Copenhagen 1917.

90. *Saxonis Grammatici Gesta Danorum,* ed. A. Holder, Strassburg 1886. English translation: *Saxo Grammaticus, The History of the Danes,* trans.P. Fischer, ed. H. Ellis Davidson, Cambridge 1979, Vol. I (text) and II (commentary). This edition contains only books I-IX. There is a translation of the other books in *Saxo Grammaticus, Books X-XVI,* translated with a commentary by Eric Christiansen (3 vols), Oxford 1980.

91. Saxo is also honest in his remark about the subjection of the newly Christianized Saxons by the Danish king Grotik, 'although they preferred the yoke of Charles and the armed might of Rome to that of Denmark' (Book VIII, 272).

92. Saxo Grammaticus, Book IX, pp.290–1.

93. Ibid., Book X, p.7.

94. *Chronicon Roskildense,* ch.VII.

95. Widukind, *Res Gestae* III, 65.

96. Adam of Bremen, *Gesta* I, 56.

97. Ibid., II, 5.

98. Ibid., II, 42 and 44.

99. The Danish conversion is in Adam of Bremen, *Gesta* I, 57–59; II, 3–4, 25–28.

100. *Olafs Saga Hins Helga. Die 'Legendarische Saga' über Olaf den Heiligen,* edited with a German translation by Anne Heinrichs et al., Heidelberg 1982.

101. Adam of Bremen about Norway and Sweden in *Gesta* II, 36–41, 57–59 and 61.

102. *Olafs Saga,* chs 29 and 30.

103. Ibid., chs 31–36.

104. Ibid., ch. 71.

105. *Anonymi Gesta Hungarorum,* ch. 57, Scriptores Rerum Hungaricarum (henceforth SRH), ed. E. Szentpetery, Budapest 1937, Vol. I.

106. *Simonis de Kéza Gesta Hungarorum,* ch. 44, SRH, Vol. I.

107. Ibid., ch.76.

108. *Legenda S. Stephani regis major et minor, atque legenda ab Hartvico*

episcopo conscripta, SRH, Vol. II, 376–440. The three versions
were all written at the end of the eleventh century and the last largely
contains the first two.

109. *Chronicon Posoniense,* ch. 33, SRH, Vol. II.
110. *Chronicon Monacense,* ch. 28, SRH, Vol. II.
111. Ibid., ch. 29.
112. *Legenda minor,* ch. 7.
113. *Libellus de Institutione Morum,* SRH, Vol. II, 619–27. It is to be compared with the mediaeval genre of *speculum regale* (king's mirror).
114. *Chronicon Monacense,* ch. 39.
115. Thietmar of Merseburg, *Chronicon* IV, 59, AQDG, Vol. IX.
116. Adam of Bremen, *Gesta* II, 44.
117. Thietmar of Merseburg, *Chronicon* VII, 72.
118. Ibid. IV, 55–57.
119. Ibid. IV, 58.
120. *Cronica Galli Anonymi* I, 5. Monumenta Poloniae Historica (henceforth MPH), ed. A. Bielowski, Warsaw 1960, Vol. I.
121. *Chronica Polonorum Vincentii Cracoviensis Episcopi* II, 8, MPH, Vol. II.
122. *Cronica Galli* I, 9 and 11–16.
123. *List S. Brunona do Henryka II Cesarza,* MPH Vol. I, p. 227.
124. *Cronica Galli* I, 6 and 11.
125. Ibid. I, 7. Cf. the Russian chronicle *Povest' vremennych let* under the year 1018. Thietmar of Merseburg mentions this war in *Chronicon* VIII, 31–32, where he also stands by his negative judgment about Boleslav. He calls him *antiquus fornicator,* in connection with the cause of the war, which is also presupposed by Gallus Anonymus: the refusal of Jaroslav to give his sister as wife to Boleslav.
126. Adam of Bremen, *Gesta* II, 35. In doing so, Adam therefore differs from his fellow countryman Thietmar of Merseburg's negative judgment about Boleslav.
127. Ibid., II, 39.
128. *Vita S. Clementis Bulgariae archiepiscopi,* PG, Vol. 126, 1194–1239, here 1201.
129. *The Ecclesiastical History of Orderic Vitalis,* ed. M. Chibnall, Oxford 1980, Vol. I, 130.
130. A modern example is the book of the Metropolitan of St Petersburg, Ioann, who died in 1995, *Samoderžavie ducha. Očerki russkogo samosoznanija* [The Self-control of the Spirit. Sketches of the Russian Self-Consciousness], St Petersburg 1994, 35–6. Metropolitan Ioann sees Ilarion as the founder of the Russian 'idea of the state' (*gosudarstvennost', deržavnost'*), the national 'integralism' (*celostnost'*) and the church *sobornost'*. A Western book in which all the ideologi-

cal readings-into Ilarion's work occur in abundance is K. Rose, *Grund und Quellort des Russischen Geisteslebens. Von Skythien bis zur Kiewer Rus,* Berlin (East) 1956.

131. *Slova Serapiona Vladimirskogo* [Sermons of Serapion of Vladimir], PLDR, Vol. 3, 440–56.

132. *Povest' o razorenii Rjazani Batjem* [The Account of the Devastation of Rjazan by Batu], PLDR Vol. 3, 184–99.

133. *Skazanie ob ubienii v orde knjazja Michaila Černigovskogo i ego bojarina Feodora* [Account of the Murder in the Horde of Prince Michail of Černigov and his boyar Feodor], PLDR, Vol. 3, 228–36.

134. John of Piano Carpini, *Geschichte der Mongolen und Reisebericht 1245–1247,* translated into German by F. Risch, Leipzig 1938, 67–70.

135. *Povest' o vzjatii Cargrada krestonoscami v 1204 godu* [Account of the Capture of Constantinople by the Crusaders in the Year 1204], PLDR, Vol. 3, 106, 110.

136. *Žitie Aleksandra Nevskogo* [Life of Aleksandr Nevskij], PLDR, Vol. 3, 426–40.

137. P. Hauptmann and G. Stricker (eds), *Die Orthodoxe Kirche in Russland. Dokumente ihrer Geschichte (860–1980),* Göttingen 1988, 156–7.

138. Ibid., 157–8.

139. *Matthaei cracoviensis episcopi epistola ad s Bernardum abbatem clarevallensem,* MPH, Vol. II, 15.

140. *Russkaja Mysl',* 29 August 1998, 8.

141. *Skazanie o Dovmonte* [Narration about Dovmont], PLDR, Vol. 4, 50–8.

142. *Slovo o žitii velikogo knjazja Dmitrija Ivanoviča* [Narrative about the life of the Grand Prince Dimitrij Ivanovič], PLDR, Vol. 4, 208–30.

143. *Povest' o našestvii tochtamyša* [Narrative about the attack of Toktamysj], PLDR, Vol. 4, 202.

144. *Povest' o Temir Aksake* [Narrative about Tamburlane], PLDR, Vol. 4, 238.

145. *Žitie sv Petra mitropolita* [Life of the Holy Metropolitan Pëtr], in Makarij, *Istorija Russkoj Cerkvi* [History of the Russian Church], St Petersburg 1886, Vol. IV, 312–16.

146. Hauptmann and Stricker (eds), *Orthodoxe Kirche* (n.137), 178.

147. Ibid., 196–9.

148. *Choždenie na Florentijskij sobor* [Journey to the Council of Florence], PLDR, Vol. 4, 486–93.

149. *Moskovskij Letopsnyj Svod konca XV veka* (Moscow codex from the end of the fifteenth century], P. Nitsche (ed.), *Der Aufstieg Moskaus: Auszüge aus einer russischen Chronik,* Graz 1967, Vol. 2, 39–58.

150. M. Cherniavsky, *Tsar and People*, New Haven 1961, 37.
151. *Povest'o vzjatii Cargrada Turkami v 1453 godu* [Narrative about the capture of Constantinople by the Turks in the year 1453], PLDR, Vol. 5, 216–67.
152. See H. Schaeder, *Moskau das Dritte Rom. Studien zur Geschichte der politischen Theorien in der slawischen Welt*, Darmstadt 1957, 40–2, 47. This also says that the name 'Roos' is a wrong translation in the Septuagint of a Hebrew word which means 'grand prince'.
153. *Poslanie na Ugru Vassiana Rylo* [Letter to the Ugra by Vasian Rylo], PLDR, Vol. 5, 532 and 534.
154. *Povest' o stojanii na Ugre* [Narrative about the standing on the Ugra], PLDR, Vol. 5, 518.
155. Russkaja istoričeskaja biblioteka, Vol. VI, St Petersburg 1880, 799. See F. Kämpfer, 'Beobachtungen zu den Sendschreiben Filofejs', *Jahrbücher für die Geschichte Osteuropas* 18, 1970, Vol. I, 40.
156. *Smirennogo inoka Fomy slovo pochval'noe o blagovernom knjaze Borise Aleksandroviče* [Eulogy of the Pious Prince Boris Aleksandrovič by the Humble Monk Foma], PLDT, Vol. 5, 2168–333.
157. *Povest' o Novgorodskom belom klobuke* [Narrative about the Novgorod White Mitre], PLDR, Vol. 7, 198–233. 'Mitre' is really not an adequate translation of *klobuk,* because the Orthodox episcopal head-dress is not pointed, but flat and round.
158. Ibid., 228.
159. V. Malinin, *Starec Eleazarova monastyrja filofej i ego poslanija* [Starets Filofei of the Eleazarov monastery and his letters], Kiev 1901, 37–66. The relevant documents are on pp.45, 50 and 63. I am grateful to Dr Arno Langeler of the University of Amsterdam for putting these *knižnaja redkost'* at my disposal and also for valuable literary advice on this topic.
160. In his article 'Beobachtungen' (n.156), F. Kämpfer gives a disputed eschatological interpretation of Filofej and also puts forward the hypothesis that Filofei had connections with the sectarian movement of Judaizers.
161. *Skazanie o knazjach Vladimirskich* [Narrative about the Vladimir rulers], PLDR, Vol. 6, 422–34.
162. H. Nolthenius, *Muziek tussen hemel en aarde. De wereld van het Gregoriaans*, Amsterdam 1981, 89. The Latin text is on 195: *Exsuperatque meum ingenium justissimus actis | rex Karolus, caput orbis, amor populique decusque | Europae venerandus apex, pater optimus, heros | Augustus; sed et urbe potens, ubi Roma secunda | flore novo, ingenti, magna consurgit ad alta | mole tholis muro praecelsis sidera tangens.*

163. Schulte Nordholt, *Myth of the West* (n.4), 39f.
164. Ibid., 40f.
165. lbid, 42.
166. Dante Alighieri, *On World Government (De Monarchia)*, trans. H. W. Schneider, New York 1957.
167. A. Dvorkin, *Ivan the Terrible as a Religious Type*, Erlangen 1992, 56.
168. *Poslanija Iosifa Volockogo* [Letters of Josif Volockij], text by A. Zimin and J. Lur'e, Moscow and Leningrad 1959, 229–32.
169. *Sočinenija I Peresvetova* [Works of I. Peresvetov], text by A. Zimin, ed. D. Lichačëv, Moscow and Leningrad 1956, 170–84.
170. 'Skazanie o Mechmet-Saltane' [Narrative about Sultan Mohammed], *Sočinenija*, 161.
171. A. Langeler, *Maksim Grek, Byzantijn en humanist in Rusland*, Amsterdam 1986, 234.
172. G. Fedotov, *Svjatoj Filipp mitropolit Moskovskij* [The holy Philip, Metropolitan of Moscow], Moscow 1991 (originally Paris 1928), 74.
173. Ibid, 75.
174. *Perepiska Ivana Groznogo s Andreem Kurbskim* [Correspondence between Ivan the Terrible and Andrej Kurbskij], text by J. Lur'e and J. Rykov, ed. D. Lichačëv, Leningrad 1979.
175. For Ivan the Terrible's view of his religious task see Dvorkin, *Ivan the Terrible* (n.167).
176. *Istorija o velikom knjazje Moskovskom* [History of the Grand Prince of Moscow], PLDR, Vol. 8, 218–399, ch.1.
177. *Perepiska*, 239.
178. Ibid, 110 and 238. In the third letter and in *The History of the Grand Prince of Moscow*.
179. Fernando Ughelli, *Italia Sacra*, a comprehensive church history in ten volumes written in 1642 to 1662. In the 1960s and 1970s another Italian history appeared under the name *Italia Sacra. Studi e documenti di storia ecclesiastica*, ed. G. Gualdo and L. Sbriziolo (twenty-eight volumes).
180. A. M. Kurbskij, *Sočinenija* [Works], ed. G. Kuncevič, Russkaja Istoričeskaja Biblioteka, Vol. XXXI, St Petersburg 1914. The original was not available to me and I have used the translation in Schaeder, *Moskau, das Dritte Rom* (n.152), 124–5. There is a study of the origin of this remarkable letter in N. Andreyev, 'Kurbsky's Letters to Vas'yan Muromtsev', *The Slavonic and East European Review* 23, 1955, 414–36.
181. Hauptmann and Stricker, *Orthodoxe Kirche* (n.137), 283–5.
182. Ibid, 293–9.
183. Ibid, 302–3.
184. *Skazanie Avraamija Palicyna* [Narrative of Avraamij Palicyni], ed. L.

Čerepnin, Moscow 1955, 110 and 113.

185. Ibid., 115.
186. Ibid., 137.
187. Ivan Chvorostinin, *Izloženie na eretiki-zlochul'niki* [Exposition against the Blasphemous Heretics], PLDR, Vol. 12, 9–17.
188. Written down in the travel account of Makarios' son Paul of Aleppo. See Hauptmann and Stricker, *Orthodoxe Kirche* (n.137), 335–45.
189. N. Zernov, *The Russians and their Church*, London 1945, 66–7.
190. *Žitie protopopa Avvakuma im samirn napisannoe* [The Life of the archpriest Avvakum written down by himself], ed. N. Gudzij, Moscow 1960, 101–2.
191. See P. Pascal, *La vie de l'archiprêtre Avvvakum écrite par lui-même*, Paris 1938, 168 n.3.
192. *Žitie protopopa Avvakuma*, 197–8.
193. Schulte Nordholt, *The Myth of the West* (n.4), 42f.
194. *Actes de la conférence des chefs et des réprésentants des églises ortho-doxes autocéphales réunis à Moscou 8–18 Juillet 1948*, Moscow 1950, Vol. 1, 31, 35, 51.
195. B. A. Uspenskij and J. M. Lotman, 'Otzvuki koncepcii "Moskva-tretij Rim" v ideologii Petra Pervogo' [The resonance of the idea of Moscow as the Third Rome in the ideology of Peter the Great], in B. A. Uspenskij, *Izbrannye trudy*, Vol. 1, *Semiotika istorii. Semiotika kul'tury*, Moscow 1996, 129–30.
196. 196. M. A. Wes, *Tussen twee bronzen ruiters. Klassieken in Rusland 1700–1855*, Baarn 1991.
197. James Cracraft, 'Feofan Prokopovich', in J. Garrard (ed.), *The Eighteenth Century in Russia*, Oxford 1971, 76.
198. Feofan Prokopovič, *Sočinenija* [Works], ed I. P. Eremin, Moscow 1961, 183, 186.
199. Ibid., 23–38.
200. Ibid., 38–48. The newborn child was Peter's intended successor in place of his older son from a first marriage, Aleksej, who was put to death on the orders of Peter himself. However, Pëtr Petrovič died at the age of two.
201. 'Slovo o vlasti i česti carskoj', ibid., 76–93. Prokopovič was later to develop this sermon into a treatise on political philosophy: *Pravda voli monaršej* [The right of the monarch's will].
202. Ibid, 60–5.
203. Ibid, 126–9.
204. Ibid, 132.
205. Ibid., 140.
206. A. Kara-Murza and L. Poljakov, *Reformator. Russkie o Petre I. Opyt*

analytičeskoj antologii [Reformer. Russians on Peter I. Attempt at an
Analytical Anthology], Ivanovo 1994, 26–8.

207. Ibid, 191.
208. Uspenskij, *Izbrannye*, 136.
209. I. Smolitsch, *Geschichte der russischen Kirche 1700–1917*, Vol. 1,
     Leiden 1964, 106. Text of the Regulation in Hauptmann and Stricker,
     Orthodoxe Kirche (n.137), 388–419.
210. Cracraft, 'Feofan Prokopovich' (n.197), 95.
211. Smolitsch, *Geschichte* (n.209), 141–6.
212. Hauptmann and Stricker, *Orthodoxe Kirche* (n.137), 478. The histo-
     rian N. Karamzin had denounced the role of eulogists of the tsar
     which the bishops had played since Peter the Great, ibid., 468.
213. Ibid, 516 and 494.
214. Ibid, 476–7.
215. The first edition of all eight 'Philosophical Letters' and a number of
     personal letters appeared in 1987: P. J. Čaadaev, *Stat' i pis'ma*
     [Articles and Letters], ed. B. N. Tarasov, Moscow. A scholarly and
     complete edition of Čaadaev's articles and the majority of his
     personal correspondence appeared in 1991: P. J. Čaadaev, *Polnoe
     sobranie sočinenij i izbrannye pis'ma* [Complete collection of works
     and selected letters], ed. Z. A. Kamenskij, Moscow 1991 (2 vols,
     henceforth cited as *Pol. sobr. soč.*). In addition to the Russian text this
     edition also gives the French original and contains an extensive
     commentary. In what follows I shall refer to this edition. In 1991 a
     new English translation also appeared: *Philosophical Works of Peter
     Chaadaev*, ed. R. T. McNally and R. Tempest, Sovietica Vol. 56,
     Dordrecht, Boston and London.
216. Peter de Great is meant.
217. Alexander I in pursuing Napoleon to Paris.
218. The reference is to the failed Decembrist revolt of 1825 which led to
     the repressive policy of Nicolas I. Čaadaev shared the political aims of
     the Decembrists but did not agree with their revolutionary method.
219. Photios (Čaadaev's note). A reference to the break between patriarch
     Photios and the pope of Rome in 867.
220. The Mongolian domination.
221. A reference to the rise of Russian serfdom in the late Middle Ages
     after the Mongolian domination.
222. A reference to Nikolaj P. Rezanov, organizer of the first Russian
     journey round the world (1803–1806).
223. Letter to F. Schelling, 1832, *Pol. sobr. soč.*, Vol. 2, 75–8.
224. Letter to A. Turgenev, October/November 1835, *Pol. sobr. soč.*, Vol.
     2, 100.
225. Letter to S. Meščerskaja of 27 May 1839, *Pol. sobr. soč.*, Vol. 2, 135.

226. Nowadays the term 'Catholicophile' is a taunt used by fundamentalist Orthodox of Orthodox priests with a leaning towards ecumenicity.
227. Sixth philosophical letter, *Pol. sobr. soč.*, Vol. 1, 178.
228. Ibid., 178 and 180. In the eighth philosophical letter Čaadaev repeats his view of the Catholic Church as the executor of divine reason with the pope and the eucharist as the most important symbols.
229. Letter to A. I. Turgenev of 20 April 1833, *Pol. sobr. soč.*, Vol. 2, 79–80.
230. Sixth philosophical letter, *Pol. sobr. soč.*, Vol. 1, 168. The agreement with Novalis is striking. There are no signs that Čaadaev knew Novalis's posthumous essay published in Germany in 1826. But for Western authors writing about Novalis to be ignorant of Čaadaev is a serious omission, which illustrates the Western European perspective among historians of the idea of Europe.
231. First philosophical letter, *Pol. sobr. soč.*, Vol. 1, 102.
232. Second philosophical letter, *Pol. sobr. soč.*, Vol. 1, 179.
233. Seventh philosophical letter, *Pol. sobr. soč.*, Vol. 1, 193–4.
234. First philosophical letter, *Pol. sobr. soč.*, Vol. 1, 102–3.
235. Second philosophical letter, *Pol. sobr. soč.*, Vol. 1, 112.
236. Fragments and thoughts, no. 190, *Pol. sobr. soč.*, Vol. 1, 254.
237. Fragments and thoughts nos 191 and 192, *Pol. sobr. soč.*, Vol. 1, 255.
238. 'Apologie d'un fou', *Pol. sobr. soč.*, Vol. 1, 299.
239. Ibid, 300.
240. lbid, 300 and 302.
241. 'Otvet na stat'ju A. S. Chomjakova "O sel'skich uslovijach"', *Pol. sobr. soč.*, Vol. 1, pp.542–5. The title of this article, which was never published by Čaadaev himself, comes from the editor, Z. Kamenskij, who in the commentary (p.746) thinks that here Čaadaev is speaking with subtle irony about Byzantium.
242. Letter from Puškin to Čaadaev of 19 October 1836, *Pol. sobr. soč.*, Vol. 2, prilozenija I, 460.
243. A. Turgenev, *Politiceskaja proza*, Moscow 1989, 10, 36, 156.
244. M. A. Alpatov, *Russkaja istoriceskaja mysl' i zapadnaja Evropa (XVIII-pervaja polovina XIX v)*[Russian historical thinking and Western Europe (eighteenth and first half of the nineteenth centuries)], Moscow 1985, 253.
245. Ibid., 254 en 256.
246. *Oeuvres choisies de Pierre Tchaadaïef publiées pour la première fois par le Père Gagarin*, Paris 1862. This contains only the first, sixth and seventh philosophical letters and the *Apologia*. Ivan Gagarin also wrote a book about Catholicism in Russia, *Tendances Catholiques dans la société russe*, Paris 1860.

247. A Dutch translation by Tom Eekman appeared in 1990: Vladimir
    Pečerin, *Van over het graf*, Amsterdam 1990. A serious mistake in the
    otherwise excellent translation is the translation of *kartezianec* with
    'Cartesian' rather than 'Carthusian' (144, 145, 146 and 159).
248. Pečerin, *Van over het graf* (n.247), 174.
249. Ibid, 201–2.
250. The Russian translation of I. Gagarin's selection appeared in 1913
    edited by M. O. Geršenzon, *Sočinenija i pi 'ma P Ja. Čaadaeva* [works
    and letters of P. J. Čaadacv], 2 vols, Moscow 1913–1914.
251. In the 1930s the *Philosophical Letters* missing from the editions by
    Gagarin and Geršenzon were published by D. I. Šachovskoj in
    Literaturnoe nasladestvo [Literary legacy], Moscow 1935, Vols
    22–24.
252. The editions by B. Tarasov and Z. Kamenskij already mentioned.
    Tarasov's translation also appeared in a popular edition (with
    reactions from Čaadaev's contemporaries under de title *Cena vekov.
    P. Ja. Čaadaev* [The value of centuries. P. J. Čaadaev], Moscow 1991,
    and in the book *Rossija glazami russkago. Čaadaev, Leont'ev,
    Solov'ëv* [Russia in the Eyes of a Russian. Čaadaev, Leont'ev,
    Solov'ëv], ed. A. F. Zamaleev, St Petersburg 1991.
253. O. B. Tarasov, 'Prostranstvo mysli Petra Čaadaeva' [The breadth of
    thought of Peter Čaadaev], *Literaturnaja gazeta*, 11 March 1992;
    Z. Kamenskij, 'O sovremennych pročtenijach P. Ja. Čaadaeva' [On
    present-day ways of reading P. J. Čaadaev], *Voprosy filosofii* 12,
    1992, 136–9. The former was reacting to the articles by V. Kantor,
    'Imja rokovoe' [A fatal name], *Voprosy literatury* 3, 1988, and
    S. Jakovlev, 'Pravo otrečenija' [The right to foreswear], *Novyj mir* 5,
    1988, no. 5. The Western *Studies in Soviet Thought* also devoted
    extra attention to Čaadaev in a special number, Vol. 32, 1986, no. 4.
254. O. A. Platonov, *Russkaja civilizacija* [Russian civilization], Moscow
    1995.
255. S. N. Bulgakov, *U sten Chersonisa* [At the Walls of Cherson], edited
    with an introduction by A. M. Mosin, St Petersburg 1993.
256. Bulgakov, *U sten Chersonisa* (n.255), 11.
257. From the various studies I would mention Andrej Walicki, *The
    Slavophile Controversy. History of a Conservative Utopia in
    Nineteenth-Century Russian Thought*, Oxford 1975. Assen Ignatow,
    *Das russische geschichtsphilosophische Denken: Grundmotive und
    aktuelle Resonanz*, Berichte des Bundesinstituts für ostwissenschaft-
    liche und internationale Studien 5, Cologne 1996, is a recent good but
    short account of Slavophile ideas.
258. Alpatov, *Russkaja istoričeskaja mysl'*, 246–7.
259. Schulte Nordholt, *Myth of the West* (n.4), 192–3 and 201–2.

260. Ignatow, *Das russische geschichtsphilosophische Denken* (n.257), 4 and 32.
261. 'Vizantizm i slavjanstvo' [Byzantinism and Slavdom], XII, in K. Leont'ev, *Izbrannoe* [Selected Works], Moscow 1993, 111 and 112.
262. Ibid, 112 and 113. Italics, exclamation marks and commas in the original.
263. Walicki, *Slavophile Controversy* (n.257), 528.
264. Ibid, 529.
265. Thus a contemporary Russian cultural scholar, quoted in Ignatow, *Das russische geschichtsphilosophische Denken*, 38.

Index